DALÍ

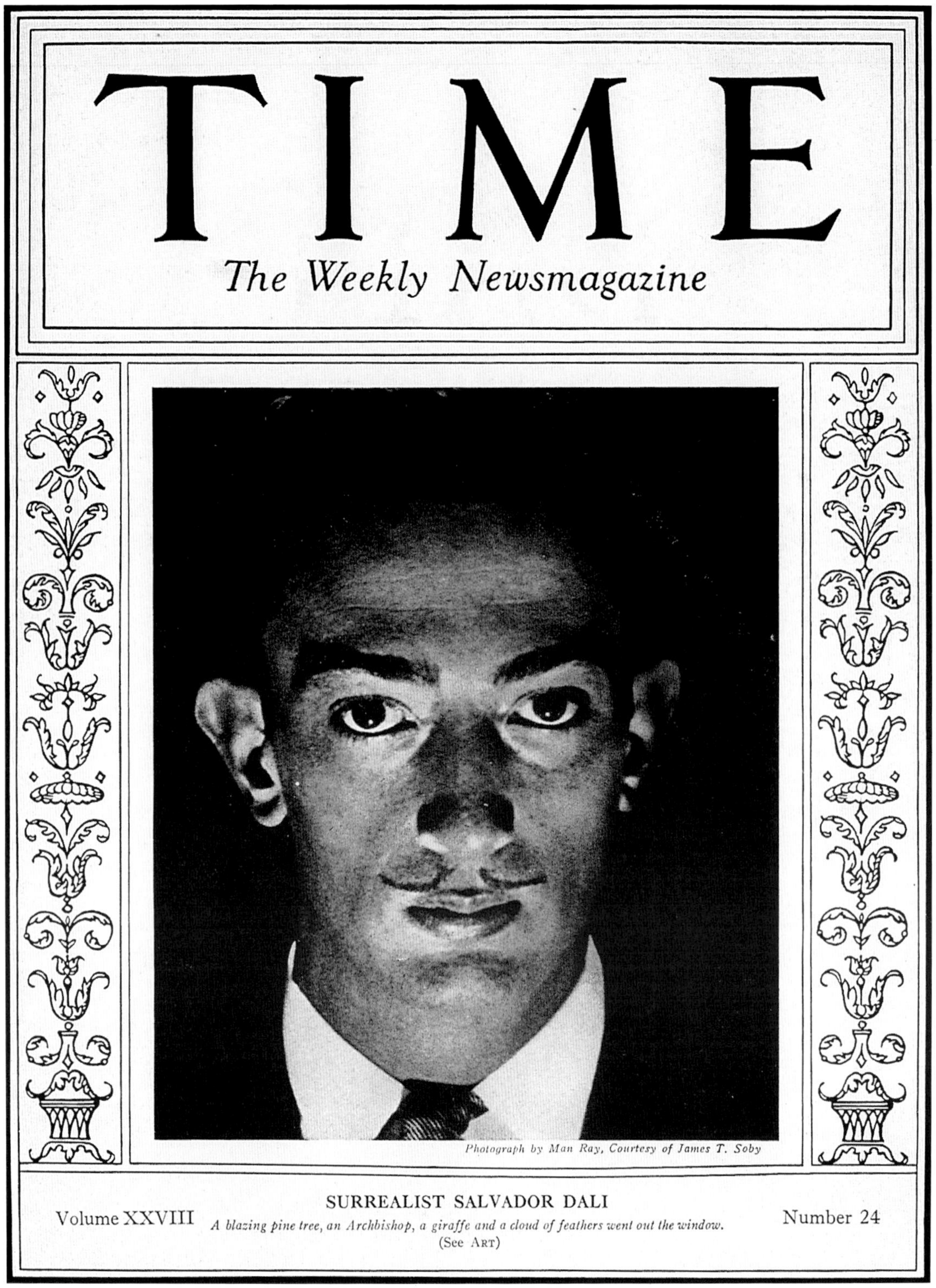

Cover of Time *magazine, 14 December 1936, featuring*
'Surrealist Salvador Dali', photo taken by Man Ray.

DALÍ

Eric Shanes

STUDIO EDITIONS
LONDON

For Peter Hodes and Jenny Walker, my two favourite realists

First published in Great Britain in 1990 by Studio Editions Ltd
This revised edition published 1994 by Studio Editions Ltd
Princess House, 50 Eastcastle Street,
London W1N 7AP, England

ISBN 1 85891 103 6

Printed and bound in China

INTRODUCTION

It is perhaps unsurprising that Salvador Dalí has proven to be one of the most popular artists of the twentieth century, for his finest works explore universal and timeless states of mind, and most of his pictures were painted with a mastery of traditional representation that has proven rare in our era. For many people, that control of representationalism in itself would have attracted them to Dalí's work, and it has certainly served to mask any gradual lessening of quality in his art. Moreover, Dalí was also probably the greatest artistic self-publicist in a century in which (as Igor Stravinsky commented in 1970), publicity has come 'to be about all that is left of the arts', and in this respect Dalí, along with his brilliant wife and co-publicist, Gala, was in a class of his own for much of his lifetime.

Yet Dalí's immense popularity is also rather ironic, for his work – in its finest phase, at least – constitutes an attack on the social, sexual and cultural values of the very society that fêted him. The notion that an artist should be culturally subversive has proven central to modernist art practice, and it was certainly central to Surrealism, which aimed to subvert the supposedly rational basis of society itself. In time, Dalí's subversiveness softened, and by the mid-1940s André Breton, the leading spokesman for Surrealism, was perhaps justifiably dismissing the painter as a mere showman and betrayer of Surrealist intentions. But although there was a sea-change in Dalí's art after about 1940, his earlier work certainly retains its ability to bewilder, shock and intrigue us, whilst also dealing inventively with the nature of reality and appearances. Similarly, Dalí's behaviour as an artist after about 1940 throws light on the superficiality of the culture that sustained him, and this too seems worth touching upon, if only for what it can tell us about the man behind the myths that Salvador Dalí so ably projected about himself.

Salvador Felipe Jacinto Dalí y Domenech was born on 11 May 1904 in Figueras, a small town in the Catalan province of Gerona, northern Spain, the son of Salvador Dalí i Cusi and Felipa Domenech. Dalí senior was the public notary of Figueras and, as such, an important and widely respected local official. He was a very forceful man, and it was rumoured that he had been responsible for the death of Dalí's elder brother, also named Salvador, who had been born in 1901 and who died in 1903; officially the death was caused by catarrh and gastroenteritis but according to Dalí his older brother died of meningitis, possibly brought on by a blow to the head. Certainly that death left Dalí's parents with an inescapable sense of anguish, and the young Dalí was always aware of the demise simply because both parents constantly projected his lost brother onto him, every day making comparisons between the two boys, dressing the younger Salvador in his dead brother's clothes, giving him the same toys to play with, and generally treating him as the reincarnation of his dead brother, rather than as a person in his own right.

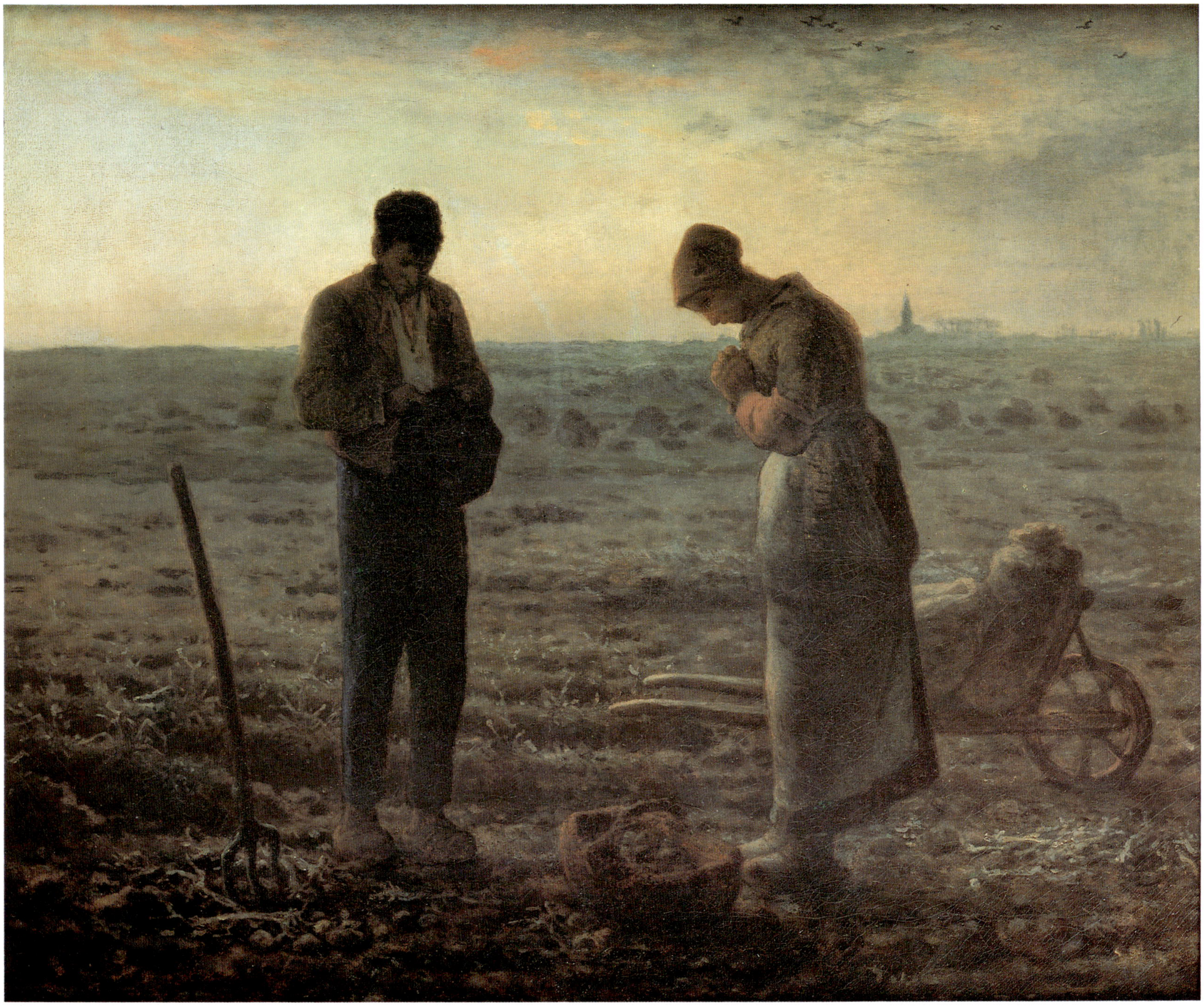

The Angelus
By Jean François Millet, 1857–59.
Oil on canvas, 55.5 × 66 cm
Musée d'Orsay, Paris

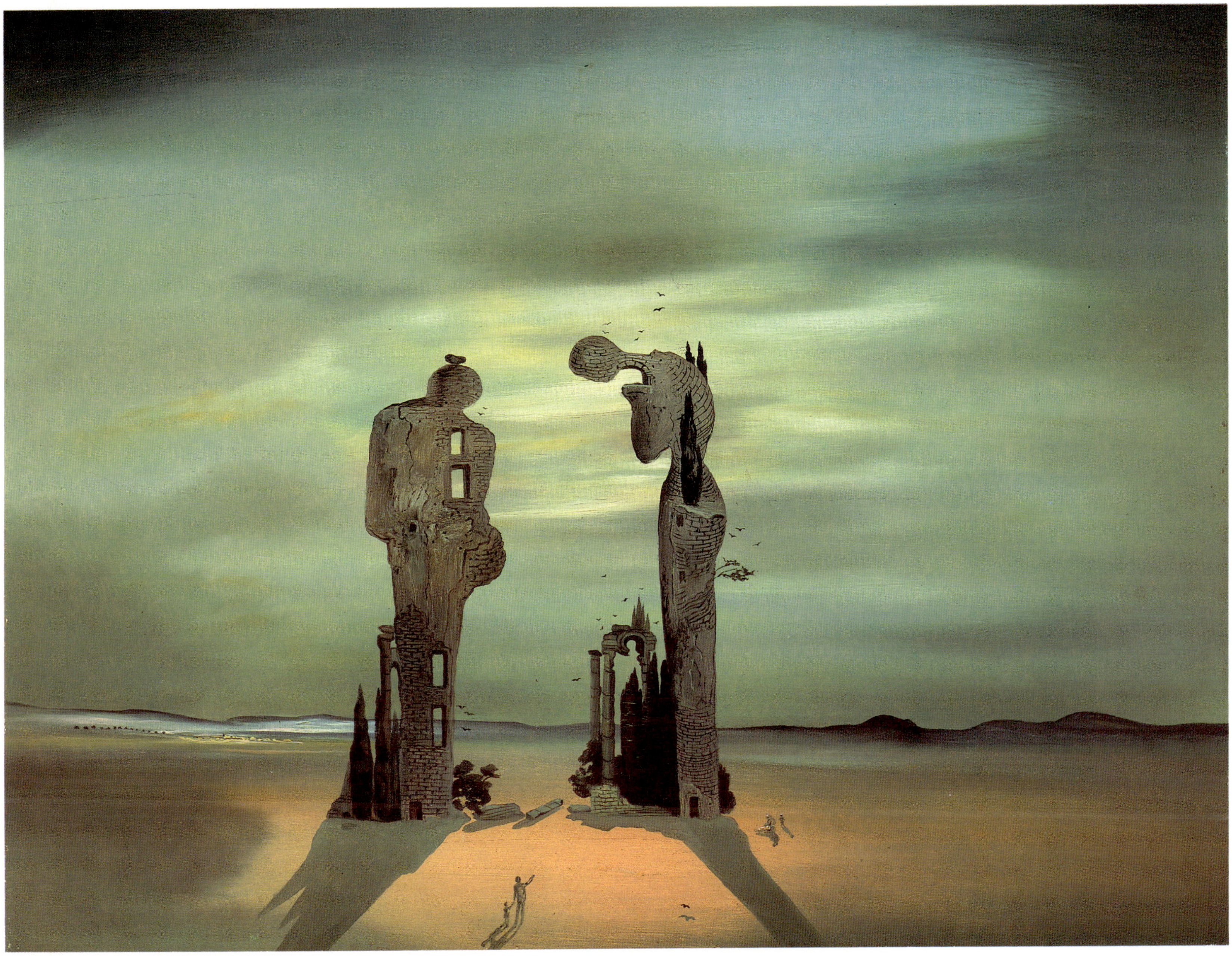

Archaeological Reminiscence of Millet's Angelus,
1933–35.
Oil on panel, 31.7 × 39.3 cm
Salvador Dalí Museum, St Petersburg, Florida, USA

Faced with such a denial of self, Dalí understandably rebelled in order to assert his own identity, while equally rebelling against the perfected image of the dead brother that his parents tried to impose upon him. Thus the painter later recounted:

Each day I looked for a new way of bringing my father to a paroxysm of rage or fear or humiliation and forcing him to consider me, his son, me Salvador, as an object of dislike and shame. I threw him off, I amazed him, I provoked him, defied him more and more.

Among other things, Dalí's rebelliousness involved him in deliberate bed-wetting, simulated convulsions, prolonged screaming, feigned muteness, jumping from heights, and acts of random aggressiveness such as flinging another little boy off a suspension bridge or kicking his younger sister in the head for no apparent reason. Dalí also frequently over-compensated for the suppression of his identity by indulging in exhibitionist behaviour, as on the occasion when he placed a dying, ant-covered bat in his mouth and bit it almost in half. Eventually both Dalí's rebelliousness and his exhibitionism would serve him in good stead artistically.

Dalí received his schooling in Figueras, first at a state school where he learned nothing, and then at a private school run by Marist friars, where he learned little more but from which he did retain certain images (such as Millet's *Angelus*, a reproduction of which hung in the school, as well as the cypress trees visible from the classroom) that would frequently reappear in his pictures. But the main educational input of these years clearly derived from Dalí's home life, for his father was a relatively cultured man, with an interest in literature and music, a well-stocked library that Dalí worked through even before he was ten years old, and decidedly liberal opinions, being an atheist and a Republican. This political nonconformism initially rubbed off on Dalí, who as a young man regarded himself as an anarchist and who professed a lifelong contempt for bourgeois values.

More importantly, the young Dalí also received artistic stimulation from his father, who bought the boy several books in a popular series of artistic monographs. Dalí pored over their reproductions, and they helped form his long-term attraction to nineteenth-century academic art, with its pronounced realism; among the painters who particularly impressed him were Manuel Benedito y Vives, Eugène Carrière, Modesto Urgell and Mariano Fortuny, one of whose works, *The Battle of Tetuan*, would inspire Dalí to paint a companion picture in 1962. And Dalí also received artistic encouragement from a friend of his father, the Figueras lawyer Pepito Pitchot, whose brother Ramón was a fluent Impressionist painter living in Paris and known to Picasso. It may have been in the Pitchot summer residence in an old mill-tower near Figueras that the young Dalí took his first steps as a painter, for when he was about nine years old he produced a still-life of cherries on the back of an old, worm-eaten door, using merely vermilion and carmine for the fruits, and white for the highlights. (Dalí also later claimed that in this work he first blurred the dividing lines between differing realities, initially by gluing the stems of the real cherries to the bases of the painted ones, and then by transferring several worms from their holes in the door – and thus within his painted cherries – to the worm-holes in various real cherries.)

Quite naturally the young Dalí was influenced by the numerous impressionistic and pointillist canvases of Ramón Pitchot that hung in the old mill-tower, and his precociousness was such that Pepito Pitchot soon persuaded Dalí senior to allow his son to study drawing with Professor Juan Nuñez at the Municipal School of Drawing in Figueras, where the boy enrolled in 1917. He remained under Nuñez's tuition for about two years, and freely admitted that he learned much from him. And in the summer of 1918 the fourteen-year-old Salvador Dalí exhibited his first pictures publicly, in a show of local art held in the Municipal Theatre, Figueras, a building that would later become a museum devoted entirely to his

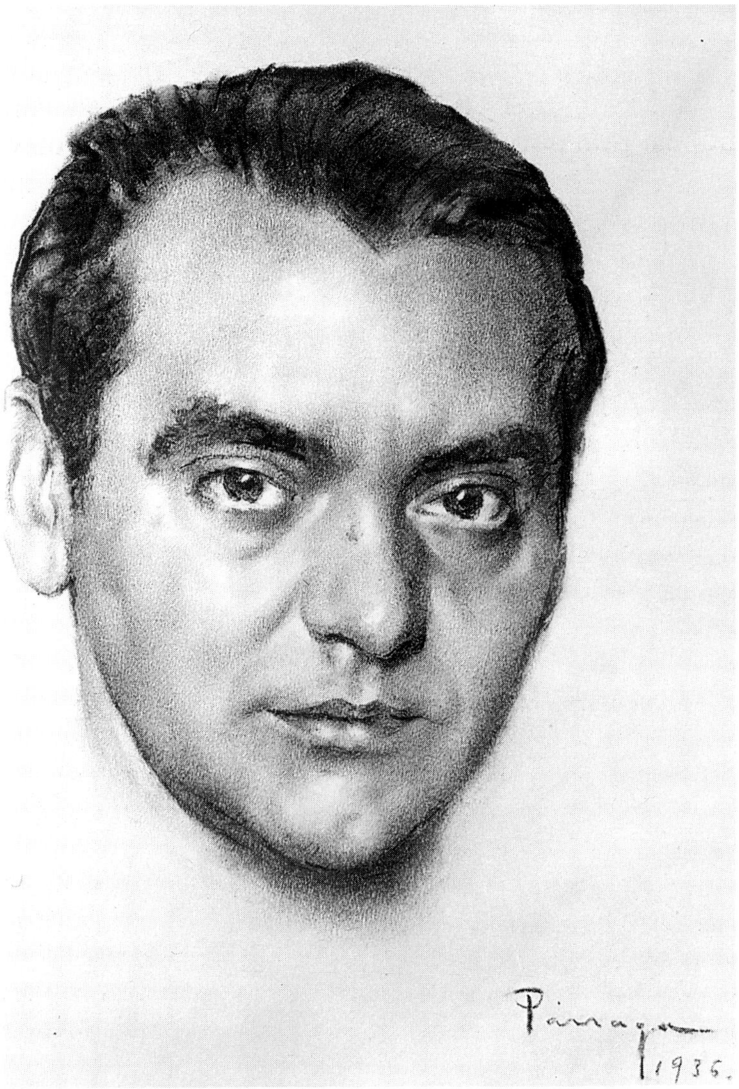

Federico García Lorca, 1898–1936.

works. The following winter Dalí exhibited further pictures there and he was then singled out for praise as someone 'who will attain fame'.

In September 1921* Dalí was accompanied by his father and sister to Madrid in order to apply for admittance to the leading art school there: the San Fernando Academy of Fine Arts. The boy had long wanted to devote himself to art, and although his father harboured the usual reservations about such an uncertain career, clearly he was relieved that his unstable son had some set target in mind. The entrance examination for the Academy of Fine Arts involved spending six days drawing a cast of Jacopo Sansovino's *Bacchus*, and although Dalí failed to make his drawing to the required size, his facility was such that the size of his work was ignored and he was accepted.

Dalí was not to be happy with the tuition he received at the San Fernando Academy, mainly because Impressionism was still the prevailing artistic mode there and it was a style he had already worked through and exhausted. Instead, he took an interest in more advanced visual thinking, such as Cubism, whilst equally being attracted to traditional artistic techniques which unfortunately were now barely being taught at the Academy because of the prevailing taste for Impressionism. But if the San Fernando Academy made only a passing contribution to Dalí's artistic development, his choice of accommodation in Madrid gave him much more creative stimulation, for he stayed in the university residence and his sojourn there coincided with that of some particularly brilliant minds in Spanish culture. Most importantly for Dalí these included Luis Buñuel, then a philosophy student and later to be an outstanding film director with whom he would collaborate, and the finest modern Spanish poet and playwright (and arguably the greatest poet of the twentieth century), Federico García Lorca. At first Dalí was somewhat distanced from his more advanced fellow students in the Residencia by his assumed, defensive haughtiness and bohemian way of dressing, but when his modernist sympathies were discovered he was readily admitted to the circle of Buñuel and Lorca, with whom he had become firm friends by early 1923.

* The Dalí literature gives 1921 for the date of Dalí's entry to the Madrid art school but Ian Gibson, the biographer of Federico García Lorca, has perused Dalí's admission records in the files of Madrid University, to which the San Fernando Academy of Fine Arts belongs, and established that he entered the school in 1922. However, there exists a Dalí drawing of Lorca which is dated 1921, and this suggests that the university record may be incorrect, for Dalí undoubtedly first met Lorca in Madrid and he had not visited the city before entering art school.

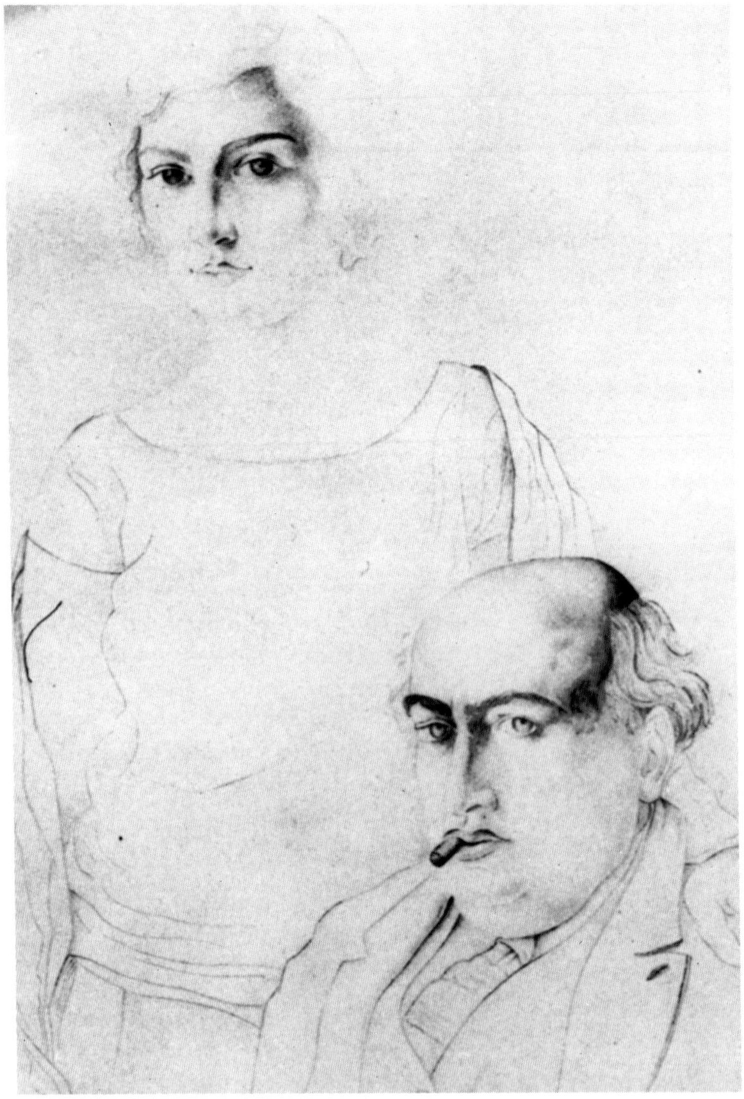

Pencil on paper, 49 × 74.5 cm
Museo de Arte Moderno, Barcelona

Dalí's dissatisfaction with the San Fernando Academy moved onto a new plane in the autumn of 1923 when he was rusticated for a year for supposed insubordination. He had supported the appointment of a progressive painter to the post of teacher of painting, and when his favourite failed to obtain the job, in protest he had walked out of the meeting at which the news of the failure was announced; this was followed by a vociferous student protest, for which it was assumed that Dalí's walkout had been the starting signal. Dalí thereupon returned to Figueras. Soon afterwards, in May 1924, he unwittingly found himself in further trouble with authority because of the political leanings of other members of the Dalí family; as a consequence Dalí was imprisoned without trial in Figueras and later transferred to the provincial capital of Gerona before being released.

By this time Dalí had experimented with a variety of artistic styles. Picasso was one influence, Derain another, while in 1923 Dalí had painted pictures of groups of nudes in the open air that were heavily indebted to pointillism and the flowing, linear style of Matisse. By the autumn of 1924, when Dalí returned to Madrid and his formal studies, he had also begun to assimilate more recent developments in Cubism and Purism. Yet simultaneously he started exploring a highly detailed representationalism, and here too the influence of Picasso (of the neo-classical style of the late 1910s and early 1920s) is again apparent, as well as that of earlier, Romantic painters such as Caspar David Friedrich. Clearly, Dalí was searching for a style that could express his innermost self, without yet being able to find it.

Back in Madrid Dalí resumed his friendship with Buñuel and Lorca. On the creative level the relationship of Dalí and Lorca was to be especially important, for eventually it strengthened their mutual attraction to Surrealism. However, the sympathy between them also led the homosexual Lorca to fall in love with Dalí who, being perhaps bisexual but more usually asexual, could not return his affections in the same way. Possibly in the spirit of sexual experimentation, on two occasions (probably in

Venus and a Sailor, *1925.*
Oil on canvas, 216 × 147 cm
Ikeda Museum of Twentieth-Century Art, Shizuoka, Japan

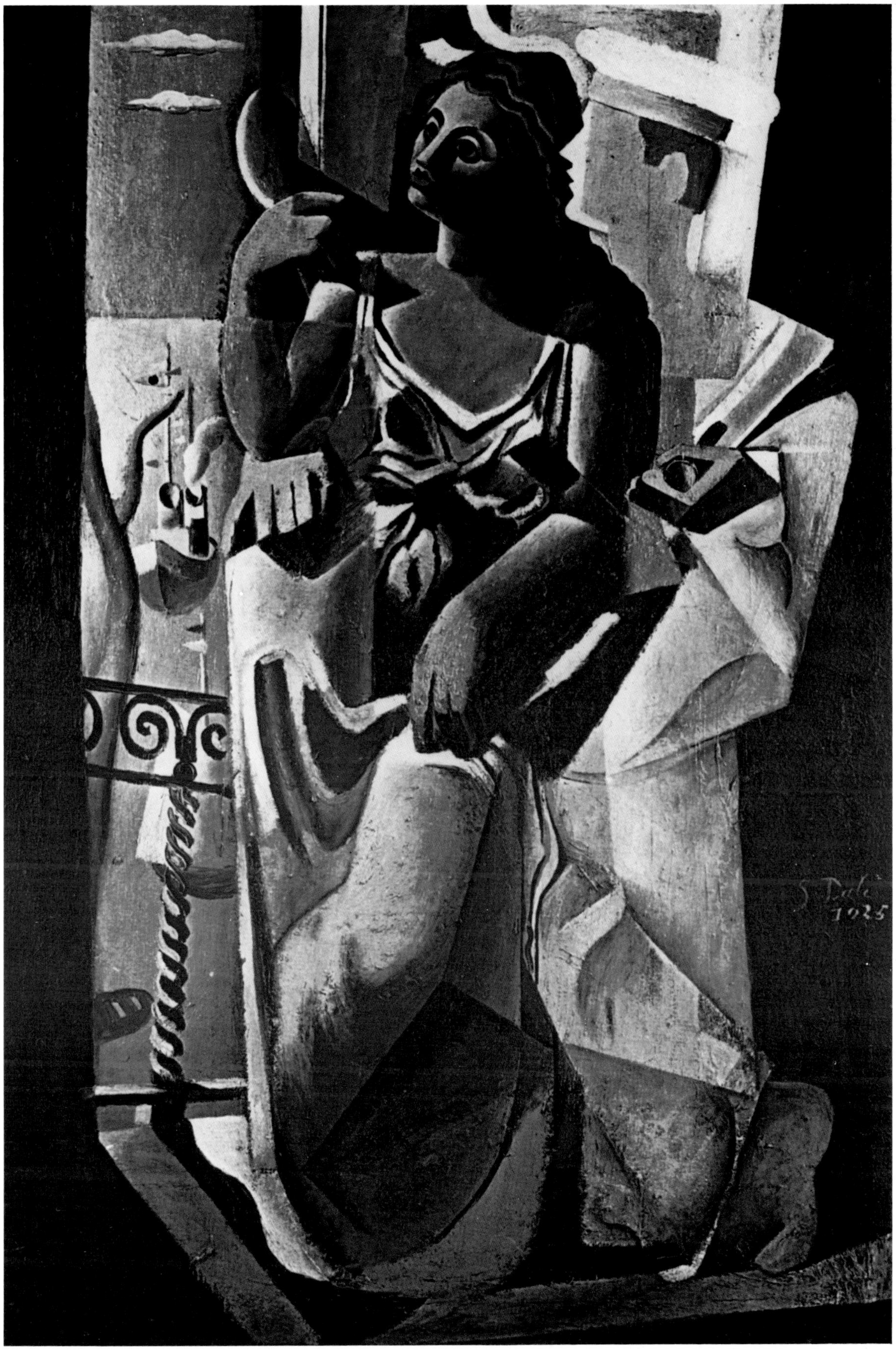
S. Dalí
1925

1926) Dalí passively allowed Lorca to try making love to him. The experiment was unsuccessful, although Dalí later commented: 'I felt awfully flattered *vis-à-vis* the prestige. Deep down, I felt that he was a great poet and that I did owe him a tiny bit of the Divine Dalí's asshole.'

In November 1925 Dalí held his first one-man exhibition, at the Delmau Gallery in Barcelona, showing seventeen mostly recent paintings that ranged stylistically across the visual spectrum from Cubist semi-abstraction, as in the *Venus and a Sailor* (see page 11), to a low-keyed realism, as in the *Girl Standing at a Window* (see page 13). The show was well received by the critics, although some of them were understandably puzzled by the stylistic diversity of the pictures. The exhibition also indirectly aided the establishment of Dalí's reputation in Paris, for it was visited by Picasso who especially admired a portrait of Dalí's sister viewed from the rear.

In April 1926 Dalí received an overwhelming testimonial to his talents through the publication of Lorca's *Ode to Salvador Dalí*, a poem that has been described as 'perhaps the finest paean to friendship ever written in Spanish'. And later that month Dalí, accompanied by his step-mother and sister, at last visited Paris for the first time, as well as Brussels. The trip was paid for by Dalí's father, who had been delighted by the success of the Delmau Gallery exhibition the previous autumn. In Brussels, Dalí was attracted to Flemish painting, with its microscopic attention to detail, while in Paris he met up again with Buñuel. The family took excursions to Versailles, to the studio of Jean-François Millet in Barbizon, and to the Grévin waxworks museum, but the high point of the entire trip was Dalí's visit to Picasso, which was arranged by another Spanish artist living in Paris. Dalí later recalled:

When I arrived at Picasso's on Rue de la Boétie I was as deeply moved and as full of respect as though I was having an audience with the Pope.

'I have come to see you', I said, 'before visiting the Louvre.'

'You're quite right,' he answered.

I brought a small painting, carefully packed, which was called The Girl of Figueras. *He looked at it for at least fifteen minutes, and made no comment whatever. After which we went up to the next storey, where for two hours Picasso showed me quantities of his paintings. He kept going back and forth, dragging out great canvases which he placed against the easel. Then he went to fetch others among an infinity of canvases stacked in rows against the wall. I could see that he was going to enormous trouble. At each new canvas he cast me a glance filled with a vivacity and an intelligence so violent that it made me tremble. I left without in turn having made the slightest comment.*

At the end, on the landing on the stairs, just as I was about to leave, we exchanged a glance which meant exactly.

'You get the idea?'

'I get it!'

The influence of Picasso stemming from this visit can be detected in many of the paintings that Dalí made upon his return to Spain. In them we see the assimilation of Picasso's latest Cubist style of the mid-1920s, with elongated figures, flat shapes and crisp silhouettes, of the type that is evident in Picasso's *Three Dancers* (see page 14) of 1925 (London, Tate Gallery). Yet simultaneously Dalí also continued to develop the romantic realism that Picasso had so admired in the portrait of his sister viewed from the rear. Clearly he was still searching for his true self.

Girl Standing at a Window, *1925.*
Oil on board, 155 × 74.5 cm
Museo Español de Arte Contemporáneo, Madrid

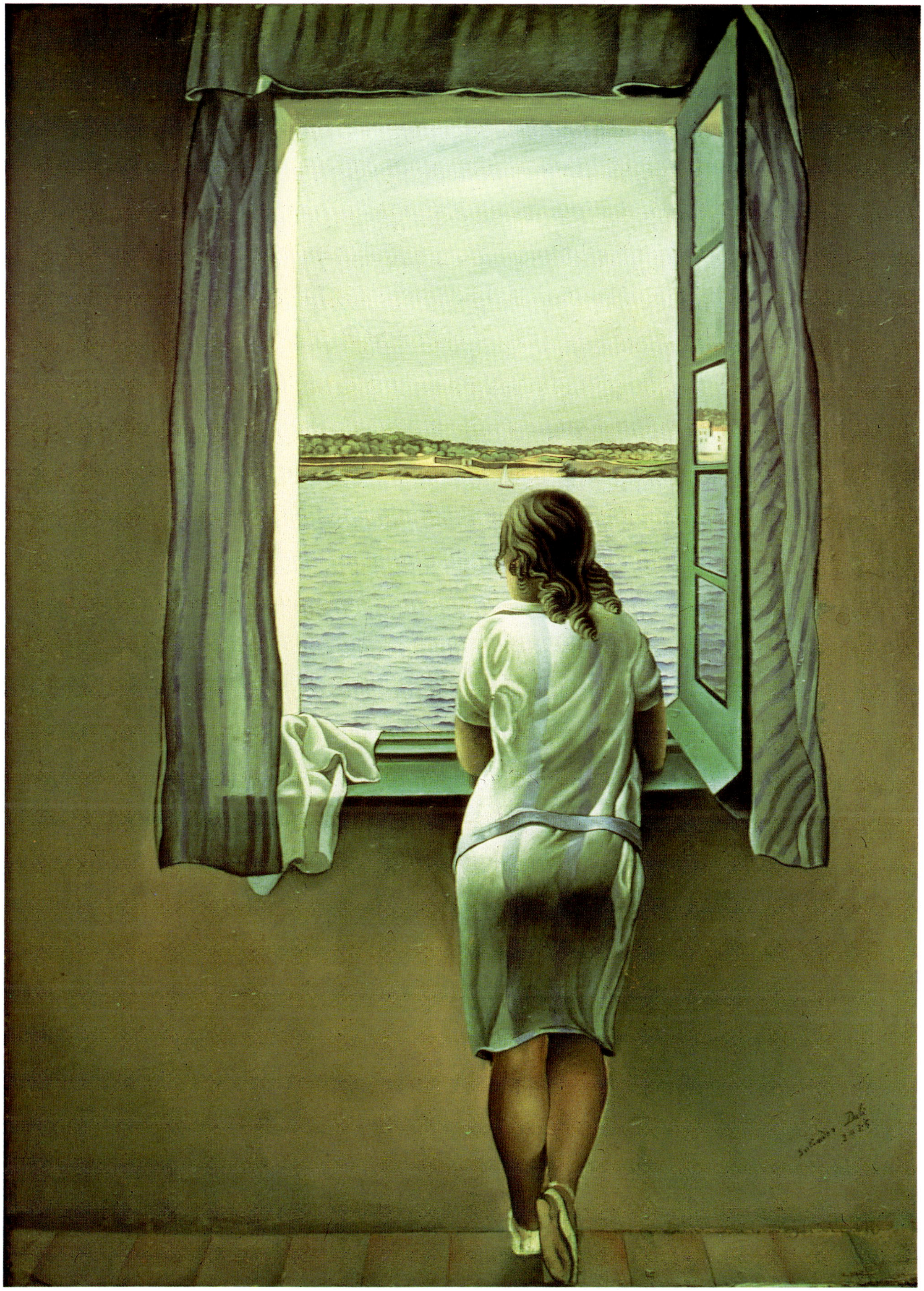

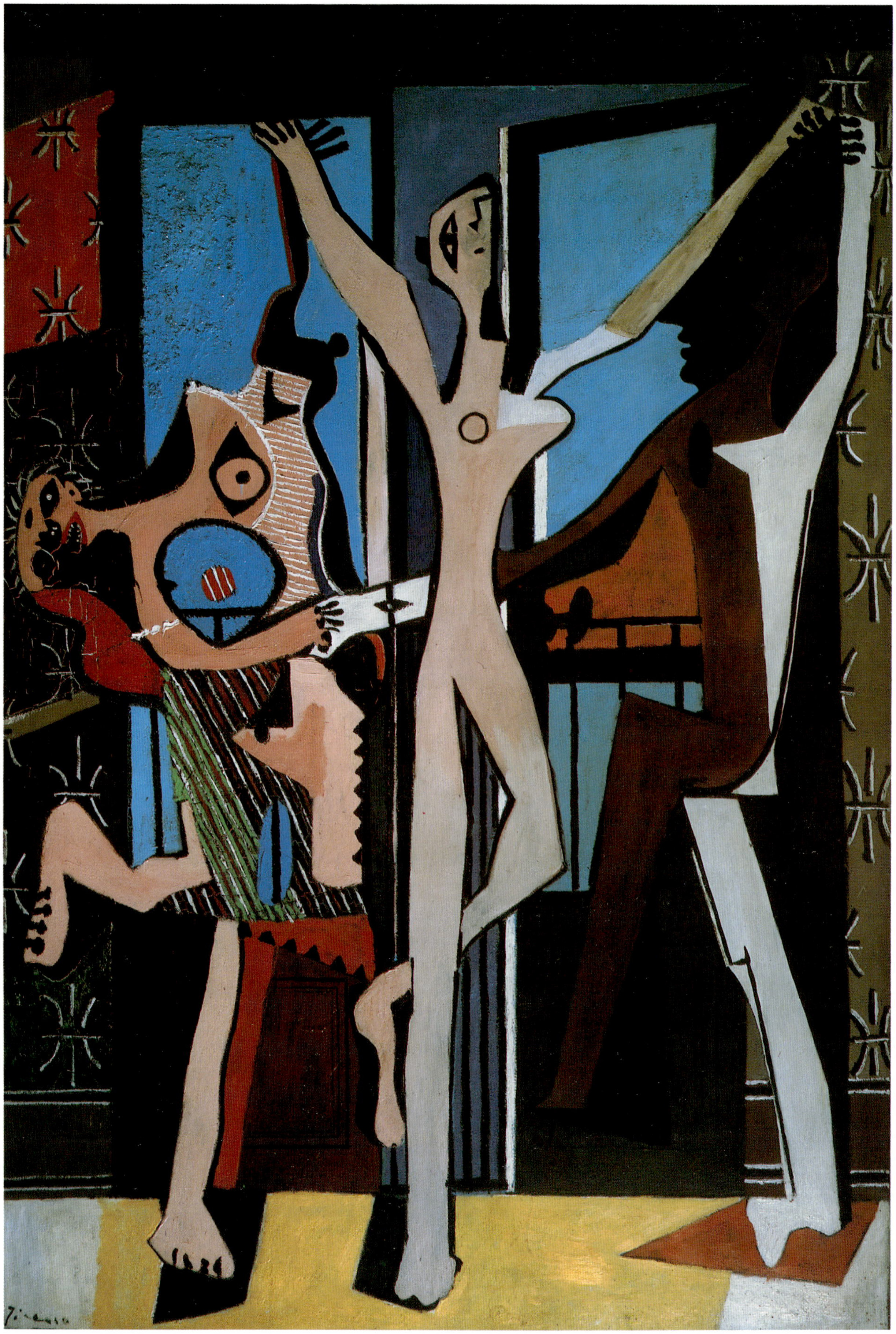

The welcome that Dalí had encountered in Paris led him to think of moving there, and in order to do so he evolved a crafty, long-term strategy that involved engineering his own expulsion from the Academy of San Fernando in Madrid. As he later stated:

The motives for my action were simple: I wanted to have done with the School of Fine Arts and with the orgiastic life of Madrid once and for all; I wanted to be forced to escape all that and come back to Figueras to work for a year, after which I would try to convince my father that my studies should be continued in Paris. Once there, with the work that I should take, I would definitely seize power!

By being 'forced to escape all that', Dalí surely meant his need to overcome a seemingly insuperable obstacle, namely that if he obtained his academic degree his father would expect him to support himself by teaching for a living rather than support him financially in Paris. And with his talents how could he fail to win his degree?

Dalí chose a typically outrageous way of solving the problem. In mid-June 1926, when he was summoned for the art history component of his final examination, he refused to be examined, stating: 'None of the professors of the School of San Fernando being competent to judge me, I retire.' The ploy was successful, for the professors were infuriated, and eight days later Dalí was expelled from the institution without obtaining his degree.

Dalí's father was shattered by the expulsion, which closed an official career in Spain to his son, but he grudgingly allowed the younger Salvador to return once again to Figueras where the boy embarked on his plan to 'work for a year'. A show of the results was held at the Delmau Gallery in Barcelona at the very end of 1926 when twenty paintings displayed an even wider range of styles than had been apparent in the works exhibited in the previous show. Once again Dalí was a huge success, with his pictures drawing a largely enthusiastic response from the press. But in his long-term planning to 'work for a year', Dalí had forgotten to take into account the Spanish army, and from February 1927 he had to spend nine months performing his compulsory military service, although the duties do not appear to have been too irksome. During that time Dalí managed to finish only a few pictures, but he did design the sets and costumes for the première of Lorca's *Mariana Pineda*, which opened in Barcelona on 24 June 1927, and he also contributed drawings, poetry and prose to the highly esteemed Sitges journal *L'Amic de les Arts*. Amongst the prose pieces was his 'Saint Sebastian', containing frequent allusions to Lorca, who that summer stayed with the painter at Cadaqués, about twenty miles to the east of Figueras on the Mediterranean, where the Dalí family had its summer villa.

Dalí's professional contact with Lorca continued in the following year when the painter contributed to a newly founded journal entitled *Gallo* that was published in Lorca's Andalusian home town of Granada, a review in which Lorca also took an active interest. In the second issue of *Gallo* in April 1928 Dalí republished an attack on Catalan cultural complacency and anti-modernism that he had co-authored with the writers Lluis Montanyà and Sebastià Gasch. This was the 'Catalan Anti-Artistic Manifesto' or 'Yellow Manifesto' that had first been published in Barcelona the previous month. In tone the essay resembles the manifestoes published over a decade earlier by the Italian Futurist poet Marinetti, for it similarly praises the machine age and attacks anti-modernist provincialism. Later that year Dalí published a further, similar *feuilleton* in which again

The Three Dancers
By Pablo Picasso, 1925.
Oil on canvas, 215 × 142 cm
Tate Gallery, London

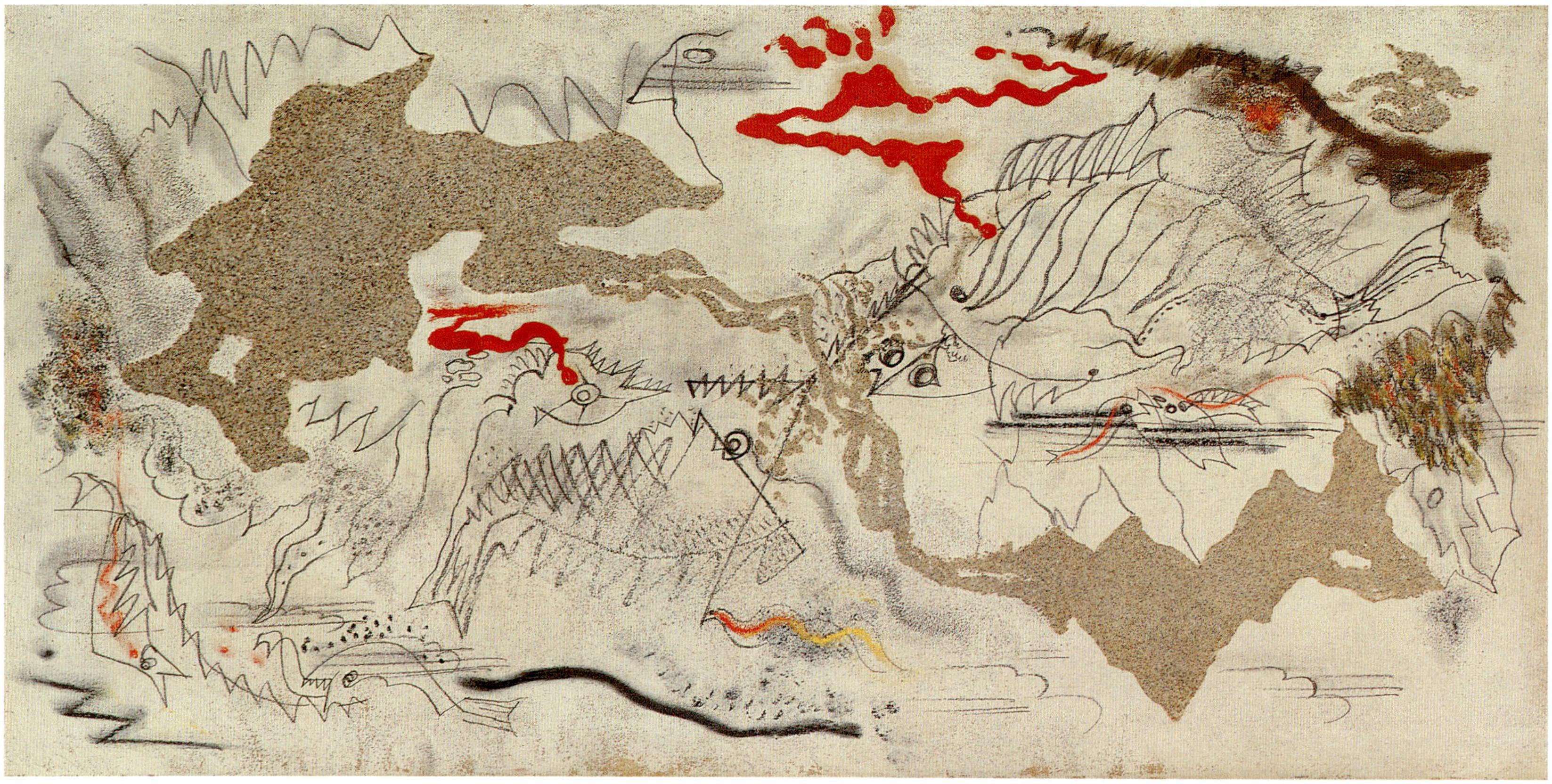

Battle of Fishes
By André Masson, 1926.
Sand, gesso, oil, pencil and charcoal on canvas,
36.2 × 73 cm
Museum of Modern Art, New York

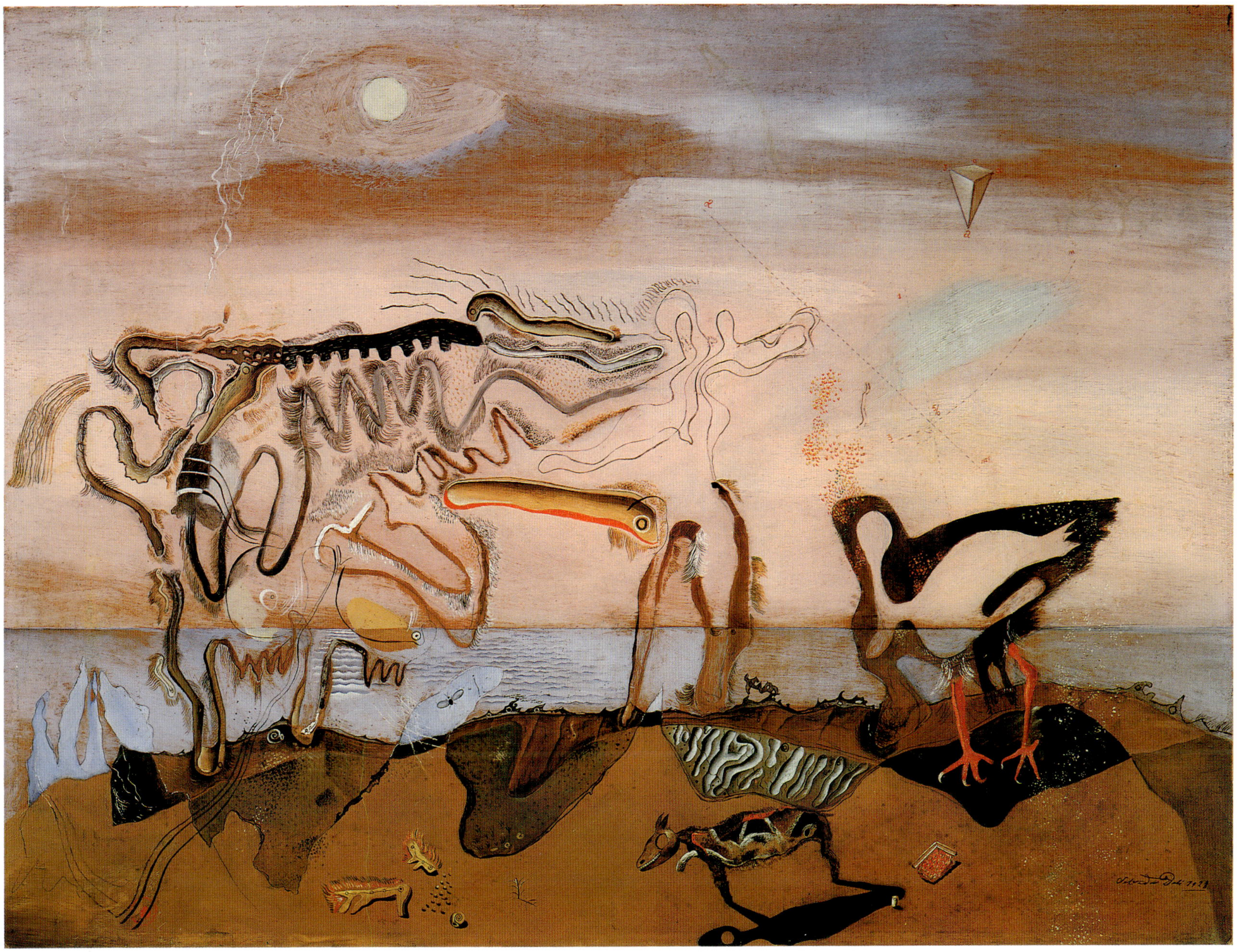

The Spectral Cow, *1928.*
Oil on laminated panel, 49.8 × 64.4 cm
Musée National d'Art Moderne, Centre Georges Pompidou, Paris

he renounced Spanish provincialism and regionalism, in favour of modernity and the new.

In the autumn of 1927 Dalí had written to Lorca:

Federico, I am painting pictures which make me die for joy, I am creating with an absolute naturalness, without the slightest aesthetic concern, I am making things that inspire me with a very profound emotion and I am trying to paint them honestly. . . .

The works in question are pictures in which Dalí had begun wholeheartedly to explore Surrealism. Dalí's engagement with Surrealist ideas had grown apace as he kept in touch with the latest developments in Paris through reading the journal of the French Surrealists, *La révolution surréaliste*, and other similar literature, and in Surrealism he sensed a form of expression that would finally liberate his inner self.

Surrealism had evolved out of an earlier artistic grouping, known as Dada, which had been founded in Zurich in 1916 by the Romanian poet Tristan Tzara and by the German writer Hugo Ball. Isolated in Switzerland physically by the Great War, and intellectually by the assault on reason epitomized by that conflict, the Zurich Dadaists had turned their backs on rationalism altogether. Although Tzara established Dada in Paris after 1919, Dadaism soon lost impetus there, for it was essentially a nihilistic response to the world, preaching the destruction of all reason and rational communication. Surrealism, however, represented something more positive, for it wanted actively to liberate the subconscious into articulating responses to the world that were more direct than those created by rational thought. To this end, from the early 1920s onwards a group of leading artists, poets and intellectuals in Paris, led by André Breton, set out to explore the vast realms of thought and response that lay behind the irrational, which they held to be a more truthful mirror to reality than rationalism.

By the late 1920s knowledge of Surrealism was widespread in Spanish intellectual circles, and of course awareness of the work of Spanish Surrealist painters living in Paris such as Miró (and Picasso, who was also influenced by Surrealism at this time) contributed greatly to that growth of interest. Thus several articles on Miró appeared in 1927–28 in *L'Amic de les Arts*, and throughout 1927 and 1928 Dalí worked through Miró's influence, as well as that of other Surrealist painters and sculptors such as Yves Tanguy, Max Ernst, André Masson (as in *The Spectral Cow*, see page 17, which especially demonstrates Masson's influence) and Jean Arp, in addition to that of proto-surrealist artists like Giorgio de Chirico and Carlo Carrà. In 1927 Dalí even experimented with automatic drawing, in which the conscious mind played no part whatsoever other than beginning and ending a seemingly random process of mark-making. Not until the American painter Jackson Pollock explored the automatic process as an end in itself a decade and a half later would this major strand in Surrealism receive fulfilment, but for Dalí in the late 1920s such a direct means of articulating the irrational was unsatisfactory. Instead, he gradually moved towards forging a new union between the normal appearances of things and unreality. In this respect the influence of Tanguy, Ernst and de Chirico proved to be of seminal importance.

A particular feature of the imagery of these three artists is the degree to which they married rational space – the traditional, perspective-based space found in Renaissance and post-Renaissance painting – and realistic landscape settings, with strange and unreal objects placed in those lifelike surrounds. Usually Tanguy created a kind of vague, desert-like landscape in which to locate his weird, polymorphic creatures and objects, while de Chirico created semi-deserted cityscapes as, occasionally, did Ernst. Dalí took over the rational use of space and realistic-looking settings, and he also assimilated the polymorphic forms of Tanguy in the paintings he made after 1927. Moreover, it was a small step for him to identify the type of desert-like landscape background that Tanguy commonly used with the fantastic geological formations, vast spaces and limitless skies of his native Catalonia, and particularly those of the vast Ampurdán plain around Figueras that he had known since his childhood. By using such backgrounds Dalí gained an efficient vehicle with which to deal with his own experiences. In time this employment of landscape would become one of the major strengths of his art, contributing greatly to the sense of disturbing unreality in his pictures and simultaneously making him one of the foremost landscape painters of the twentieth century.

In the winter of 1928 Dalí also began working in another important area: the cinema. A year earlier he had written an essay on the subject entitled 'Film-Art, Anti-Artistic Thread' which he had dedicated to his friend from the Madrid Residencia, Luis Buñuel, who by that time was working in the Paris film industry. In the essay, Dalí extolled the freedom of visual imagery and movement that film enjoys, and deprecated the way that the medium was usually employed simply to recount a narrative, instead of cutting across normal meanings. Moreover, Dalí rejected the way that modernist artists who had experimented with cinema, such as Man Ray and Fernand Léger, had employed abstracted cinematic imagery in their films. For Dalí the power of film lay in its potential to place ordinary objects and surroundings in non-rational dramatic situations, so as to create a new dimension of meaning and thereby open up hitherto unexplored ways of perceiving the world in all its variety.

Dalí soon got the chance to turn his theories into practice, for during the winter of 1928 Buñuel visited him in Figueras to show him the outline for a movie. Dalí instantly rejected this script as being too conventional, and in the following week he and Buñuel wrote a new scenario together, bouncing ideas off each other in a most vivacious way. As Buñuel later recalled:

Our only rule was very simple: no idea or image that might lend itself to a rational explanation in any way would be accepted. We had to open all doors to the irrational and keep only those images that surprised us . . . The amazing thing was that we never had the slightest disagreement; we spent a week of total identification.
'A man fires a double bass', one of us would say.
'No', replied the other, and the one who'd proposed the idea accepted the veto and felt it justified. On the other hand, when the image proposed by one was accepted by the other, it immediately seemed luminously right and absolutely necessary.

The result was to be a film that took Surrealist cinema into a wholly new dimension of psychological disturbance and cultural subversion: *Un Chien andalou*.

In order to help Buñuel with the shooting of the film, Dalí travelled to Paris in March 1929. In many ways this visit marked a turning point in his career, for he not only received artistic stimulus from it; ultimately his cultural and sexual existence was to be transformed by it as well. Buñuel shot *Un Chien andalou* very quickly, and Dalí assisted the proceedings in various ways, such as by pouring glue into the rotting carcasses of donkeys placed inside grand pianos to add to their sense of putrefaction, by giving the animals extra sets of teeth to make them appear more leering, and by enlarging their eye sockets to make them look more decomposed. In one scene, in which the donkey-laden pianos are hauled into sight, Dalí even appears dressed as a Jesuit priest, dragged along behind the pianos. Naturally, the film defies rational analysis in terms of plot, and there is certainly no symbolism in it, but it has been suggested that the 'Andalusian Dog' of the title was Lorca, and this interpretation receives some support from the fact that the extremely homophobic Buñuel clearly had it in for his old Andalusian friend once he discovered his sexual proclivities, and wanted to wean Dalí away from friendship with him (Lorca himself had no doubts as to the identity of the 'Dog'). The tone of the film is set near its outset by the revolting sight of a girl having her eye sliced open with a razor blade; clearly Dalí and Buñuel wanted to test our sensibilities from the beginning. Yet Dalí felt that *Un Chien andalou* was not nearly disgusting enough, and both he and his collaborator were disappointed by the public reception of the work, for they had intended it to be a major assault on bourgeois values. Instead, as Dalí stated,

the public who applauded Un Chien andalou *is a public stupefied by the reviews and 'disclosures' of the avant-garde, who applaud everything that seems new or bizarre to them because of snobbism. This public did not understand the moral depth of the film, which is aimed directly at them with total violence and cruelty . . . .*

Similarly, Buñuel saw in that selfsame public 'an idiotic crowd which finds *beautiful* or *poetic* what is, after all, simply a desperate, impassioned call to murder'. Naturally, because of its calculated offensiveness, *Un Chien andalou* caused a sensation when it was premièred in October 1929, and it did much to further Dalí's reputation as an *enfant terrible*. Although this was not the first time he had reaped the benefits of scandal, there was a slight difference between offending a few old professors in Madrid and taking the artistic capital of the world by storm, and the value of such scandal was certainly not lost on someone who would soon become the twentieth century's greatest artistic self-publicist.

Equally, *Un Chien andalou* had vital side-effects on Dalí's development as a painter: it sharpened his visual imagery and caused a greater reliance upon visual transformation in his work. To take the first: the filmic conjunction of photographic reality and an irrational, inexplicable narrative demonstrated to Dalí a way forward in his painted imagery, for in the paintings he made in 1929 after returning to Figueras from Paris (such as *The Lugubrious Game*, page 49), the heads, bodies and all manner of objects became far more highly detailed than they had been previously. And although elements in the pictures of 1929 remained abstracted to a degree (as in the 'soft', polymorphic self-portraits that appear in works like *The Great Masturbator* and *The Enigma of Desire*, pages 51 and 53), those forms are modelled and lit so as to suggest that they are real objects as we would perceive them three-dimensionally in the real world. Because of this more sharply focused imagery and greater degree of illusionism, the bizarre or inexplicable juxtapositions, dislocations of space and scale, and metamorphoses or emphases within the pictures seem even more unreal by contrast with the very naturalistic backgrounds in which they occur. Moreover, the photographic dissolves of cinema also influenced Dalí, especially in the way that from now on he would transform parts of objects into other things (as in *The Great Masturbator*, page 51, where the head and shoulders of a woman suddenly well up from the side of Dalí's polymorphic self-portrait). It is difficult to believe that such a new emphasis on realistic settings and this greater use of visual transformation did not derive from the sharper visual focus and photographic transformations that Dalí had perceived in *Un Chien andalou*.

The Parisian trip to assist with the making of *Un Chien andalou* had other beneficial side-effects. Eventually Dalí obtained an agreement with the art dealer Camille Goemans to give him an exhibition in Paris later in 1929, and while in Paris the painter first met – albeit briefly – someone who was soon to transform his life utterly: Gala Eluard.

In order to firm up their agreement over Dalí's Paris debut, in the summer of 1929 Goemans visited the painter in Cadaqués. He was joined there by Paul and Gala Eluard and their daughter Cécile, by the Belgian Surrealist painter René Magritte and his wife, and by Buñuel. Paul Eluard was a distinguished Surrealist poet who was very friendly with André Breton, and he and Gala had married in 1917. By the early 1920s the Eluards had begun living in a *menage à trois* with Max Ernst, a relationship that naturally broke up Ernst's marriage and which itself broke up by about 1925. Thereafter Eluard and Gala settled down together again, but their marriage was clearly doomed, and the visit to Cadaqués in the summer of 1929 gave it the death blow. Gala Eluard was of Russian extraction – her original name was Elena Dimitrievna Diakonova – and she was born in 1895, the daughter of a failed Siberian gold prospector. She grew up in Kazan and as an adolescent suffered from some form of tuberculosis which had eventually necessitated treatment in Switzerland. Indeed, she had first met Eluard at a sanatorium in Switzerland where he too had been sent to receive treatment for the same disease, and later she followed him to France where they married.

At Cadaqués in the summer of 1929 Dalí appears to have been in a state of acute sexual hysteria, expressed both in bouts of prolonged, uncontrollable laughter and, less directly, in the emphasis he gave to the subject of masturbation in the painting *The Lugubrious Game* (page 49), which he had begun immediately after returning from Paris. The visit of Gala Eluard to Cadaqués and Dalí's attraction to her, which outwardly had to be suppressed because she was with her husband, obviously heightened the painter's emotional and sexual frustration. But Gala was equally attracted to Dalí, and perhaps she also sensed that here was a rising star to whom she could profitably hitch herself – not an unnatural thought for a woman with a failing marriage and no visible means of support. At any rate, Gala stayed on after Eluard returned to Paris in September, and soon afterwards she began an affair with Dalí. Clearly she was on the same unusual psychological wavelength as the painter, if the following anecdote told by Dalí of his first physical contact with her is to be believed:

I kissed her on the mouth, inside her mouth. It was the first time I did this. I had not suspected until then that one could kiss in this way. With a single leap all the Parsifals of my long bridled and tyrannized erotic desires rose, awakened by the shocks of the flesh. And this first kiss, mixed with tears and saliva, punctuated by the audible contact of our teeth and furiously working tongues, touched only the fringe of the libidinous famine that made us want to bite and eat everything to the last . . . I threw back Gala's head, pulling it by the hair, and, trembling with complete hysteria, I commanded,
'Now tell me what you want me to do to you! But tell me slowly, looking me in the eye, with the crudest, the most ferociously erotic words that can make both of us feel the greatest shame!'
'I want you to kill me!' [she replied].

Dalí desisted from carrying out such a macabre request, but the story may indicate the calculated side of Gala's personality, for it is hard to take her demand seriously – obviously she was just trying to match Dalí in eccentricity. Upon the onset of their relationship Dalí's hysteria disappeared, which demonstrates its psycho-sexual origin, and his love-making with Gala was probably the first sexual relationship he had ever had with a woman (as his unfamiliarity with deep kissing attests), as well as possibly being his last, for thereafter the painter appears to have preferred masturbation to direct sexual relations with his wife. As a child he had come across a medical textbook illustrating the clinical effects of venereal diseases, and this appears to have put him off having direct sexual relations for life, although he did sample such contacts on occasion. But in time Gala would easily find numerous substitutes with which to satisfy her healthy libido.

Dalí remained convinced ever afterwards that Gala had saved him from outright madness that summer. After she had returned to Paris in late September 1929 Dalí threw himself further into his work in preparation for the forthcoming Paris exhibition. He produced some of his finest masterpieces that autumn, pictures such as a portrait of Paul Eluard (now in a private collection), which Dalí freely admitted was a means of salving his conscience over his affair with the poet's wife; *The Enigma of Desire* (page 53), in which the painter dealt with his relationship with his mother; and *The Great Masturbator* (page 51), a work that he called 'the expression of my heterosexual anxiety'. The show itself, held in the Camille Goemans Gallery between November and December 1929, included eleven paintings and was a great success, finally consolidating Dalí's reputation. Breton wrote an introductory essay for the catalogue (although he had his doubts even then about whether Dalí would fulfil his promise as a Surrealist artist), and that put the seal upon the painter's acceptance by the Surrealist movement, with which he had aligned himself fully on the earlier visit to Paris that spring. The exhibition was a sell-out, and Breton bought a painting (*Accommodations of Desire*, page 55), as did a leading collector, the Vicomte de Noailles, who hung the work (*The Lugubrious Game*, page 49) between pictures by Lucas Cranach and Antoine Watteau. Yet although the show was a success, Camille Goemans was deeply in debt and he was unable to pay Dalí what he owed him from the sale of his pictures. The Vicomte de Noailles thereupon stepped in and advanced 29,000 francs for another painting. With the money Dalí bought himself a fisherman's cottage in Port Lligat, near Cadaqués.

In addition to buying pictures, the Vicomte de Noailles was to be important to Dalí in others ways as well. Subsequently he introduced Dalí to his next Parisian dealer, Pierre Colle, and he also gave Buñuel and Dalí the money to make a further film, although Dalí was far less happy with Buñuel's efforts this time. The resulting film, *L'Age d'or*, was even more violent and subversive than its predecessor, but Buñuel also made it into more of a specific attack upon clericalism, and this narrowing of meaning led Dalí to feel betrayed by his collaborator. Shortly after the première of *L'Age d'or* in 1930, right-wing thugs smashed up the cinema in which it was being shown and destroyed works of art that were hanging in the foyer, including a painting by Dalí.

After returning to Paris in 1929, Gala Eluard briefly went back to her husband, but by the following year she had moved in with Dalí, despite the very dim view taken by the painter's father of this liaison with a married woman and mother who was, moreover, almost ten years older than his son. Additionally, Dalí senior had been enraged by a print made by the painter which depicted the Sacred Heart and bore the caption 'Sometimes I spit with pleasure on my mother's portrait.' Dalí's mother had died in 1921, and his father interpreted this gloss on the picture as a gross insult to the memory of his dead wife. The ensuing rows culminated in Dalí senior disowning his son completely. Soon afterwards Dalí began using the story of William Tell's shooting of an apple from his son's head as a means of dealing with his strained relationship with his own father, and in such comparatively direct treatments of the painter's most deep-seated anxieties and preoccupations it is possible to detect a new-found psychological focusing of his art.

Dalí had long been familiar with the writings of Sigmund Freud, having read *The Interpretation of Dreams* when still a student in Madrid. The book made a profound impression on him, for as he recorded:

This book presented itself to me as one of the capital discoveries in my life, and I was seized with a real vice of self-interpretation, not only of my dreams but of everything that happened to me, however accidental it might seem at first glance.

By the end of the 1920s Dalí had also read Richard Krafft-Ebing's *Psychopathia Sexualis*, with its exploration of sado-masochistic tendencies. Such writings were to prove fruitful for the painter not as subjects to be directly illustrated but as means of exploring his own fantasies pictorially. Within such a process the association of ideas and images became crucial, even if Dalí purposely employed those associations in a loose way so as not to imply specific meanings (it is the very ambiguity of meaning in his works that gives the pictures their unusual imaginative potency).

Moreover, in 1930 Dalí also began to build upon his immensely imaginative propensity for associating images through visual simile, the acute similarity that can exist between very different types of objects, and for creating composite objects out of subsidiary objects, as well as double or multiple images. Thus in the *Apparition of Face and Fruit Dish on a Beach* of 1938 (page 101), we can see numerous visual similes, as well as composite imaging, whereby different components serve to make up a head, while in *Slave Market with the Disappearing Bust of Voltaire* of 1940 (page 103) we can perceive in the centre either two people dressed in antique costumes or a bust of Voltaire (but not both at once).

According to Dalí himself, this faculty for perceiving more than one image in the appearance of things derived from his schooldays; as he stated in *The Secret Life of Salvador Dalí*, published in 1941:

The great vaulted ceiling which sheltered the four sordid walls of the class was discoloured by large brown moisture stains, whose irregular contours for some time constituted my whole consolation. In the course of my interminable and exhausting reveries, my eyes would untiringly follow the vague irregularities of these mouldy silhouettes and I saw rising from this chaos, which was as formless as clouds, progressively concrete images which by degrees became endowed with an increasingly precise, detailed and realistic personality.
From day to day, after a certain effort, I succeeded in recovering each of the images which I had seen the day before and I would then continue to perfect my hallucinatory work; when, by dint of habit, one of the discovered images became too familiar, it would gradually lose its emotive interest and would instantaneously become metamorphosed into 'something else', so that the same formal pretext would lend itself just as readily to being interpreted successively by the most diverse and contradictory configurations, and this would go on to infinity.
The astonishing thing about this phenomenon (which was to become the keystone of my future aesthetic) was that, having once seen one of these images, I could always thereafter see it again at the mere dictate of my will, and not only in its original form but almost always further corrected and augmented in such a manner that its improvement was instantaneous and automatic.

In time such an ability was augmented by other experiences, such as the discovery of a postcard view of an African village which, if looked at sideways, resembled the visage of Picasso (in 1935 Dalí turned that image into a painting). Eventually Dalí's employment of visual simile, composite, and double and multiple imaging would become one of the mainstays of his art, but it was certainly not based on anything as passive as dreaming. Dalí may have occasionally used dreams as the starting points for pictures, but more usually it was his highly developed and profoundly imaginative wakeful 'inner-eye' that served to provide him with his imagery. Such an ability to connect the appearances of things was to prove integral to the 'Paranoid-Critical Method' that Dalí began to evolve after about 1930, whereby association, when taken to an extreme, could generate wildly imaginative and hallucinatory (or 'paranoid') states of mind.

In June 1931 Pierre Colle gave Dalí his second Paris exhibition and introduced the painter to a New York dealer, Julien Levy, who in 1933 would give him his first one-man show in America. The 1931 Pierre Colle Gallery exhibition comprised twenty-one works, including the painting that was undoubtedly to become Dalí's most popular picture, *The Persistence of Memory* (page 63), which Colle later sold to Levy at the trade price of $250. This work was exhibited again in a group show of Surrealist paintings, drawings and photographs held early in 1932 by Levy in New York, and on that occasion it was bought by the New York Museum of Modern Art in what would turn out to be a particularly shrewd and far-sighted piece of collecting.

By 1932 Dalí was busier than ever. His customary method of work was to paint with the aid of a bril-

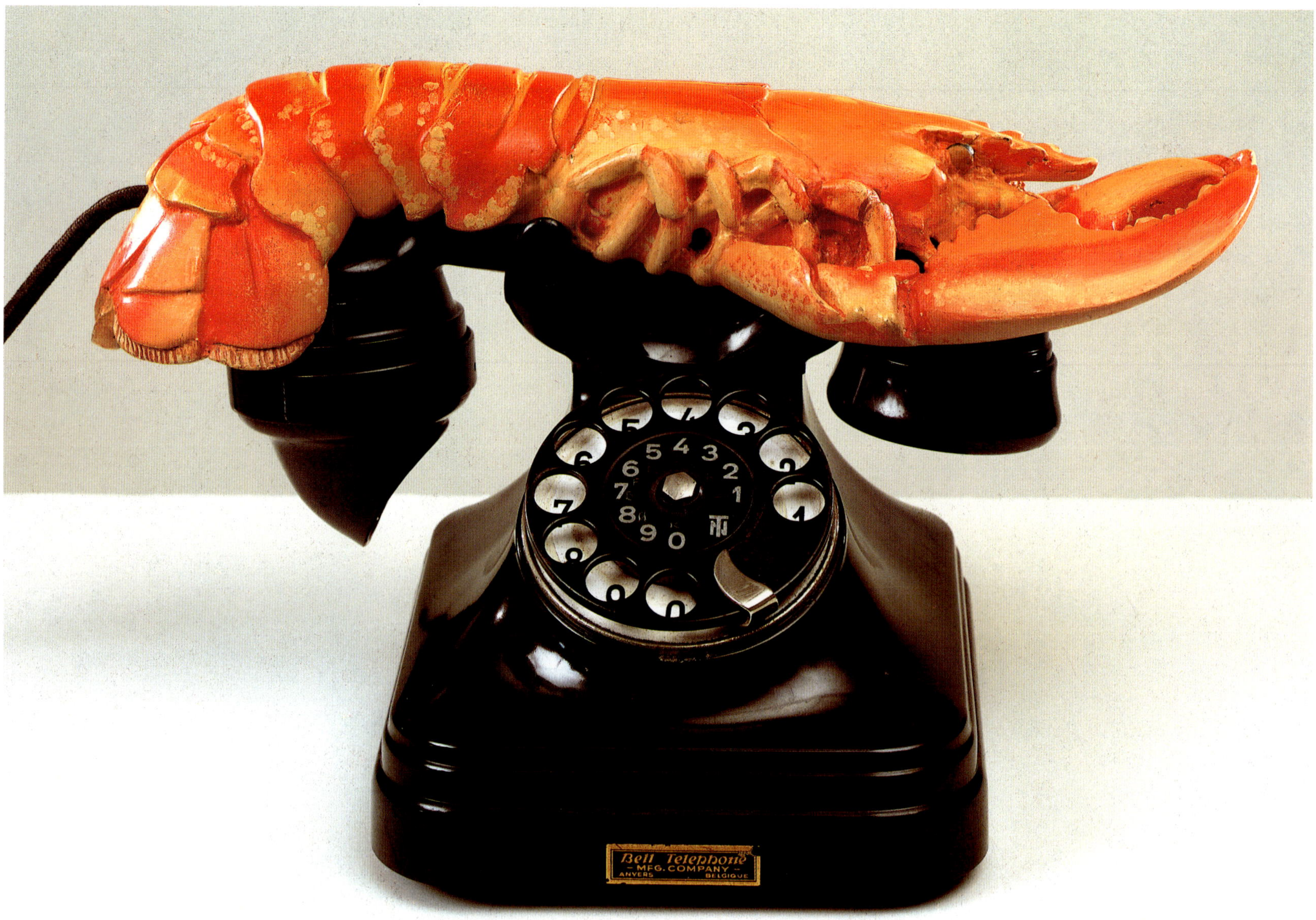

Lobster Telephone, *1936.*
Assemblage, 30 × 15 × 17 cm
Tate Gallery, London

liant artificial light and a jeweller's magnifying glass placed in one eye. A good number of the canvases produced at this time are extremely small – *The Persistence of Memory* (page 63) measures only 24.1 × 33 cm (9½ × 13 ins), for example – which allowed the painter to work over much of the image with the finest of sable brushes, while the canvas itself has a very minute tooth so as to allow Dalí to create a high degree of detail without breaking up the brushmarks. And Dalí was not only creating fine paintings at this time. In 1933 he made perhaps his best set of etchings, namely the designs to illustrate a new edition of *Les Chants de Maldoror* by Isidore Ducasse, Comte de Lautréamont, which was commissioned by the Swiss publisher Albert Skira. Moreover, during the early 1930s Dalí also began creating objects, such as those he displayed in a group exhibition of Surrealist objects held in 1933 at the Pierre Colle Gallery.

Dalí's first Surrealist objects had been created in answer to a loss of direction felt by the Surrealists in 1929, when André Breton had instituted a commission comprising Dalí and a young Marxist critic, in order to propose new paths for the movement to follow. Dalí had suggested the creation of Surrealist objects, and his idea was subsequently taken up enthusiastically by other members of the group. Throughout the 1930s Dalí made a great number of objects, perhaps the most famous being his *Lobster-Telephone* (see page 24) and his sofa in the shape of Mae West's lips. The latter object evolved as the natural offshoot of one of Dalí's most witty dual-image composites, the *Face of Mae West (Usable as a Surrealist Apartment)* of 1934–35 (page 75), in which the painter's inventiveness in creating visual puns reached new heights of genius.

In January 1933 another wealthy patron of the arts, the Prince Jean Louis de Faucigny-Lucinge, was induced by Gala to persuade eleven other rich collectors (including the Vicomte and Vicomtesse de Noailles and an artistically inclined, wealthy American widow, Caresse Crosby) to form a syndicate to be known as the 'Zodiac' group to support Dalí financially. Each member undertook to contribute the sum of 2,500 francs annually in exchange for the right to choose a large painting or a smaller picture and two drawings, the month in which the choices were to be made to be decided by lots drawn at a pre-Christmas dinner. This syndicate remained in existence until Dalí went to America in 1940.

Gala had divorced Paul Eluard in 1932, and at the end of January 1934 Dalí married her in a civil ceremony in Paris, with her ex-husband as one of the witnesses. (Dalí remarried her in a religious ceremony in Spain in 1958.) The year 1934 was a frantically busy one for the painter, for in it he held no less than six one-man shows: two in Paris, two in New York (one of them comprising the *Chants de Maldoror* etchings), one in London and one in Barcelona. Just before the Barcelona exhibition opened in October, Dalí travelled to Figueras with Gala and sought forgiveness from his father, which was finally forthcoming after the painter's uncle had pleaded on his behalf. Soon afterwards a political uprising in Barcelona forced the panic-stricken couple to make a headlong flight back to France by car (their driver was killed by a stray bullet on his return journey to Barcelona). This taste of the unsettled state of Spanish politics shook the very unworldly painter considerably and it profoundly coloured his attitude to later political events in Spain.

In November 1934 the Dalís sailed for the United States, where they stayed until mid-January. The first showing of Dalí's work in America had taken place in 1931, at a group exhibition held at the Wadsworth Atheneum in Hartford, Connecticut, and his first one-man show there had followed at Julien Levy's Gallery in the autumn of 1933. For Dalí's second one-man exhibition in New York in 1934, the painter overcame his fear of travel, and the trip to America was assisted financially by Picasso who had continued to take an interest in his unusually talented compatriot (whom he once described wittily as 'an outboard motor continually running'). Dalí's characteristically eccentric social ineptitude surfaced on this trip, for on the train out of Paris he sat surrounded by all his canvases with strings connecting them to himself lest they be stolen *en route*, and with his back to the engine so as to arrive sooner at his destination. On board ship Dalí wore a lifejacket continuously, although he remained balanced enough to prepare for his disembarkation in New York in a suitably provocative manner by getting the ship's baker to prepare a bread loaf over two metres long with which to face reporters, who untypically ignored the unusual object. But apart from that initial setback, Dalí found in America an ideal homeland for his exhibitionism, and at an ideal time. The Depression was in full swing by 1934, but of course it barely touched the rich who sought ever more elaborate ways of spending their money and more inventive diversions from the harsh realities around them. Despite his anti-bourgeois stance of some years earlier, Dalí – and perhaps even more so Gala – loved money, and from this time onwards a fundamental change of attitude began to come over the artist, one that would eventually lead to a change in the direction of his work.

Early in 1935 Dalí lectured in Hartford and at the Museum of Modern Art in New York, and it was during these talks that he made the much quoted claim: 'The only difference between a madman and myself is that I am *not* mad.' And before the Dalís sailed back to Europe, Caresse Crosby organized a farewell fancy-dress party, the 'Dream Betrayal Ball' ('Bal Onirique') at a fashionable New York restaurant. Dalí wore a pair of spotlit breasts supported by a brassière for this event, but for once the other participants appear to have outdone him in the surreality of their costumes. Indeed, Gala nearly caused a scandal because her headdress sported the effigy of a baby's corpse, possibly in an allusion to the kidnapped Lindbergh baby that had been murdered a few months earlier. Confronted by a reporter with this act of calculated offensiveness, the Dalís denied it, although later they privately confessed their intention.

In the summer of 1935 Dalí also published an important essay, 'The Conquest of the Irrational', in which he outlined his aesthetic:

My whole ambition in the pictorial domain is to materialize the images of concrete irrationality with the most imperialist fury of precision. – In order that the world of imagination and of concrete irrationality may be as objectively evident, of the same consistency, of the same durability, of the same persuasive, cognitive and communicable thickness as that of the exterior world of phenomenal reality. – The important thing is what one wishes to communicate: the concrete irrational subject. – The means of pictorial expression are placed at the service of this subject. – The illusionism of the most abjectly arriviste *and irresistible imitative art, the usual paralysing tricks of* trompe-l'oeil, *the most analytically narrative and discredited academicism, can all become sublime hierarchies of thought, and the means of approach to new exactitudes of concrete irrationality.*

Unfortunately, what Dalí overlooked in this cogent statement of aims was the possibility that the visual academicism would take over from any need to find something new to say.

In September 1935 Dalí had his last meeting with Lorca when the poet passed through Barcelona. The painter had written to Lorca suggesting that they should collaborate on an opera which would bring together Ludwig II of Bavaria and Leopold Sacher-Masoch, but the poet was evidently unresponsive. And although Lorca was overjoyed to see Dalí again – they had not met since 1927 – he was puzzled by the painter's marriage, for as he later told a friend, Dalí could never be sexually satisfied by any woman when he hated breasts and vulvas, was terrified of venereal disease, and was sexually impotent and anally obsessive.

On this trip to Spain Dalí was accompanied by an important English art collector, Edward James, who claimed descent from King Edward VII and who had built up a superb collection of Surrealist art after inheriting a fortune as a young man. Dalí had agreed to sell James his most important works, an agreement that would continue until 1939, by which time the collector had acquired over forty of Dalí's best pictures. In 1935 James also employed Dalí to redesign his house in Sussex in the Surrealist style, for which the painter suggested that the drawing-room should re-create the feel and appearance of the inside of a dog's stomach. The architect who supervised the project, Hugh Casson, worked out how to implement such a request but the outbreak of World War II meant that the project had to be shelved, although by that time several of Dalí's other, less ambitious proposals for the house had been carried out.

In the summer of 1936 Dalí visited London for the International Surrealist Exhibition at the New Burlington Galleries, where he also agreed to give a lecture and requested a friend, Lord Berners, to hire him a deep-sea diving suit in which to deliver the talk. When Berners telephoned a hire shop for such apparel he was asked 'to which depth does Mr Dalí wish to descend?', to which he replied 'To the depths of the subconscious'. He was then told that because of that requirement the suit would have to be fitted with a special helmet, instead of the normal one. But on this occasion Dalí's flamboyant exhibitionism nearly killed him, for he had forgotten to request some means of obtaining air in his outlandish garb, and as a result he almost suffocated before his companions on the lecture platform realized that something was amiss and freed him from the suit (the audience thought that it was calculated behaviour and enjoyed it immensely).

Shortly afterwards, in mid-July 1936, the Civil War broke out in Spain. Dalí had anticipated the conflict in the *Soft Construction with Boiled Beans – Premonition of Civil War* (page 79) completed just a few months earlier, and later that year he painted *Autumn Cannibalism* (page 81); in both works food figures significantly, perhaps as a realization of Dalí's stated thinking:

When a war breaks out, especially a civil war, it would be possible to foresee almost immediately which side will win and which side lose. Those who will win have an iron health from the beginning, and the others become more and more sick. The ones [who will win] can eat anything, and they always have magnificent digestions. The others, on the other hand, become deaf or covered with boils, get elephantiasis, and in short are unable to benefit from anything they eat.

Dalí's own response to the war was typically uncommitted, for again he fled Spain, although he was probably right to panic, for modernist artists such as himself – and especially those who had attacked the bourgeoisie and Catholicism, as he had done in *Un Chien andalou* and *L'Age d'or* – were not safe there. Thus, on 18 August 1936 Lorca was murdered by the fascists in Granada. When Dalí heard the news he tried to make light of it by saying 'Olé!', the response to a successful pass in bullfighting, but this was thrown back at him for the rest of his life. (Later he attempted to justify the glib remark by stating that he had uttered it in order to show how Lorca's 'destiny was fulfilled by tragic and typically Spanish success'.)

When he was in London in the summer of 1936, Dalí almost certainly visited the National Gallery and looked carefully at Andrea Mantegna's *Agony in the Garden*. Later he recreated the conjuction of cityscape and unusual rock formations seen in that work, in paintings such as *Sleep* (page 93) and *Swans reflecting Elephants* (page 95). And soon after the outbreak of the Spanish Civil War, Dalí visited Italy at the invitation of Edward James, who had rented a villa near Amalfi; from there he went on to stay with Lord Berners in Rome. It seems highly likely that on his way back to Paris (where he had settled after fleeing from Spain), Dalí stopped off in Arezzo and

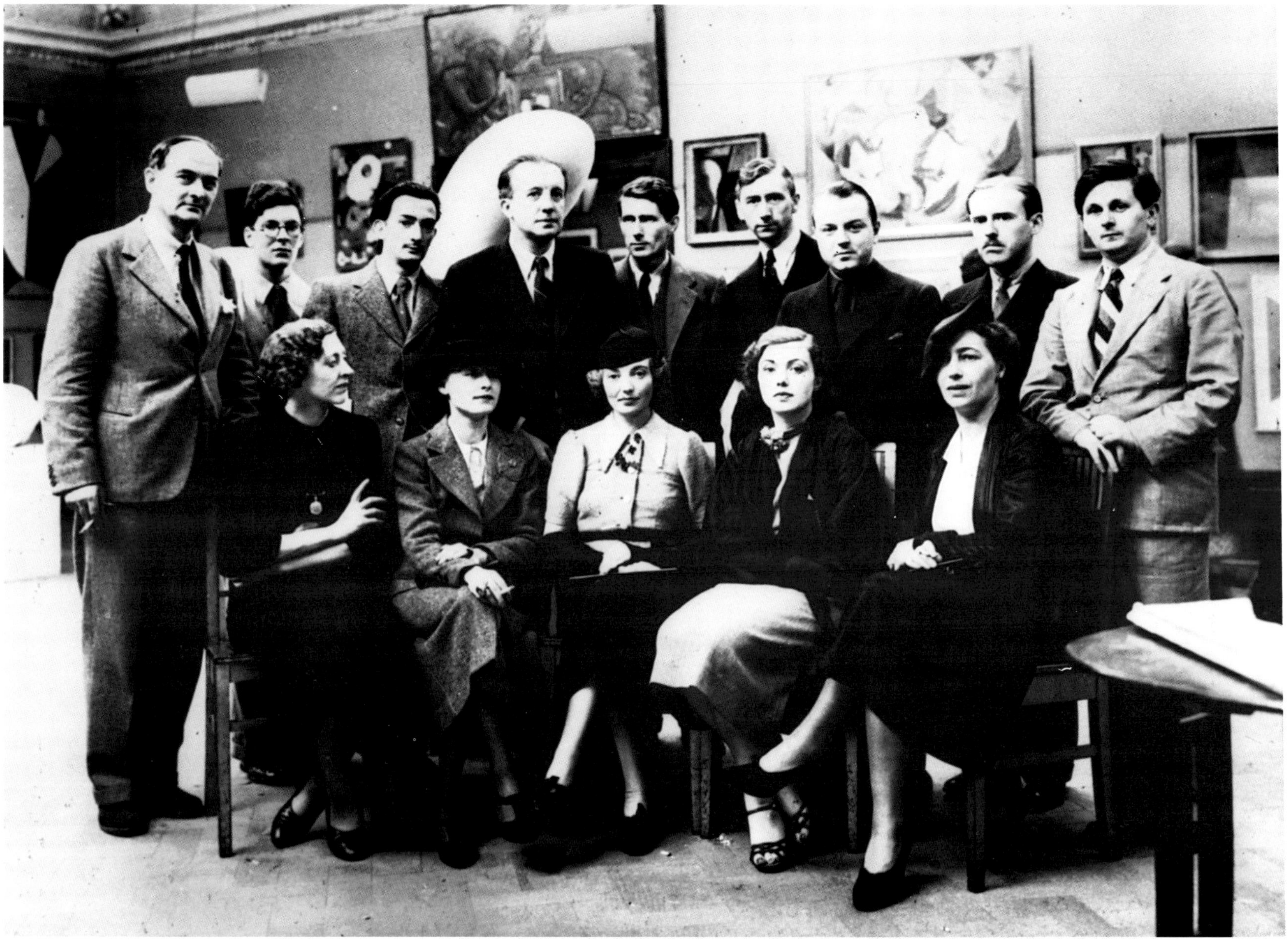

At the International Surrealist Exhibition in London, 1936. From left, back row: Rupert Lee, Ruthven Todd, Dalí, Paul Eluard, Roland Penrose, Herbert Read, E.L.T. Mesens, George Reavey, Hugh Sykes Davies. Front row: Diane Lee, Nusch Eluard, Eileen Agar, Sheila Legge, unidentified woman.

Florence to examine the works of Piero della Francesca, for he referred to them in print in 1937. The imagery of Piero's linked renderings of the Duke of Montefeltro and his wife in the Uffizi Museum, Florence, later conditioned the exact form of Dalí's 1945 portrait of Isabel Styler-Tas (page 117).

The Dalís visited America again in December 1936, and it was on this trip that the painter received that supreme accolade of American culture, namely an appearance on the cover of *Time* magazine (see Frontispiece). The compliment was certainly an indication of the fundamental harmlessness of his cultural subversion. That Christmas, Dalí sent the comedian Harpo Marx a harp strung with barbed wire which Harpo evidently appreciated, and subsequently the painter visited Hollywood to sketch out a scenario with the funnyman, a script entitled *Giraffes on Horseback Salad*, although this was never turned into a film.

In the same year Dalí also began designing dresses and hats for the leading couturier to the *haut monde*, Elsa Schiaparelli, who had worked with Picasso and Jean Cocteau amongst others. Dalí was his usual inventive self as a designer, creating hats in the shape of upturned shoes, imitation chocolate buttons covered in bees, a handbag in the guise of a telephone, and the like.

Early in 1938 Dalí took part in the International Exhibition of Surrealism held at the Beaux-Arts Gallery in Paris. For this he concocted perhaps his most elaborate object: the *Rainy Taxi*, a Paris taxicab whose roof was pierced so as to admit the rain and which contained a shop-window mannequin wearing a sordid cretonne print dress decorated with Millet's *Angelus*, over which two hundred live snails were freed to roam. And later that year Dalí visited Sigmund Freud in London, where he made a small pen-and-ink drawing on blotting-paper of the great Viennese psychoanalyst, a work that he later developed into some other fine portrait drawings. That autumn Dalí visited Monte Carlo to work with Coco Chanel, for whom he designed the ballet *Bacchanale* on behalf of the Ballets Russes de Monte Carlo. The painter called this entertainment 'the first paranoiac ballet based on the eternal myth of love in death', and in it he realized his intention, expressed to Lorca some years earlier, of creating a stage work around the persona of the mad King Ludwig of Bavaria, Richard Wagner's great patron. The ballet was choreographed by Léonide Massine and accompanied by Wagner's music, and it transferred to New York towards the end of 1939.

Dalí had revisited New York in February 1939 for a further exhibition at the Julien Levy Gallery, and it was on this occasion that he was engaged by the Bonwit Teller department store on Fifth Avenue to design window displays, earning nationwide notoriety in the process. What the store had expected of Dalí is not known but what it got was a window revealing an astrakhan-lined bathtub filled with water and complemented by a mannequin wearing only green feathers and a red wig, while another window displayed a black satin bed supporting a mannequin resting her head on a pillow of live coals, over which stretched a canopy created out of a buffalo's head, with a bloody pigeon stuffed in its mouth. Not surprisingly, pedestrians began complaining about this comely display as soon as it went on view early one morning and it was hastily altered by the Bonwit Teller management. When Dalí turned up to survey his work later in the day he was so enraged by the unauthorized changes that he overturned the bath through a plate-glass window, and for his pains found himself hauled into court by a passing policeman, charged with disorderly conduct. He received a suspended sentence, but the publicity much enhanced his reputation for eccentricity, and the ensuing Levy Gallery show was almost a sell-out, greatly boosting Dalí's prices in the process. Clearly, scandal paid.

Dalí stayed on in America that summer in order to create a work for the New York World Fair, his

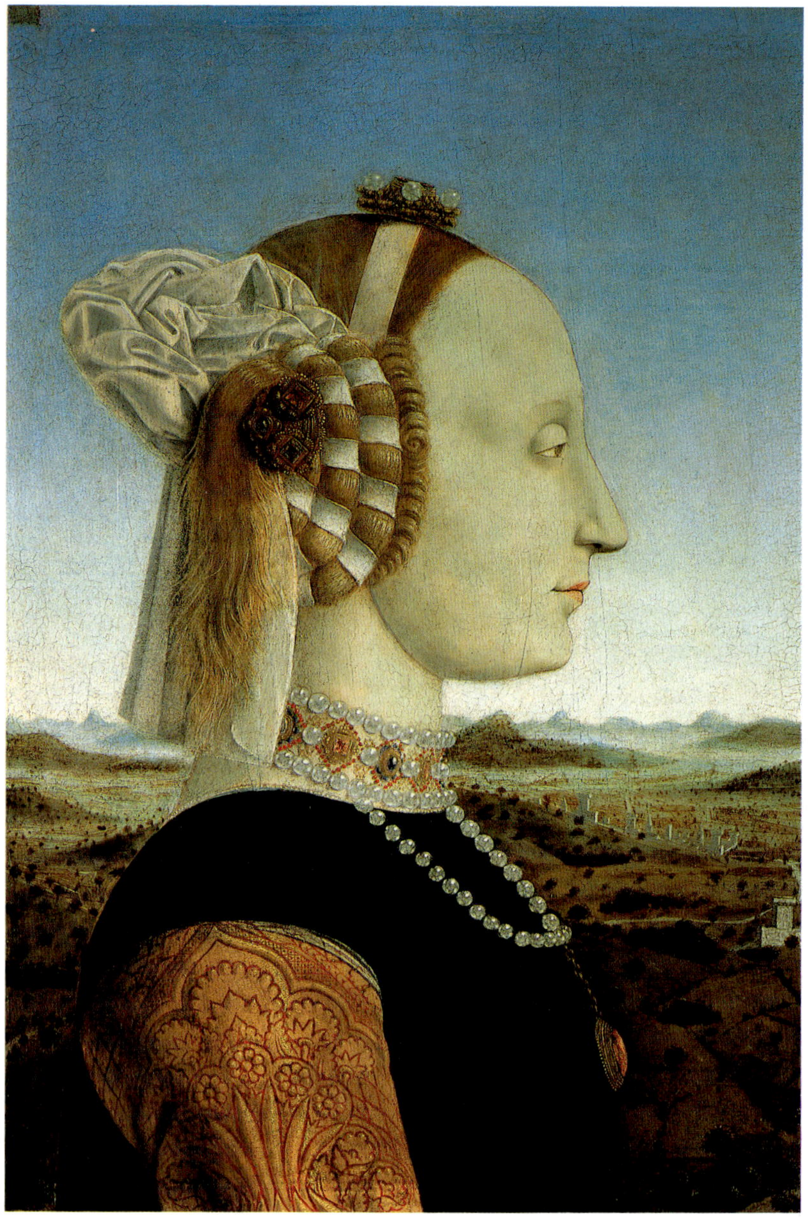

Portrait of Battista Sforza
By Piero della Francesca, c. *1460–72.*
Panel, 47 × 33 cm
Galleria degli Uffizi, Florence

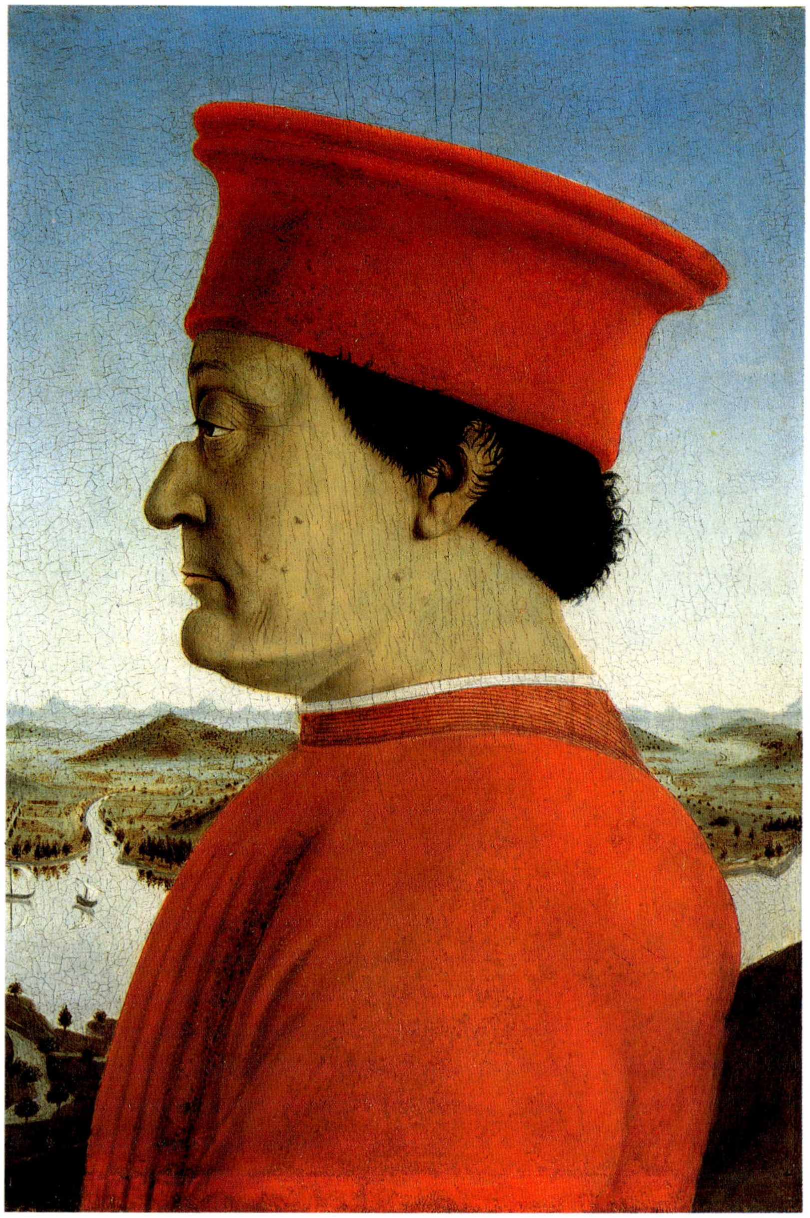

Portrait of Federico da Montefeltro
By Piero della Francesca, c. *1460–72.*
Panel, 47 × 33 cm
Galleria degli Uffizi, Florence

Dream of Venus; it was unrealized, due to disagreements between Dalí and the World Fair management. But soon after he returned to France World War II broke out and the painter vacated Paris, eventually to settle in Arcachon, in the south-west of France, a locale he chose for its good restaurants. Following the fall of France in June 1940 the Dalís returned via Spain and Portugal to the United States, where they arrived on 16 August 1940 and where they sat out the rest of the war.

Salvador Dalí's move to America in 1940 marked a watershed in his career, for his artistic achievements before that date were far richer than they ever were to be after it. Until then the painter had genuinely and inventively grappled with his innermost responses to the world, and produced his greatest masterworks in the process. Moreover, his occasionally madcap antics seemed the natural offshoot of those responses, especially where a genuinely Surrealist subversion of accepted standards of 'civilized' behaviour was concerned. But after 1940, and especially because of the need to make money once the financial support of the Zodiac group had disappeared, Dalí the showman took over, which was not difficult given his love of publicity. After the end of the war a newfound interest in scientific, religious and historical subject matter meant that the authenticity of Dalí's exploration of the subconscious began to drain away, to be replaced by something far more calculated in effect. Moreover, after 1940 a new banality often entered into Dalí's work, as his imagery was made to bear a more rationally comprehensible load and a more directly symbolic meaning. Of course there is nothing innately invalid about Dalí's enthusiasm for scientific, religious and historical subject matter; the painter had as much right to pursue such interests as anyone else. But the question arises as to whether those concerns led to any creative enhancement of Dalí's imagery and its development into new areas of aesthetic experience, and for the most part the answer has to be a negative one, for too often Dalí's later quasi-scientific, religious and historical pictures lack any innovatory aesthetic dimension, and thus seem merely illustrative. And sadly, financial greed – in which Gala played a major part – would also determine much of Dalí's artistic sense of direction after 1940, eventually making the painter into the willing accomplice to one of the biggest and most prolonged acts of financial fraud ever perpetrated in the history of Western art.

Once safely across the Atlantic in 1940, the Dalís at first settled with Caresse Crosby in Hampton, Virginia, where they lived for a year, virtually taking over the widow's mansion and holding court there in the process. Later they went westwards and settled in Monterey, south of San Francisco. In 1941 Dalí produced his first volume of autobiography, *The Secret Life of Salvador Dalí*, a work in which he greatly furthered the myths about himself as a madman who was not mad. This book was later analysed by George Orwell in one of his most brilliant essays, 'Benefit of Clergy' (1944), in which he took at face value the Dalinian myth but argued that 'One ought to be able to hold in one's head simultaneously the two facts that Dalí is a good draughtsman and a disgusting human being.' He also questioned the right of an artist like Dalí to claim exemption from the normal moral constraints of mankind (hence the title of the essay).

The American years were busy ones, with Dalí living the high life and building upon his realization that at a time in which a booming war economy was bringing into being a new moneyed class in the country, people who had never before had the time, money or inclination to purchase works of art now began to buy it on a massive scale, and often in order to boost their social status. To reach out to such a new economic force, Dalí optimized the value of self-publicity, becoming in the process the darling of that section of the American *haut monde* who wanted the delicious thrill of dallying with danger, although of course he presented no real threat to them at all, and would do so less and less as time went by.

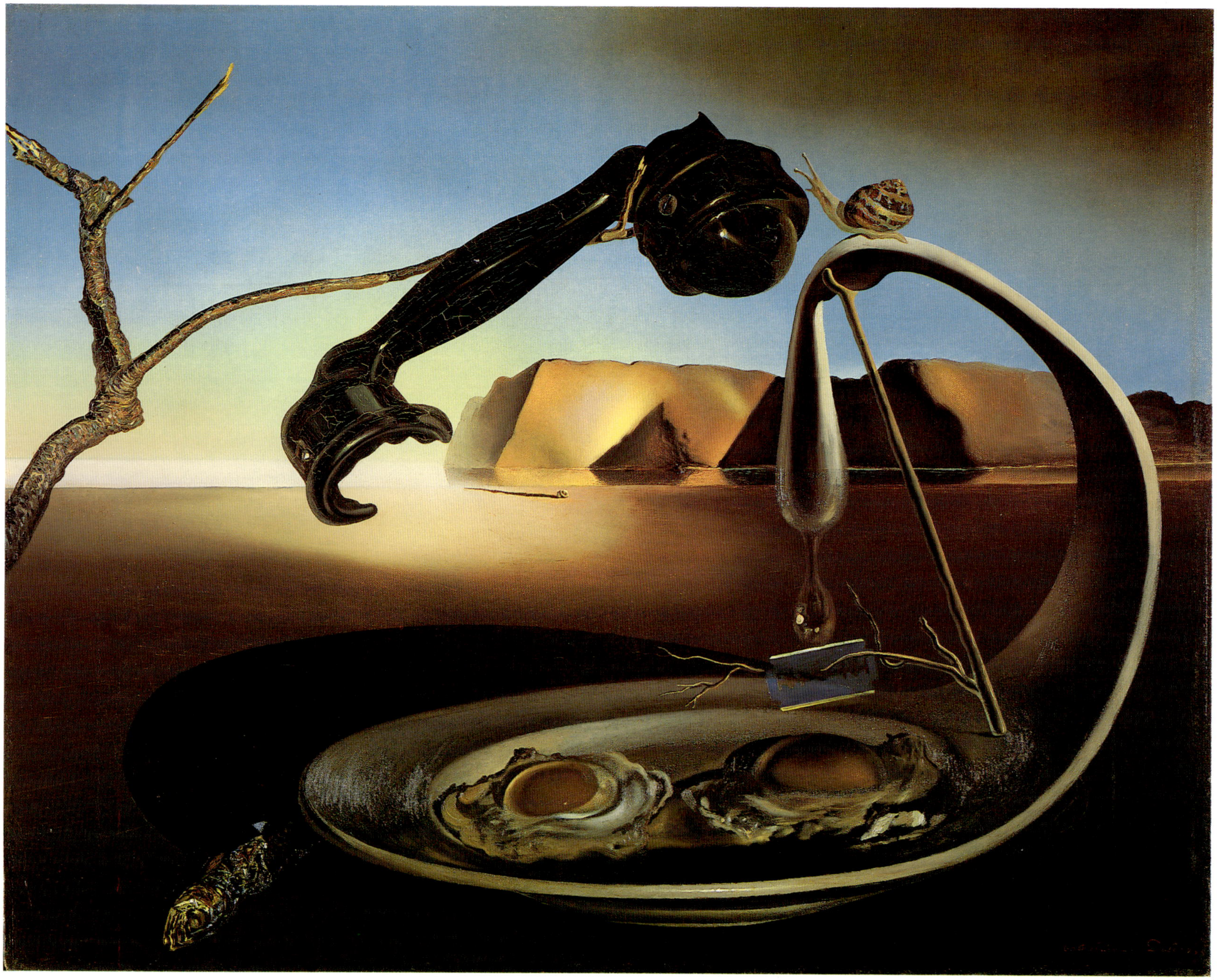

The Sublime Moment, *1938.*
Oil on canvas, 38 × 47 cm
Staatsgalerie, Stuttgart

In these years Dalí painted society portraits, holding an exhibition of such pictures in New York in 1943; he designed a charity dinner to raise money for wartime refugees, for which event he had 5,000 jute sacks suspended above the banquet to create a sense of suffocation, in the process re-creating in the USA an environmental sculpture that had originally been created by Marcel Duchamp for the 1938 Paris Surrealist exhibition; he designed an apartment for Helena Rubinstein, as well as painting her portrait (page 111); he wrote a novel entitled *Hidden Faces*, published in 1944; he created ballets; he began publishing his own self-promotional newspaper, *Dalí News*, which ran to only two issues; and in 1945 he went to Hollywood to work with Alfred Hitchcock on the dream sequence of his film *Spellbound*. Hitchcock wanted a Dalinian type of sharply focused surreal imagery because he apprehended that dreams and nightmares are often not visually vague affairs but quite the contrary. Dalí duly provided some very resonant images indeed, including a sequence of painted eyes being cut open by scissors that clearly stemmed from the eye-cutting sequence in *Un Chien andalou*. And in 1946 Dalí and Walt Disney collaborated on a short animated sequence intended to form part of a full-length film called *Destino*, although this was never developed further.

In 1948 the Dalís at last returned to Europe. Thereafter they regularly spent part of each winter in New York and the rest of the year in Paris and Port Lligat. By this time André Breton had expelled Dalí from the Surrealist movement, thus bringing to a conclusion his long-lived dissatisfaction with the artist. Earlier, in 1934, Breton had been enraged by Dalí's portrayal of Lenin in *The Enigma of William Tell* (page 69), and had attempted to attack the painting physically but failed. Equally he had been disgusted at Dalí's lack of enthusiasm for Marxism, and by his professed admiration for Hitler, a response that seems to have been motivated more by the painter's desire to offend Breton than by any genuine liking for the dictator. As a consequence of all these provocations, Breton had put Dalí 'on trial' in his Paris studio in February 1934. The event was very surrealistic, with Dalí running a temperature because of 'flu, and sucking on a thermometer that made his dialogue with Breton and his fellow jurors even more incomprehensible than usual. Eventually Breton had allowed Dalí to remain in the group. But by 1948 Dalí's avidity for money – which led Breton to coin his memorable anagram of the painter's name, 'Avida Dollars' – as well as his professed and by now genuine sympathy for another fascist dictator, General Franco, necessitated his expulsion from the Surrealist movement, although Dalí appears to have lost no sleep over it.

In many ways Breton's expulsion of Dalí from the Surrealist movement was understandable, for by the mid-1940s the painter had ceased to explore the subconscious and the irrational to the degree that he had done in the 1930s. Although the artist continued to project his fantasies, fantasy is not the same as surrealism, for it merely embroiders reality, whereas surrealism essentially works against the grain of rationalism. But after the mid-1940s Dalí's art was frequently supportive of rationally comprehensible experience, despite being couched in an imagery that might look unreal at first glance. Thus, in a picture like *The Temptation of Saint Anthony* of 1946 (page 119), the imagery does not project Dalí's psychological responses but instead simply gives us the hallucinatory vision of the saint who is portrayed at the bottom left – in other words, the unreal imagery serves a merely illustrative function. Similarly, in one of Dalí's most popular pictures of the post-war years, the *Christ of St John of the Cross* of 1951 (page 125), the cross and figure floating above the landscape serve to project the floating, mystical state of the martyr, another explicable apprehension. And in a work like *The Last Supper* of 1955 (page 131) we are but one remove from a still in a Hollywood epic, with overlaid imagery that is identical in effect to that obtained by a multi-exposure photograph. Here there is little displacement of reality, and the imagery projects a very transparent religious symbolism, with

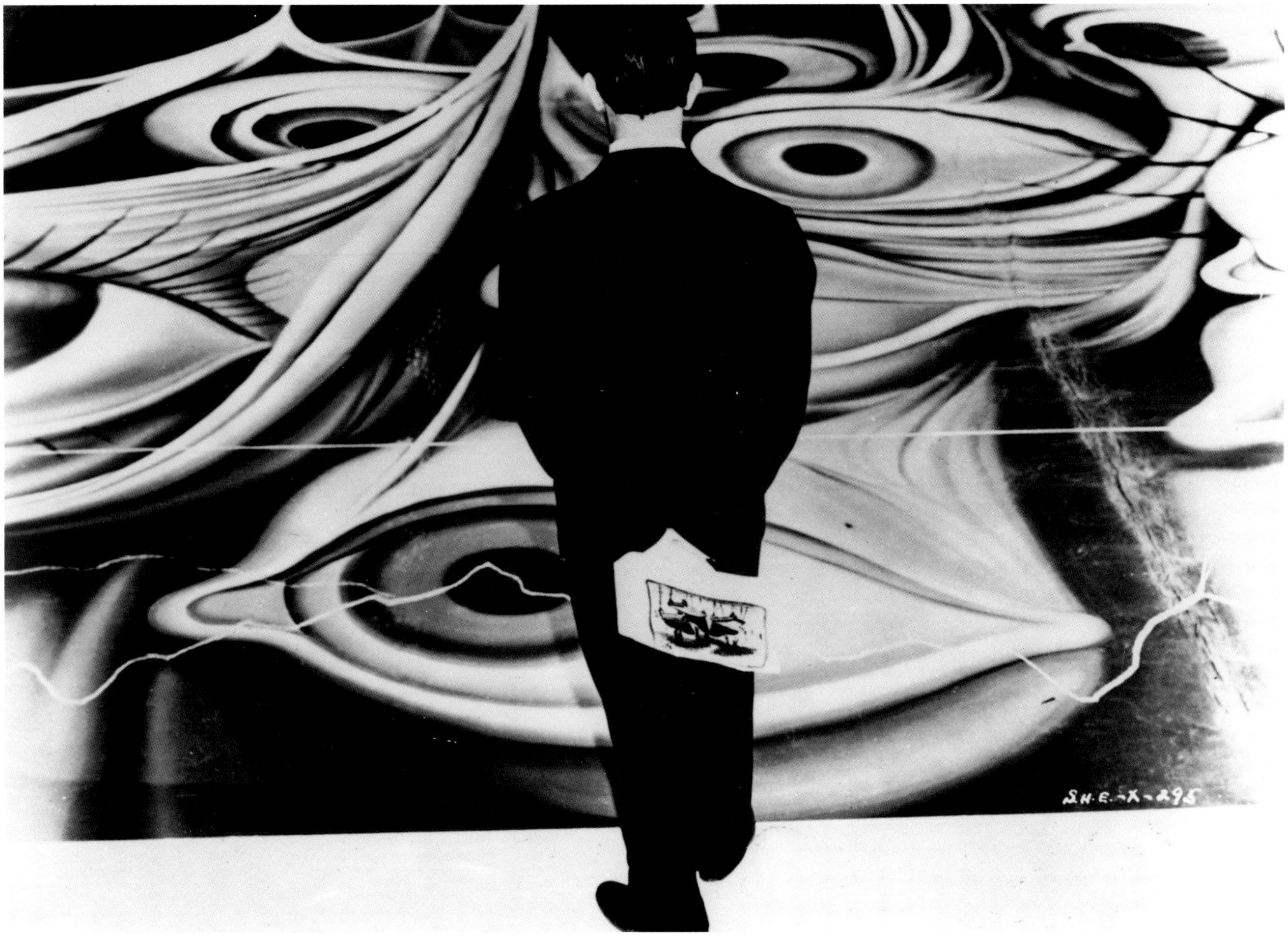

Dalí standing before one of his sets for Alfred Hitchcock's Spellbound, *1945.*

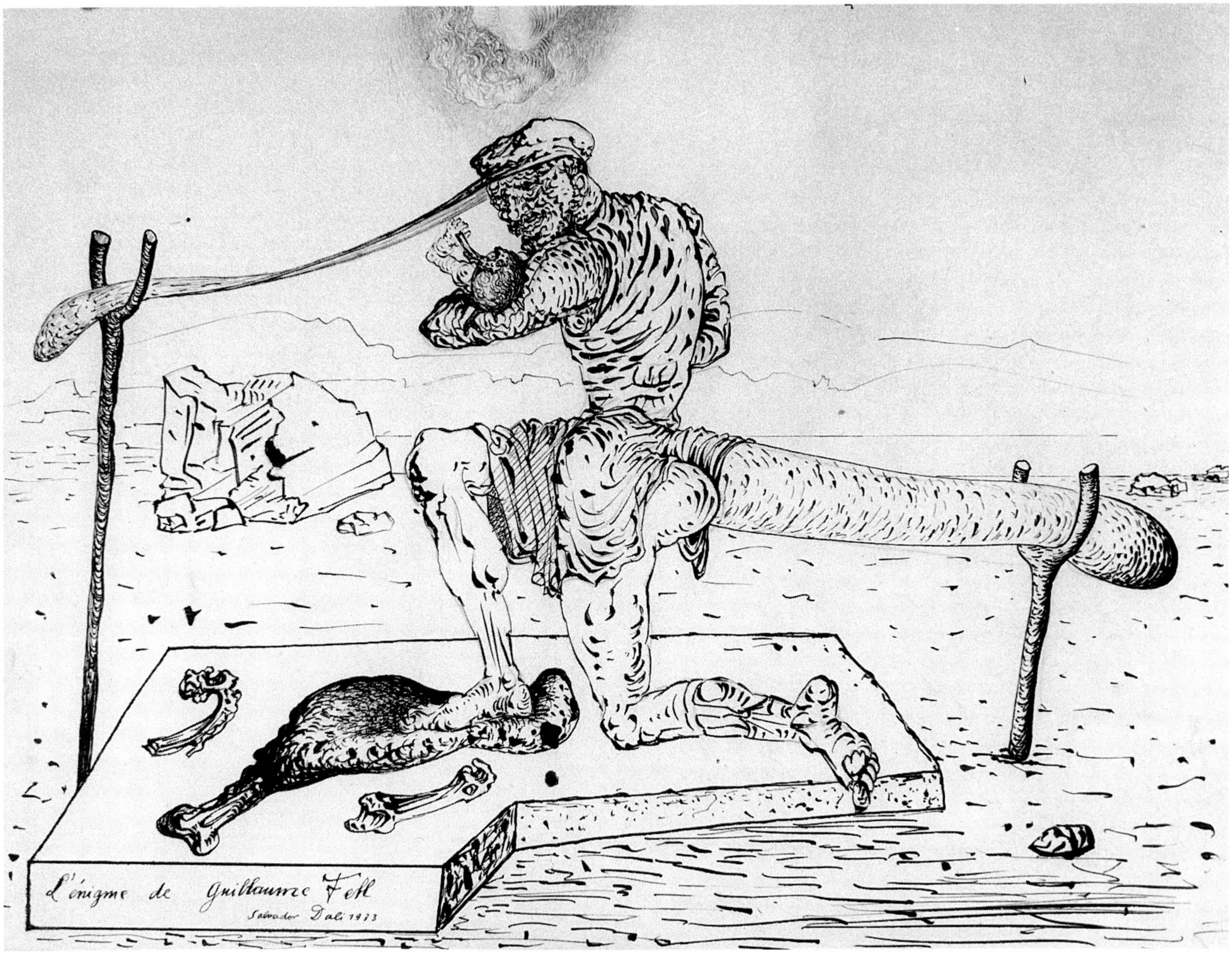

Study for 'The Enigma of William Tell', *1933.*
Ink and pencil drawing, 17.1 × 22.2 cm
Salvador Dalí Museum, St Petersburg, Florida, USA

its alignment of the bread and wine before Christ with the substance of His flesh above, to which He points with three raised digits, thus alluding to the Trinity.

In the late 1940s, and as a direct result of the growth of atomic physics in that decade, Dalí became intrigued by the latest scientific developments, stating that whereas Freud's theories had provided the intellectual basis for his earlier art, now those of the physicist Werner Heisenberg would do so. Dalí appreciated the massive progress of science in our time but also lamented the gap that had widened between our knowledge of the physical world and our appreciation of the metaphysical sphere, that which exists beyond the purely physical realm. Dalí was increasingly preoccupied by reconciling the two as he attempted to create a metaphysical system through what he called 'nuclear mysticism'. Unfortunately, however, this 'mysticism' did not necessarily provide the painter with an imagery that goes very far beyond physical appearances; instead, such imagery usually just looks rather like science-fiction illustration, albeit with a quasi-mystical bias. Moreover, after the 1950s Dalí frequently incorporated into his oeuvre different styles and techniques of painting, such as abstract expressionism in the late 1950s, optical art in the 1960s, and pointillism in the 1970s. He also experimented with new means of creating images such as stereoscopy, holography and digitalization in the 1960s and 1970s. These explorations and assimilations certainly demonstrated Dalí's acute technical adventurousness, but again they did not advance his art much in terms of its content – too frequently we see old and by now somewhat stale wine served up in new bottles.

Yet while Dalí increasingly demonstrated his technical adventurousness after the 1940s, paradoxically on a human level he moved away from the radicalism of thought and social stance that had characterized his art and behaviour in the 1930s. One milestone of that change in terms of social acceptance was the audience Dalí received in November 1949 from Pope Pius XII, an occasion on which the painter sought the blessing of the Pope for the smaller of his two versions of *The Madonna of Port Lligat* (page 123). What the Pope made of the picture is not recorded, but had he known he would surely have been shocked by the fact that Dalí did not just use Gala as a model for such religious paintings: the artist genuinely thought her divine. Such an elevation was somewhat ironic, given that Gala's highly promiscuous sexual behaviour differentiated her in every way from the supposed 'Mother of God': both in America and in Europe from the 1940s onwards, she compensated for Dalí's sexual inadequacies by maintaining a constant succession of young lovers. Ironically, one of them enjoyed 'divine' associations, for Jeff Fenholt, whom Gala acquired as a lover in the late 1960s, starred as Jesus Christ Superstar in the Broadway musical of the same name.

Nor was the Pope the only one of Dalí's new-found cultural heroes. Over the years the painter identified ever more closely with the fascist dictator General Franco, who in 1964 conferred a high civil order on him, the Cross of Isobel the Catholic. In 1974 Dalí painted a portrait of Franco's granddaughter, and the following year he sent the dictator a telegram congratulating him on executing several Basque secessionists, an act of support that caused an uproar in Spain. Dalí then poured fuel on the flames by publicly regretting that Franco had not executed more such 'terrorists'. Clearly the painter had come a long way from the irreligious, anti-social and anti-bourgeois Surrealist of the 1930s.

Throughout the 1950s and increasingly thereafter the Dalí commercial bandwagon rolled on, with the painter burnishing his reputation for eccentricity by referring to himself constantly as 'the Divine Dalí', and taking every opportunity to capitalize upon the penchant of the mass media for sensationalism. In this respect, after about 1945 Dalí was a trendsetter in his comprehension of the way that the spread of the mass media in the postwar world was changing social expectations of what an artist should be, and how he could meet and build upon those expectations commercially by striking a sensationalist pose. As a consequence of all this, by the mid-1960s the painter was at the centre of a commercial operation that was unprecedented in the history of Western art. He had acquired a manager, Peter Moore, who looked after his affairs between 1962 and 1976, and who eventually boasted that when he began working for Dalí the painter could only expect $1000 for one of his canvases, whereas by the time he left Dalí's employ his prices were in the half-a-million-dollar range. Moore himself made millions out of the commission he received from merchandizing every aspect of Dalí, from Dalí ashtrays to Dalí perfumes, and one can readily believe his claim that he had exhausted the yellow pages telephone directory finding products that he could link to Dalí. Moore was subsequently followed in the same role by Enrique Sabater and by Robert Descharnes.

The lifestyle of the Dalís obviously required vast sums of money. In New York they habitually stayed at the St Regis Hotel, in Paris at the Meurice, and they always tipped lavishly. Gala like to gamble on a big scale, and this too added to the need for income. Faced with these pressures, at some time in the mid-1960s Dalí became party to a massive fraud perpetrated on print collectors.

Normally, prints are produced in limited and numbered editions, with the signature of the artist that authenticates them added only *after* they have been printed. Once the printing is completed the printing plates are destroyed in order to maintain the limited nature of the printing, and thus the price of each print, the smaller the number of prints in each edition the greater being their resale market value. Until the mid-1960s Dalí had respected those conventions but after that date he began signing blank sheets of printing paper – the numbers have been estimated at somewhere between 40,000 and 350,000 sheets – and these were then later printed with worthless reproductions of the artist's paintings and sold as genuine prints issuing from Dalí's own hand. Moreover, it did not prove difficult to forge the painter's signature, and of course many bogus prints bearing mere printed reproductions of Dalí's signature were also sold by unscrupulous dealers. But as a result of this exploitative and/or lackadaisical attitude, the Dalí print trade is in chaos and many thousands of people have been conned into buying worthless prints. It might be argued that in debasing commercial values like this Dalí was striking a blow against the rampant commercialism of the art market, but of course the painter was the first to profit from such exploitation, and any such justifications therefore seem very hollow. Moreover, it was not only Dalí's prints that were faked. The painter also increasingly allowed his studio assistants to move from the permissible activity of filling in parts of his works, to painting entire pictures on his behalf, works that eventually he signed and authenticated as having come wholly from his own hand. For this reason, many of the paintings created in the 1980s must equally be considered very suspect.

In 1970 Dalí announced the creation of a Dalí Museum in Figueras, and in September 1974 the Teatro Museo Dalí was inaugurated. Another major foundation for the display of Dalí's works also opened to the public in these years, for in 1971 Reynolds and Eleanor Morse, American collectors who had, since they started buying in the early 1940s, built up the best private holding of Dalí's works anywhere, transferred their collection from their home town, Cleveland, Ohio, to a new museum in St Petersburg, Florida.

Further public honours came Dalí's way in the remaining years of his life. In 1972 he was elected a Foreign Associate Member of the Academy of Fine Arts of the Institut de France, while in 1982 he was presented with the Medal of Gold by the Generalidat of Catalonia and created Marquis de Pubol by the

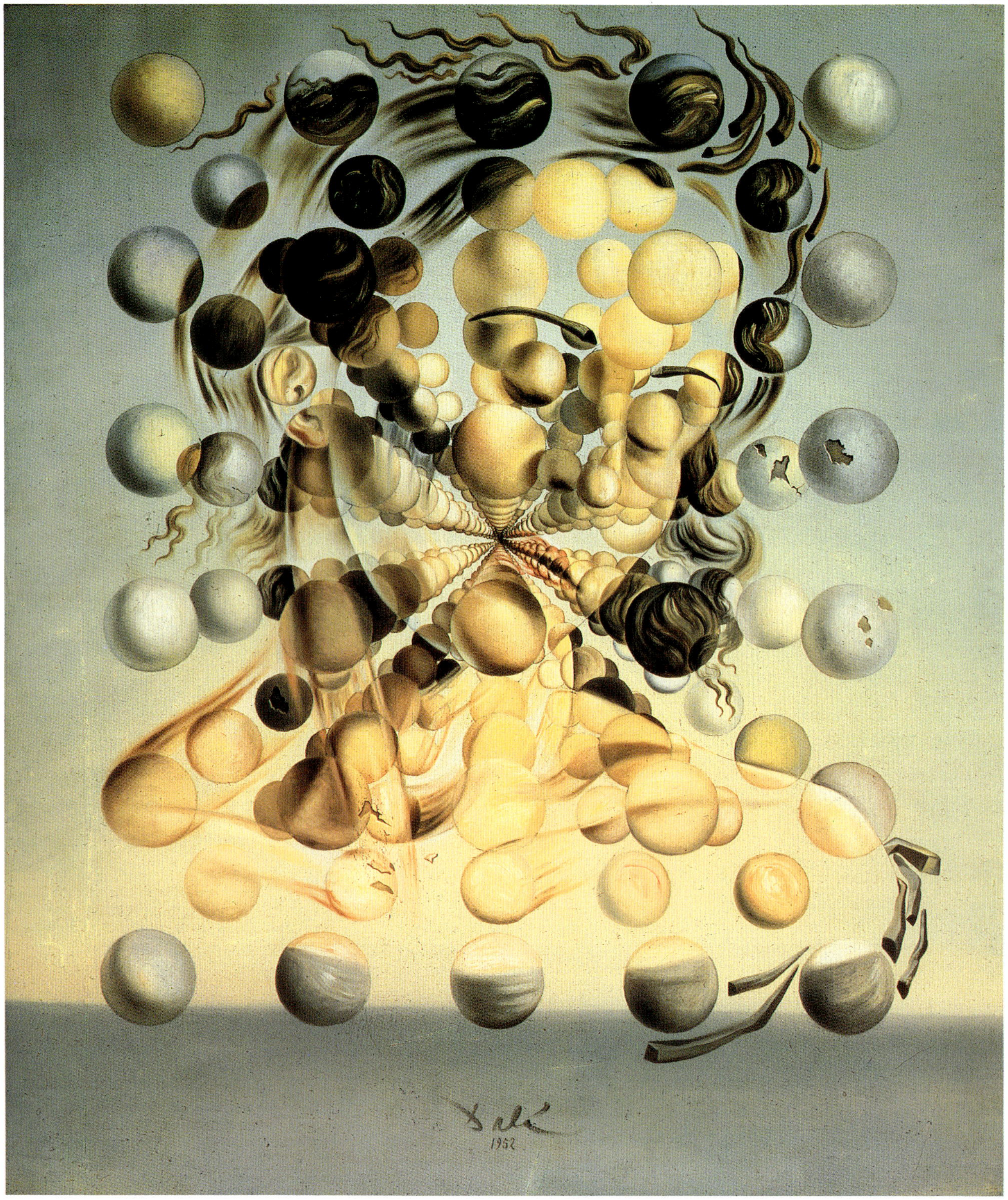

Galatea of the Spheres, *1952.*
Oil on canvas, 65 × 54 cm
Teatro-Museo Dalí, Figueras

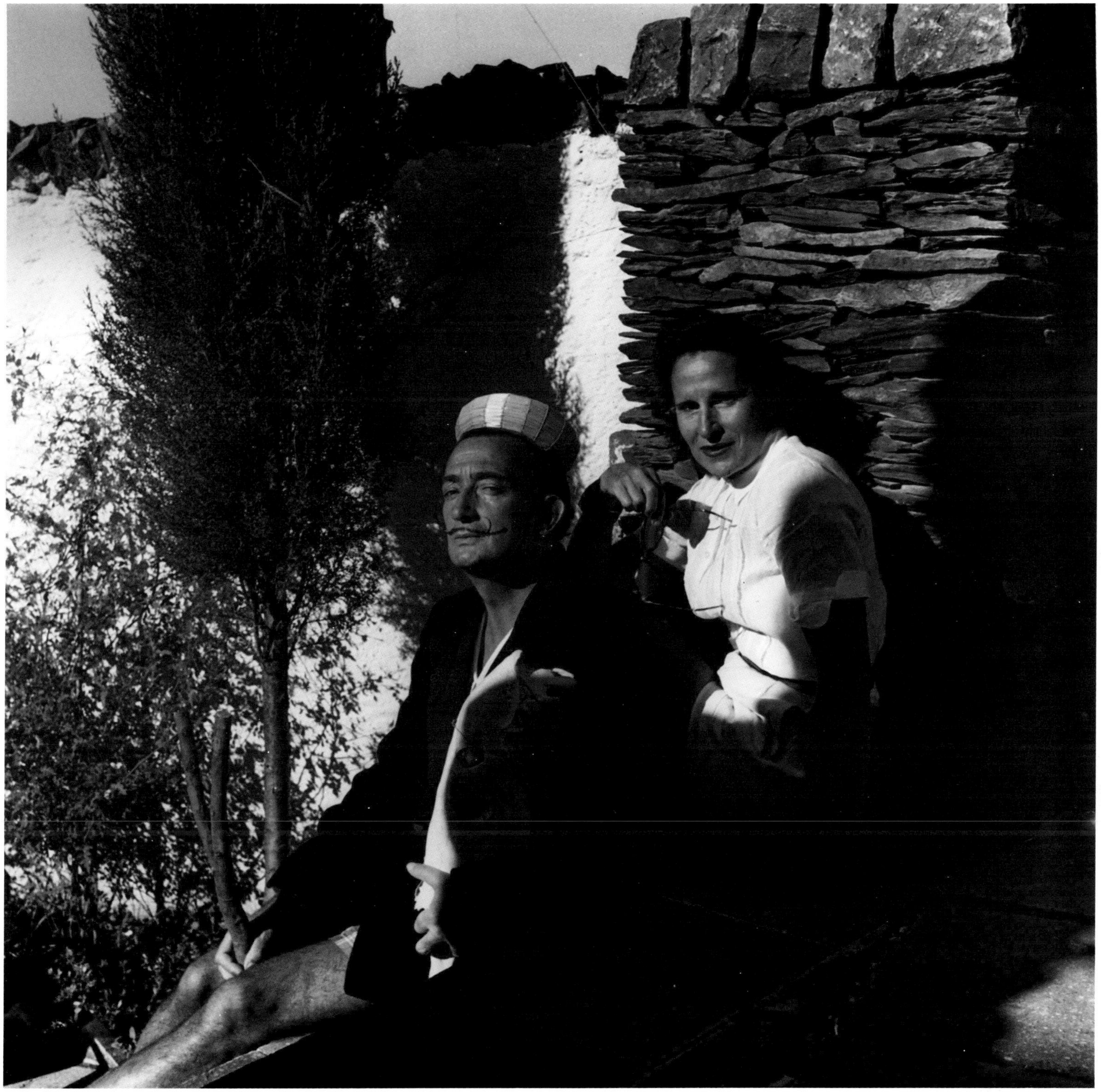

Salvador and Gala Dalí at Port Lligat, 1951.

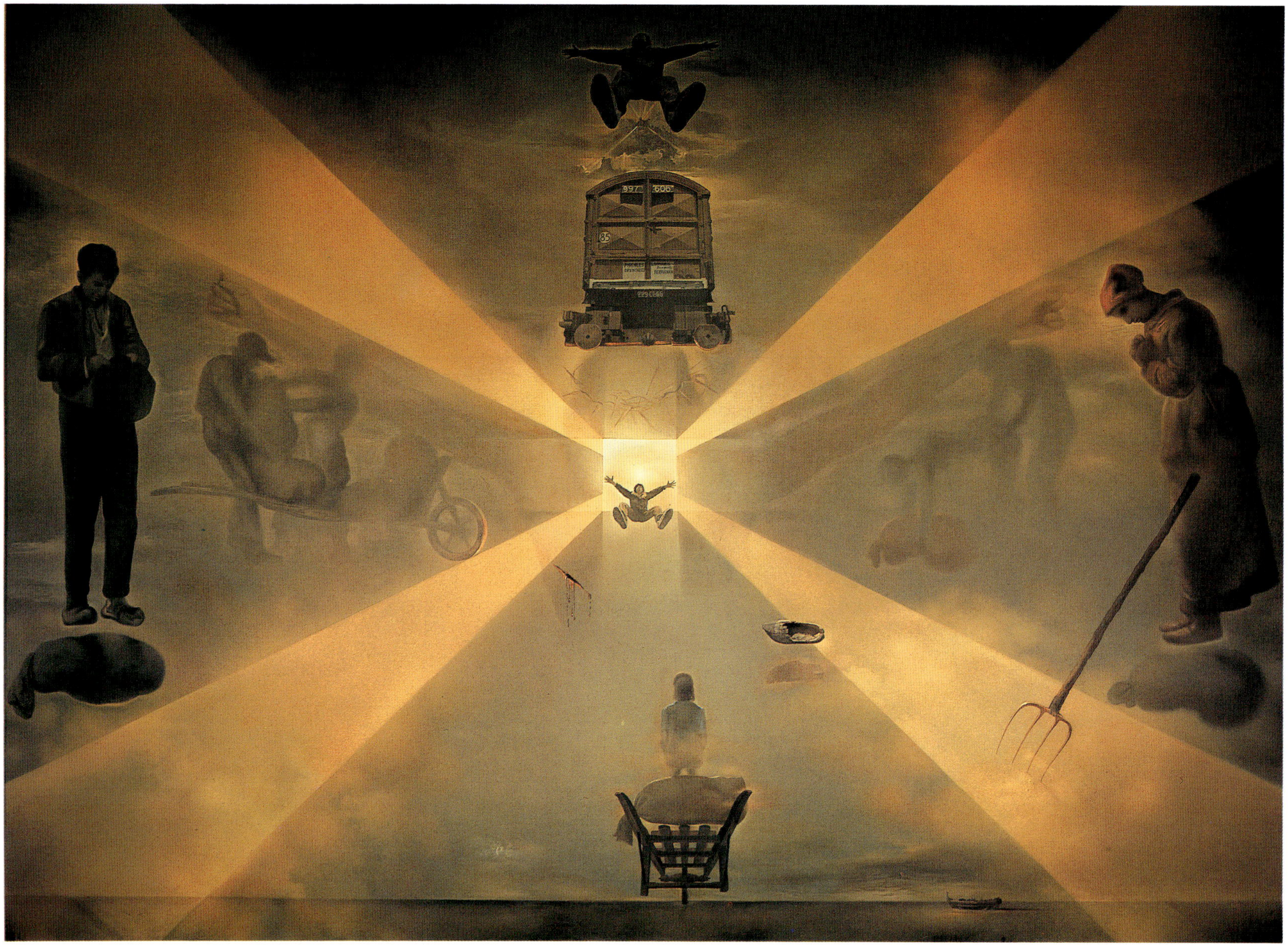

Perpignan Railway Station, *1965.*
Oil on canvas, 295 × 411 cm
Museum Ludwig, Cologne

King of Spain. Large exhibitions of his work were also held, such as the retrospective held at the Centre Georges Pompidou in Paris in 1979 (which later moved to London), and the similar survey mounted at the Museo Español de Arte Contemporáneo in Madrid in 1983. But on a personal level these were sad years for Dalí. He suffered from medical complaints that were sometimes diagnosed as Parkinson's Disease, although he does not appear to have had that illness, and he was terrified of death. He was also increasingly isolated emotionally, for despite the fact that he was surrounded by acolytes, his relationship with Gala finally broke up as she ensconced herself in the castle in Pubol, near Figueras, that he had bought for her. Here she maintained a succession of young lovers well into her eighties but refused Dalí admission unless he had written permission to visit her. Yet she continued to form the centre of the painter's emotional universe, and not surprisingly, after she died in Pubol on 10 June 1982, he disintegrated psychologically. On 30 August 1984 he was seriously injured by a fire while asleep, and it later emerged that as well as suffering from burns he was also seriously malnourished, despite having been surrounded by medical attendants, for he had simply refused to eat, suffering from the delusion that he was being poisoned. When he was finally discharged from hospital he looked a very tragic sight indeed.

Salvador Dalí died on 23 January 1989 in Figueras. For six decades after 1930 he had been a major public figure, and for at least the first of those decades he had certainly been in the forefront of the modernist experiment, creating works that have not lost their power to intrigue and disturb us. If in the final analysis much of his later output was of a lesser creative and imaginative standard, it has still proven unusually attractive to a public avid for visual meaning and stimulation, and overall his paintings have never lost their ability to engage the eye, if only because of their immense technical proficiency. For that alone, Dalí's work will stand out from much contemporary art, which may be more advanced intellectually but which all too frequently has been shoddily crafted and done little to excite the eye. But in his finest pictures and objects Dalí certainly made a major contribution to twentieth-century art, as he reached down to the depths of the subconscious in new and revealing ways. Not for nothing did he require that diving suit in 1936.

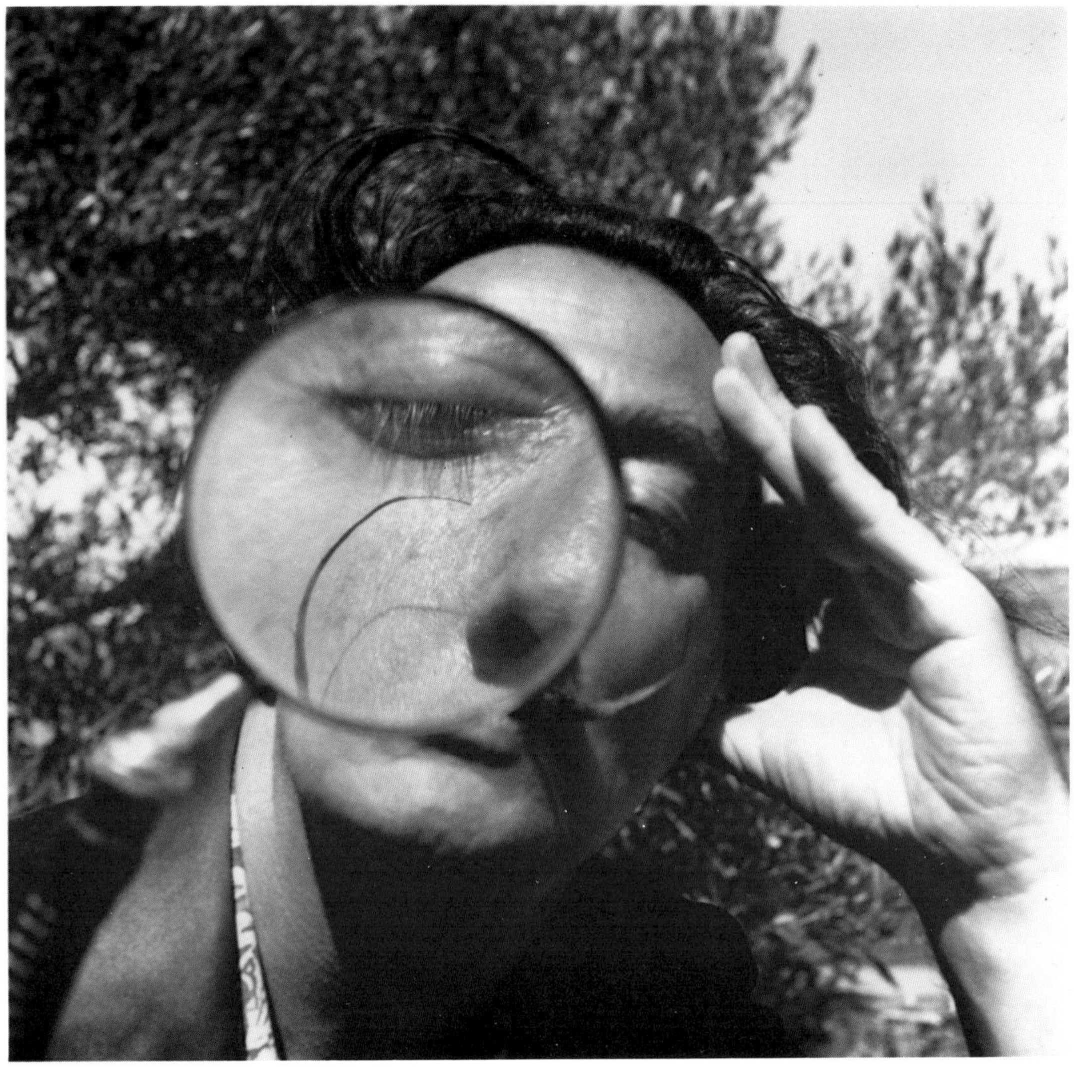

1904–1989

Dalí

THE PLATES

Apparatus and Hand

Painted 1927
62.2 × 46.3 cm
Salvador Dalí Museum, St Petersburg, Florida

This oil painting on panel was exhibited at the 1927 Autumn Salon in Barcelona, from which it was bought by Camille Goemans, who would later become Dalí's dealer in Paris.

The picture enjoys a very pronounced stylistic similarity to works by the French painter Yves Tanguy, such as the painting *He Did What He Wanted* of 1927, now in a private collection in New York. Most particularly, the likeness may be detected in the triangular shapes of the central 'Apparatus and Hand', in the placing of the 'Apparatus' in an illusionistic space, and in the location of further objects, such as the formation of birds, in the sky. Similarly, one can also detect here the influence of Giorgio de Chirico, in the use of shadows to add to the illusions of brilliant lighting and depth, in the pronounced perspective of the rectangular, platform-like area in the foreground, in the cubistic dislocations of the nude on the right, and in the objects placed around her.

Yet there are also purely Dalinian inputs here as well, such as the mountains, rock-arch and clouds on the right; the manic quality of the hand and its surrounding shapes; and most particularly, the red nude, and further, transparent and therefore liquid-looking nudes emanating from the 'Apparatus'. Given Dalí's predilection for masturbation by the mid-1920s, in this painting he may very well have been dealing with masturbatory fantasies, the expulsion of bodily fluids, and the determining role of hands in such processes.

Naturally, it would prove easy to go beyond this elementary identification and interpretation of the visual data, and attempt to use that information to analyse Dalí himself in pseudo-Freudian terms. Yet such speculation would be wrong, as well as probably missing its target, for it would obviate the more important need of the viewer to interpret the imagery in terms of his or her own experience.

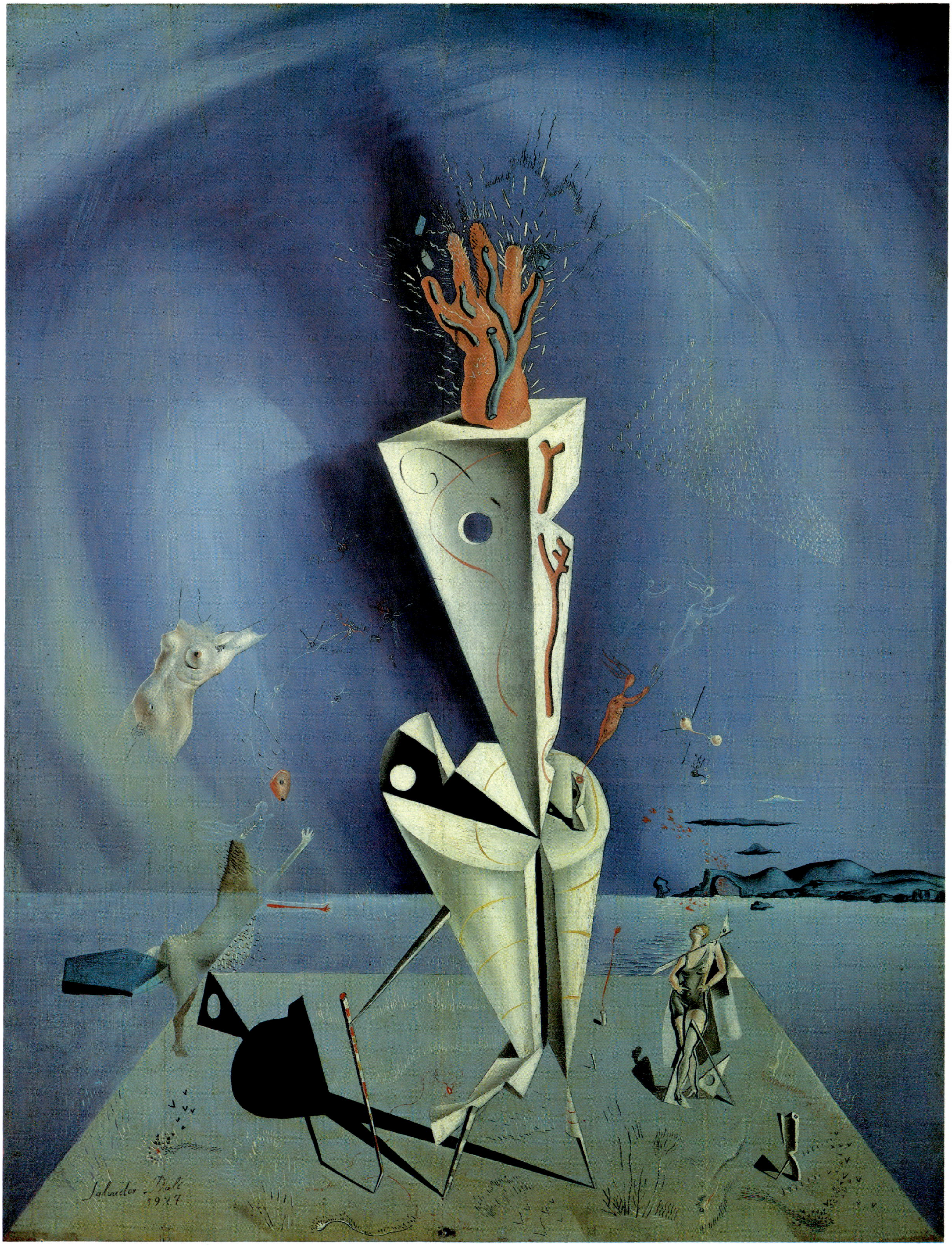
Salvador Dali
1927

Joan Miró and André Masson were clearly the stylistic influences on this oil painting, the former acting upon the shaping of the figure, the latter upon its setting (and especially the lower half of the surround, where Dalí mixed sand with his paint).

Once again Dalí demonstrated his preoccupation with sexuality here, for one hand is located over the bather's sexual apparatus and simultaneously resembles the female aperture, while the digits of the other hand equally resemble phalluses, particularly the protruding thumb and little finger. Moreover, within the palm of the hand on the left is a form that resembles a labia. The 'face' of the bather looks rather like an electrical screw-fitting, complete with further screw-holes that double as eyes, and given the sexuality of the figure, the central hole itself may equally bear a sexual connotation. In the sky we are wittily reminded that we are looking at an illusion, for Dalí went to some trouble to emulate exactly the types of highlighted cracks that may be perceived on walls or similar flat surfaces.

The Bather

Painted 1928

63.5 × 74.9 cm

Salvador Dalí Museum, St Petersburg, Florida

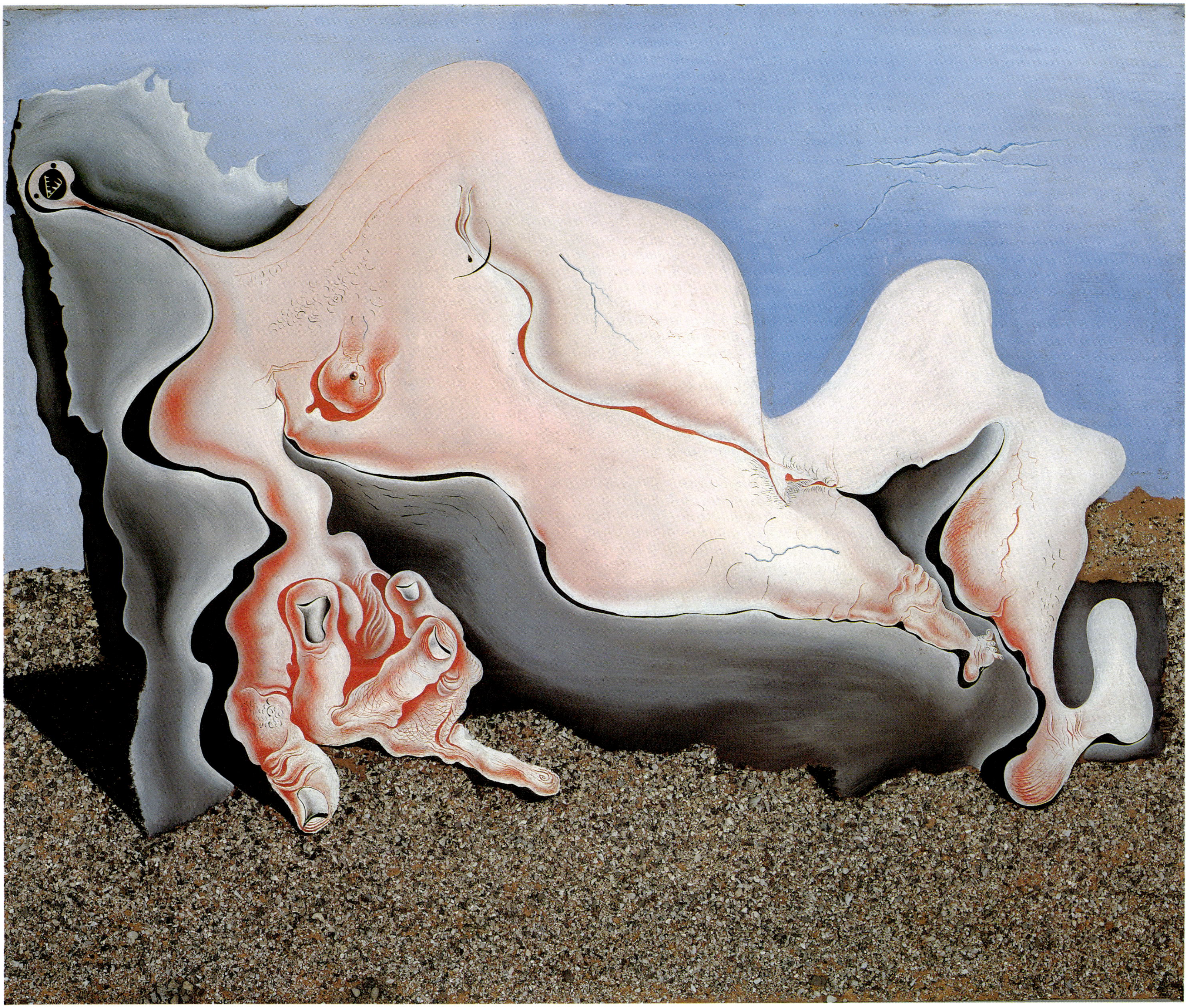

The Lugubrious Game

Painted 1929
21.3 × 34.9 cm
Private Collection

This picture (also known as *Dismal Sport*) was painted on cardboard in oils, and incorporates pieces of printed paper; there is also a drawing on the back by Lorca. The work formed the centrepiece of Dalí's first exhibition in Paris, held in November–December 1929 at the Goemans Gallery, where it was bought by the Vicomte de Noailles. With its clear-cut light, long shadows, enforced perspective and prominent statue, the picture demonstrates the continuing if diminishing influence of de Chirico, but in all other respects Dalí here moved far beyond the orbit of those painters who had earlier influenced him stylistically.

Opposite the extended, gigantic hand of the statue which hides its face in its other hand – possibly in shame – may be recognized the soft, sleeping head of Dalí himself, with a grasshopper attached to his mouth; the painter had suffered a horror of such insects since childhood. The image is studded with forms bearing sexual connotations, such as the extended, phallic finger which points towards an ant-covered anus and buttocks immediately above the sleeping head; the vulva-like vertical mouth of a bearded head to the right of the finger; and the similar form that appears above the bird-goat-cat 'ear' of the Dalinian self-portrait. The figure seated on the plinth below the statue also proffers an object that looks extremely like the female sexual organ. The pronounced perspective of the steps on the right and the inscription on the plinth further a feeling of precision in the work, against which all the fantastic, wheeling forms seem more rhythmic by contrast, thus heightening the sense of unreality.

Dalí painted this picture in Cadaqués in the summer of 1929. According to the painter himself, its title was suggested by Paul Eluard. The work was in progress when Eluard visited Cadaqués with Gala, along with Goemans, Buñuel, Magritte and his wife. In addition to Dalí's acute, sexually induced hysteria that summer, the excrement-stained underpants of the manic-looking young man at the lower right worried the visitors; they delegated Gala to enquire of the painter as to whether he was coprophagic (i.e., someone who likes eating faeces). Dalí later recorded:

I was suddenly tempted to answer her with a lie. If I admitted to her that I was coprophagic, as they had suspected, it would make me even more interesting and phenomenal in everybody's eyes. But Gala's tone was so clear, and the expression of her face, exalted by the purity of an entire and lofty honesty, was so tense that I was moved to tell her the truth.

'I swear to you that I am not "coprophagic". I consciously loathe that type of aberration as much as you can possibly loathe it. But I consider scatology as a terrorizing element, just as I do blood, or my phobia for grasshoppers.'

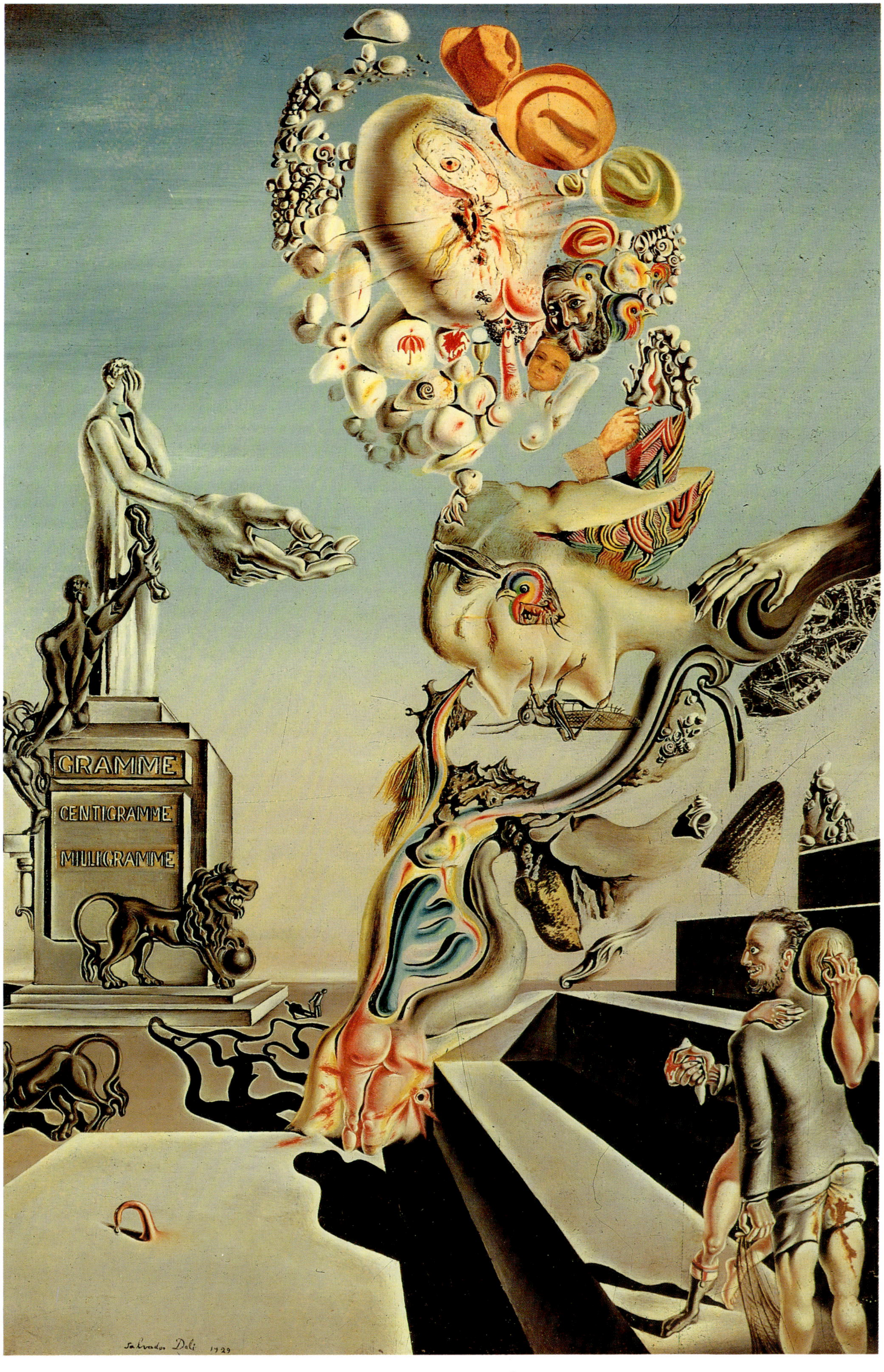
GRAMME
CENTIGRAMME
MILLIGRAMME
Salvador Dalí 1929

Dalí painted this picture in the autumn of 1929 after Gala Eluard had returned to Paris. As in *The Lugubrious Game* (page 49), here Dalí portrayed himself as a soft polymorphic object with a grasshopper attached to his mouth. According to the painter, the soft form terminates in the 'architecture and ornamentations' of a piece of 1900s furniture, and similarly the image of the woman smelling the genitals of a man derived from a cheap nineteenth-century chromolithograph of a woman smelling a lily; now the lily has been relocated below the woman's head. Naturally, the protruding stamen of the lily is very phallic in form and subtly it heightens our awareness of the sexuality of the woman, as does the lion's head with its libidinously protruding tongue nearby. In overall form, the polymorph is extremely resemblant to the fantastic shapes of the rocks around Cadaqués, from which Dalí derived its shape, and that coastal association, plus other, darker psychological associations, is brought into play by the fishhook embedded in the polymorph's scalp. The way that the woman's head and the male form above it metamorphose out of the polymorph is the type of transformation that Dalí might well have derived from the cinematic dissolves in *Un Chien andalou*, made earlier in 1929.

In his book *The Unspeakable Confessions of Salvador Dalí*, published in 1976, the painter wrote that when painting this work:

I masturbated frequently, but with great control over my penis, mentally leading myself on to orgasm but disciplining my actions so as the better to savour my ecstasy. Masturbation at the time was the core of my eroticism and the axis of my paranoiac-critical method. The prick I was hooked on, so to speak. There was me and my orgasm – and then the rest of the world . . . The Great Masturbator *. . . is the expression of my heterosexual anxiety – with its mouthless character incarnated by a grasshopper while the ants eat its belly. . . .*

The Great Masturbator

Painted 1929

110.1 × 151.1 cm

Private Collection

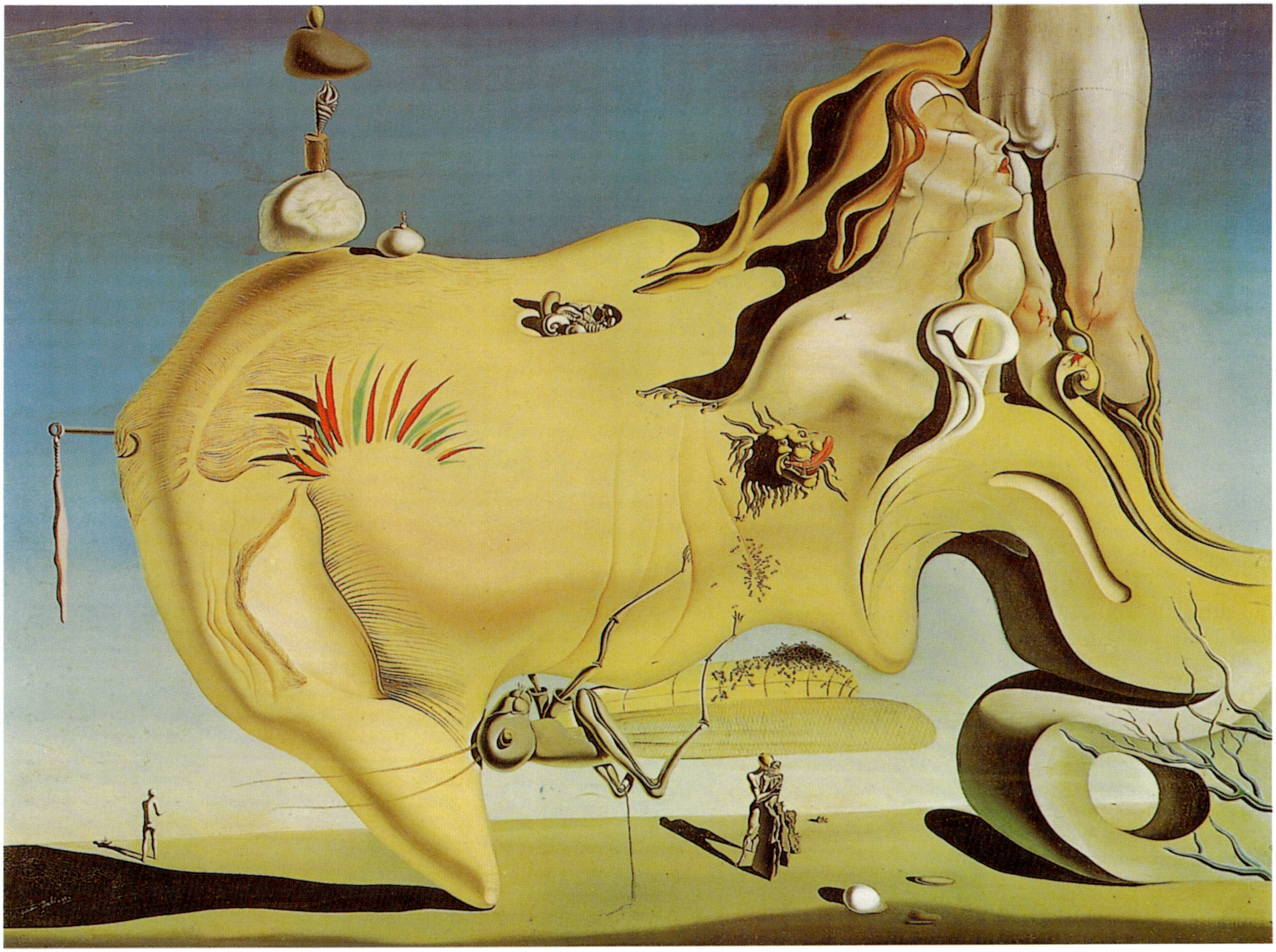

As was common in Dalí's pictures of this period, the polymorph that represents himself is asleep, which obviously projects the sense that we are looking at a dream. The dream-like unreality is subtly heightened by the fact that the words 'ma mère' only appear in under half of the eighty-one compartments pressed into the polymorph – it is as though the remaining vacant depressions are waiting to have the words written in them. On the left, directly above Dalí's diminutive head, is a further strange form comprising the heads of a lion and a woman, the ubiquitous grasshopper, an egg borne aloft by a semi-nude, a Phoenician amphora, and a hand holding a knife.

Here again Dalí derived the polymorph from the weird shapes of the rocks around Cadaqués, and that marine connection seems strengthened by the molluscs at the base of the structure. To the right of the ants feasting off Dalí's neck is an elegantly turned form that again clearly derived from the shapes of *fin de siècle* furniture. And as in *The Great Masturbator* (page 51), the lion's heads, with libidinous tongues, respectively introduce a note of furious animalism and depravity.

The Enigma of Desire: My Mother, My Mother, My Mother

Painted 1929
110.2 × 149.8 cm
Private Collection

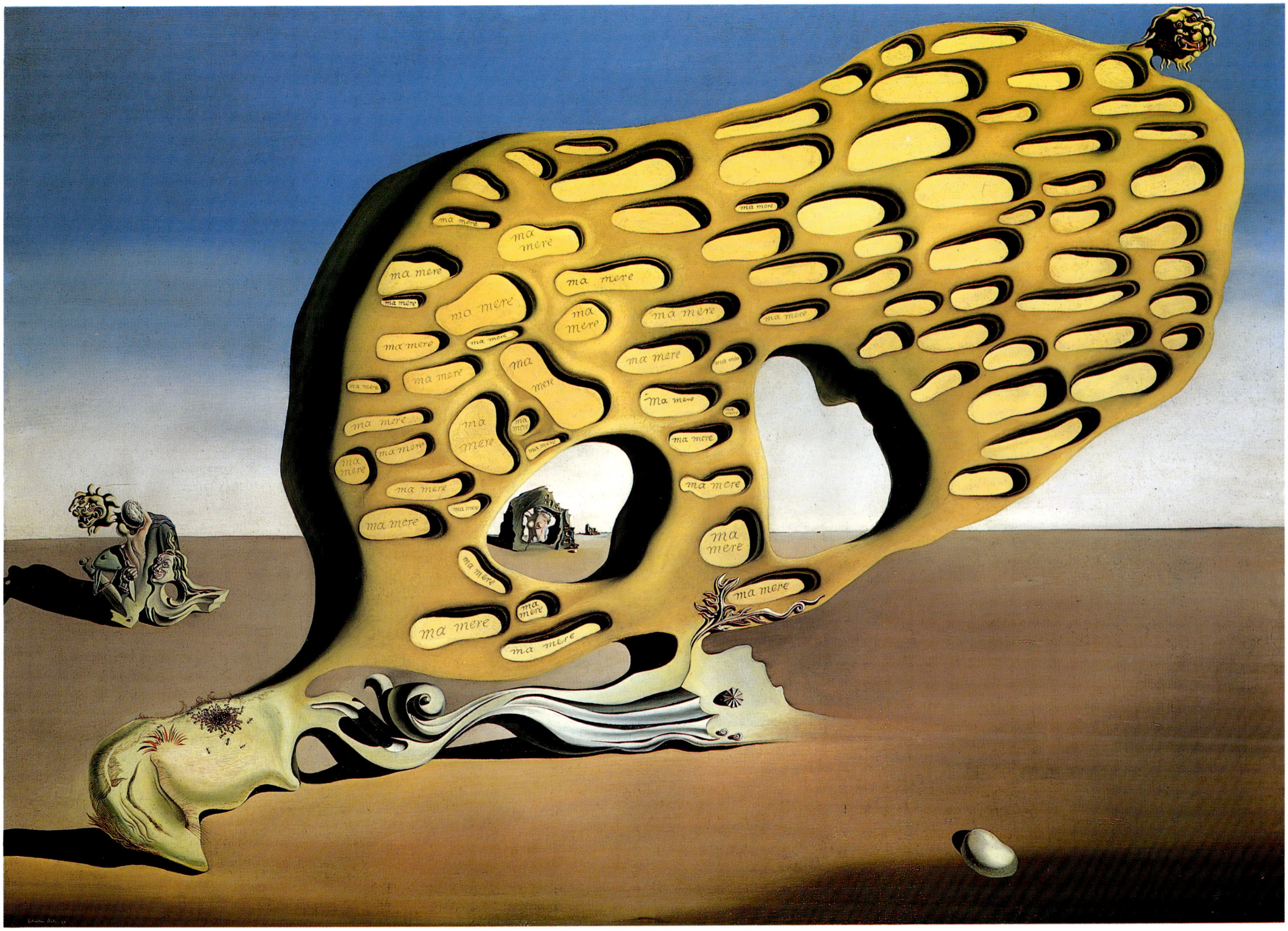
ma mère
ma mère
ma mère
ma mère
ma mère
ma mère
ma mère
ma mère
ma mère
ma mère
ma mère
ma mère
ma mère
ma mère
ma mère
ma mère
ma mère
ma mère
ma mère
ma mère
ma mère
ma mère
ma mère

Accommodations of Desire

Painted 1929
22.9 × 34.9 cm
The Jacques and Natasha Gelman Collection

This oil painting with collaged elements on wood panel was bought from Dalí's first Paris exhibition by André Breton, who had written the catalogue essay.

As we have seen elsewhere, the head of a lion was used frequently by Dalí for its animalistic connotations at this time, and here such animalism is subtly advanced by being stated in glaring colours and contained within the regular, calm forms of some pebbles whose shapes Dalí derived from stones he had seen around Cadaqués, forms which had further suggested images to him when he stared at them intently for long enough. In this work the painter brought to fruition his close scrutiny of the techniques of Flemish painting undertaken in Brussels in 1926, for the detail in this tiny picture is quite exceptional. The heads of the lions are a pair of lithographed prints stuck down on the canvas, and Dalí employed the outer edge of one of the heads as a stencil with which to outline their silhouettes in red and white elsewhere; similarly, he cut out the face of one of the lions but re-used the mouth from that cut-out on another of the pebbles. The repetition of parts of the heads of the lions, or of their entire heads, suggests a deconstruction of the image.

In *The Unspeakable Confessions of Salvador Dalí*, the painter wrote of this work that the 'lion's maws translate my terror before the revelation of the possession of a woman's cunt, that would lead to the revelation of my impotence'. The 'maws' may be seen at the lower left and midway at the upper right.

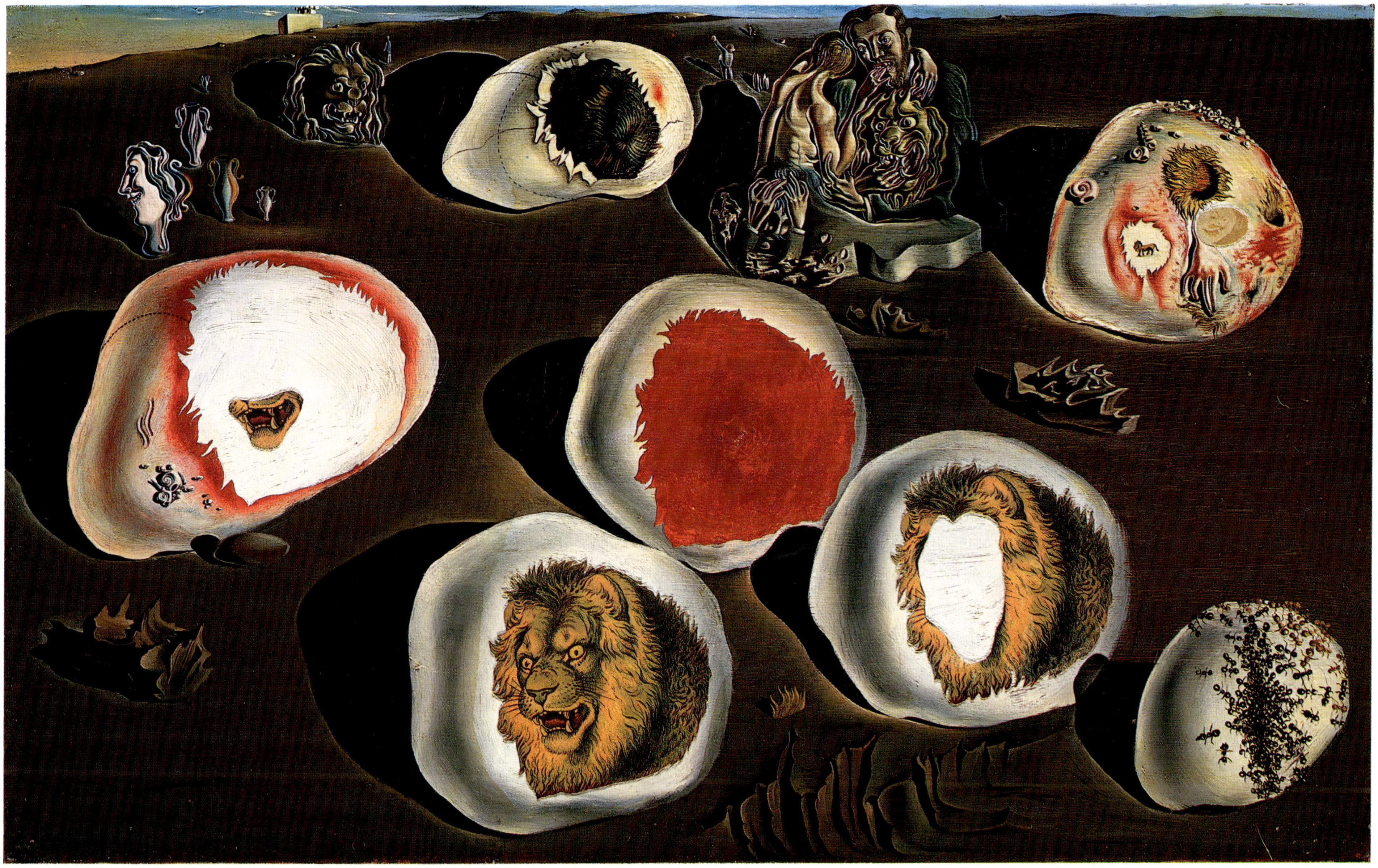

Again the influence of other artists may be seen here: Giorgio de Chirico, in the boxes containing images, the skull-like form on the horizon on the left, and in the use of perspective, light and shade; René Magritte (who stayed with Dalí at Cadaqués in the summer of 1929), in the imagery of the insertions containing the grasshopper and other objects in the central box, as well as in the cyclists bearing sugared almonds on their heads in the box on the right; and Max Ernst, in the curious bird-like forms that appear between the box on the left and the central box. The characteristic soft self-portrait of Dalí asleep is readily apparent in the central box.

Yet in addition to demonstrating the influence of de Chirico, Magritte and Ernst, this oil painting on panel with collaged elements equally demonstrates the degree to which Dalí had evolved his own particular vision of things by 1929, with the repeated rectilinearity of the boxes acting as a foil to the emotionally charged imagery of the woman being embraced by a man and threatened by a knife at the lower left.

Illumined Pleasures

Painted 1929

23.8 × 34.9 cm

Museum of Modern Art, New York

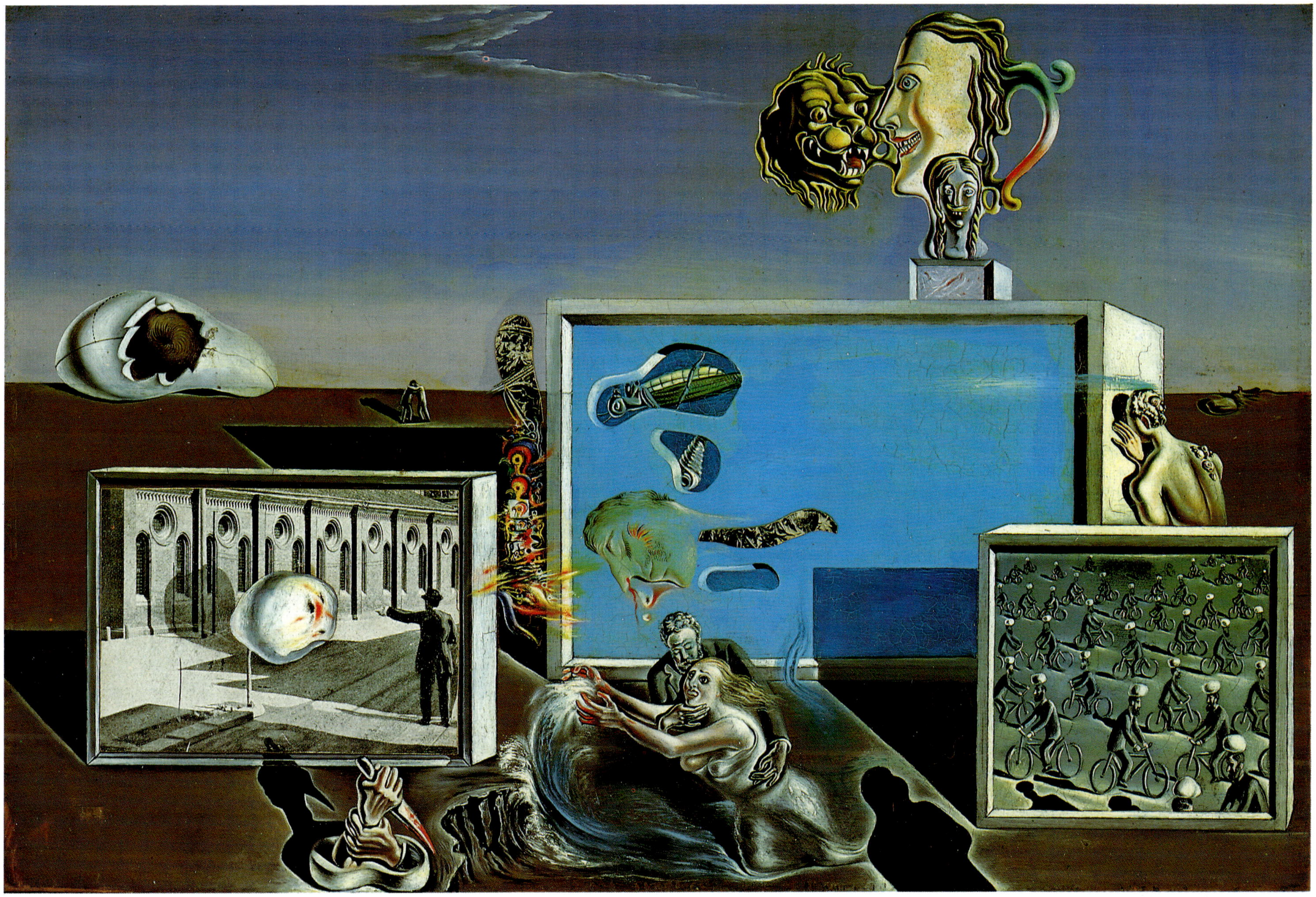

Dalí's penchant for visual simile and the creation of composite images out of subsidiary images may be seen to brilliant effect in this painting, for the central form may simultaneously be perceived as a horse with a bushy tail, as a reclining woman stretched out luxuriously, and as a lion. This multiplicity enjoys a close correspondence to the type of fragmentation and transformation we frequently encounter in dreams.

The distant buildings, statue and chimney demonstrate the continuing influence of Giorgio de Chirico, as does the colouring and internal lighting of the picture. A very similar work, also painted in 1930, was destroyed by fascist thugs on 30 December 1930 when it was being displayed at the Studio 28 cinema in Paris to complement the screening of the Dalí-Buñuel film *L'Age d'or*.

Invisible Sleeping Woman, Horse, Lion

Painted 1930
60 × 69.8 cm
Private Collection

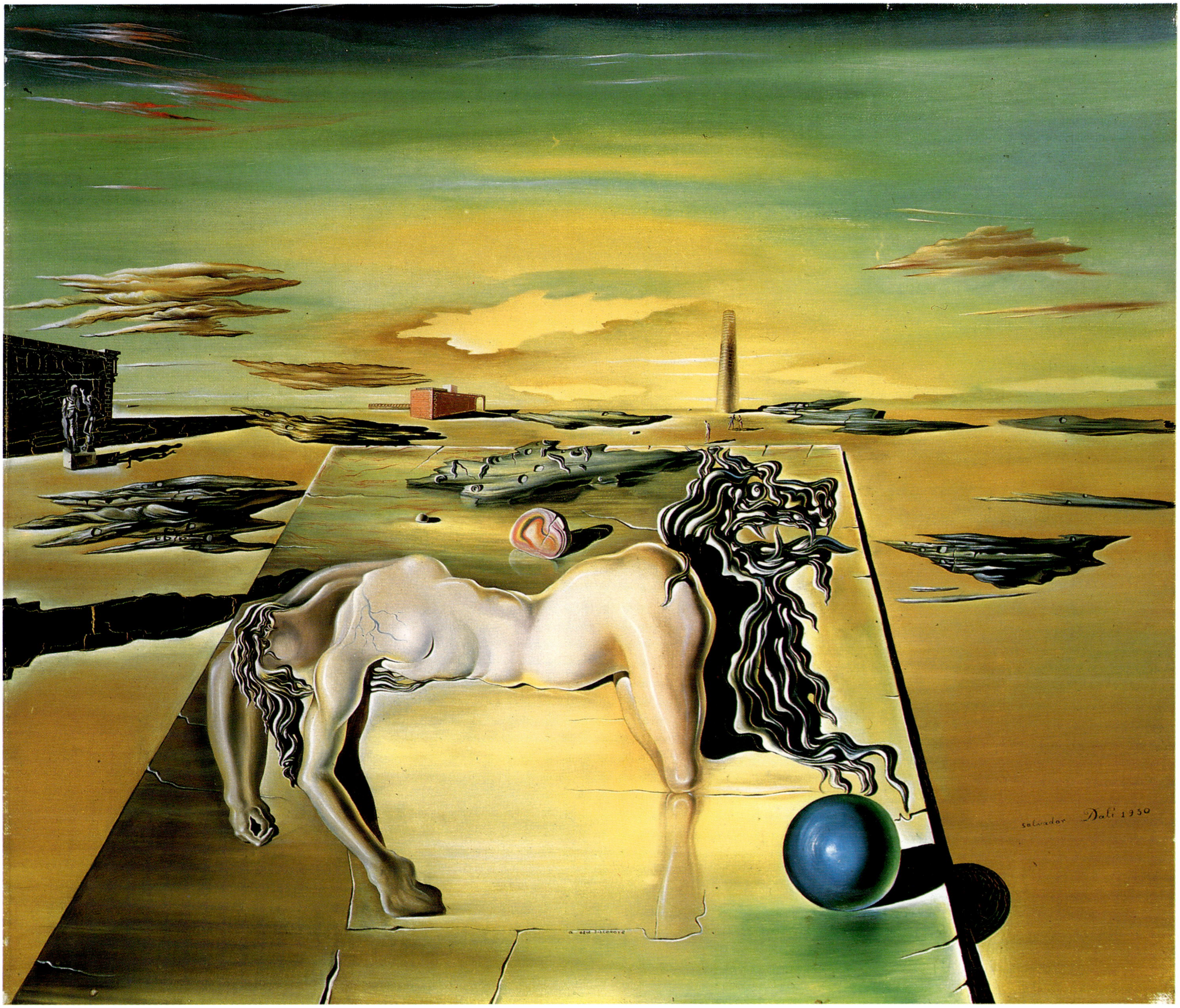
salvador Dalí 1930

Partial Hallucination. Six Apparitions of Lenin on a Grand Piano

Painted 1931

113.9 × 146 cm

Musée National d'Art Moderne, Paris

In his essay *The Tragic Myth of Millet's Angelus*, published in 1963 but written in 1941 and then misplaced, Dalí recalled the genesis of this painting:

In 1932 [sic] *at sunset, I saw the bluish, shiny keyboard of a piano where the perspective exposed to my gaze a series of miniature yellow phosphorescent haloes surrounding Lenin's visage.*

Lenin would reappear in a number of Dalí's other pictures – for an example see *Enigma of William Tell* of 1933 (page 69) – and the Russian political leader had undoubtedly entered the painter's consciousness through contact with André Breton, who was a confirmed Marxist. In the later work, however, there is a debunking element in the portrayal, whilst here Dalí was in a far more genuinely irrational frame of mind, as a man wearing an armband denoting his solidarity with the foreground cherries looks beyond Lenin dancing the light fantastic up and down the keyboard, ants swarm across (blank) sheet music, and a Catalan rock face appears through a partially open doorway.

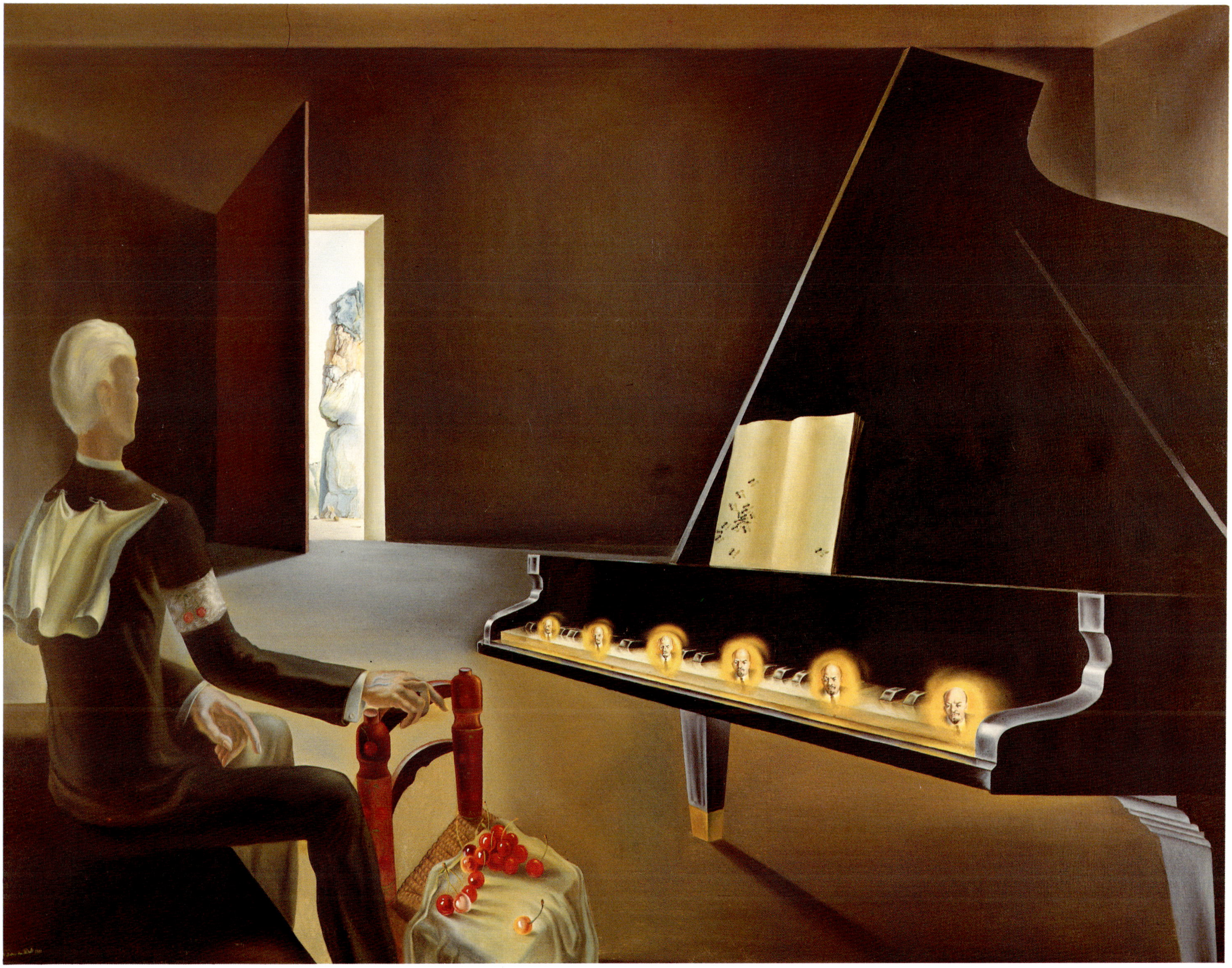

The Persistence of Memory

Painted 1931
24.1 × 33 cm
Museum of Modern Art, New York

This is undoubtedly Dalí's best-known and best-loved picture. Painted in oils on canvas, it was first exhibited at the Pierre Colle Gallery in Paris in June 1931. In *The Secret Life of Salvador Dalí*, the painter related the genesis of the image:

It was on an evening when I felt tired, and had a slight headache, which is extremely rare with me. We were to go to a moving picture with some friends, and at the last moment I decided not to go. Gala would go with them, and I would stay home and go to bed early. We had topped off our meal with a strong Camembert, and after everybody had gone I remained a long time at the table meditating on the philosophic problems of the 'super-soft' which the cheese presented to my mind. I got up and went into my studio, where I lit the light in order to cast a final glance, as is my habit, at the picture I was in the midst of painting. This picture represented a landscape near Port Lligat, whose rocks were lighted by a transparent and melancholy twilight; in the foreground an olive tree with its branches cut, and without leaves. I knew that the atmosphere which I had succeeded in creating with this landscape was to serve as a setting for some idea, for some surprising image, but I did not in the least know what it was going to be. I was about to turn out the light, when instantaneously I 'saw' the solution. I saw two soft watches, one of them hanging lamentably on the branches of the olive tree. In spite of the fact that my headache had increased to the point of becoming very painful, I avidly prepared my palette and set to work. When Gala returned from the theatre two hours later the picture, which was to become one of my most famous, was completed.

In the centre is Dalí's characteristic 'soft' self-portrait; its reclining position and closed eyes subtly augment the dreaminess of the image.

Much of the impact of the work is advanced by its contradiction of our certainty that objects made of metal cannot be soft or eaten by ants. In a century of relativity theory, such an image of the malleability of watches – and thus by a simple act of association, the malleability of time itself – remains a potent one.

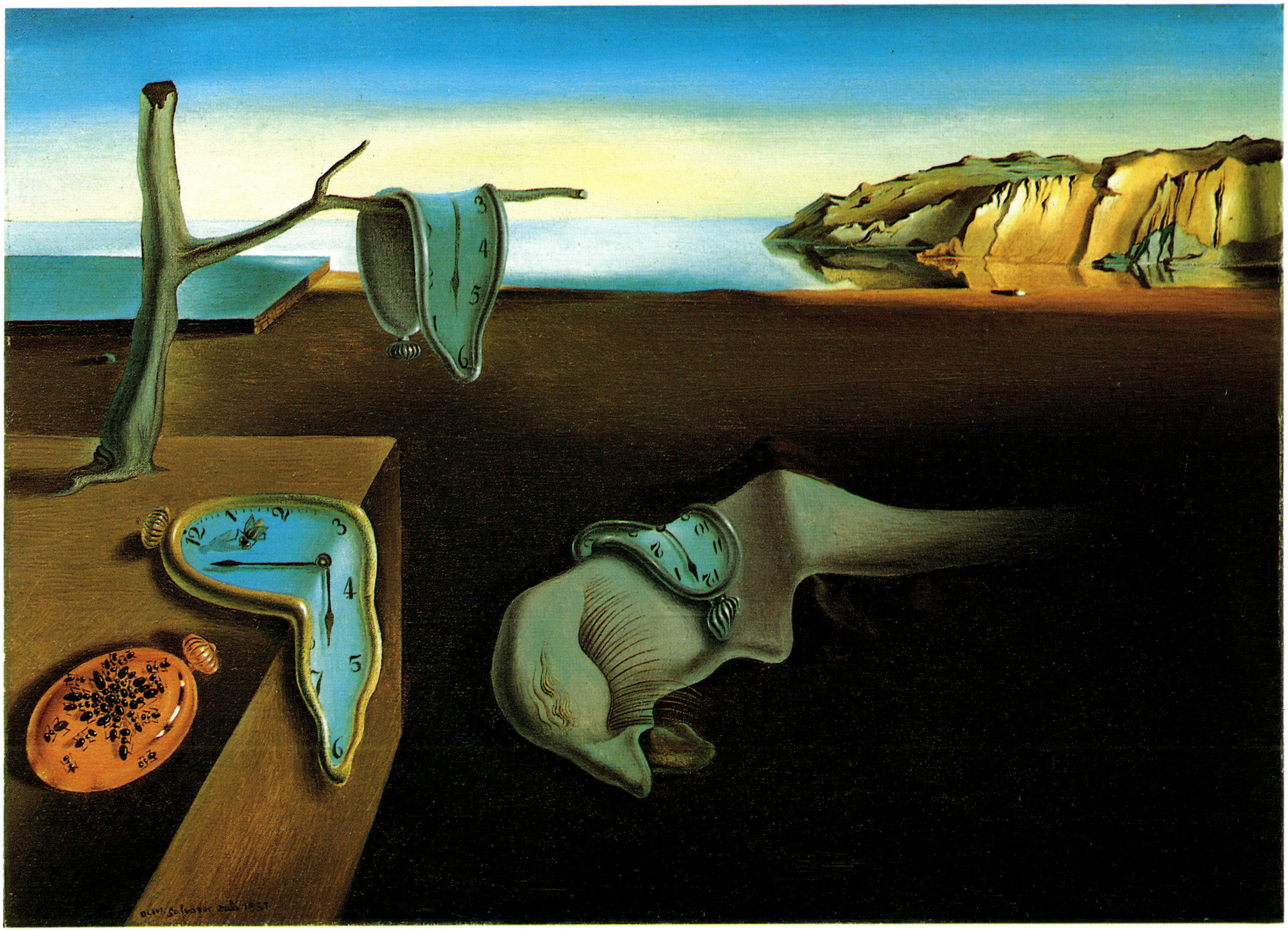

The Spectre of Sex Appeal

Painted 1932

18 × 13.8 cm

Teatro-Museo Dalí, Figueras

The little boy dressed in a sailor suit and holding an ossified penis at the lower right of this tiny oil painting represents Dalí himself, as he explained in 1969 when he was painting an identical figure in his *Hallucinogenic Toreador* (page 139). And the painter also once captioned a photograph of this work 'erotic bogie of the first order', which seems an apt description. The bogie's breasts are composed of huge sacks, while phallic-looking bones protrude from various points of her anatomy.

The way that the bogie towers over an adjacent figure directly anticipates the towering spectral form of the *Soft Construction with Boiled Beans: Premonition of Civil War* of 1936 (page 79).

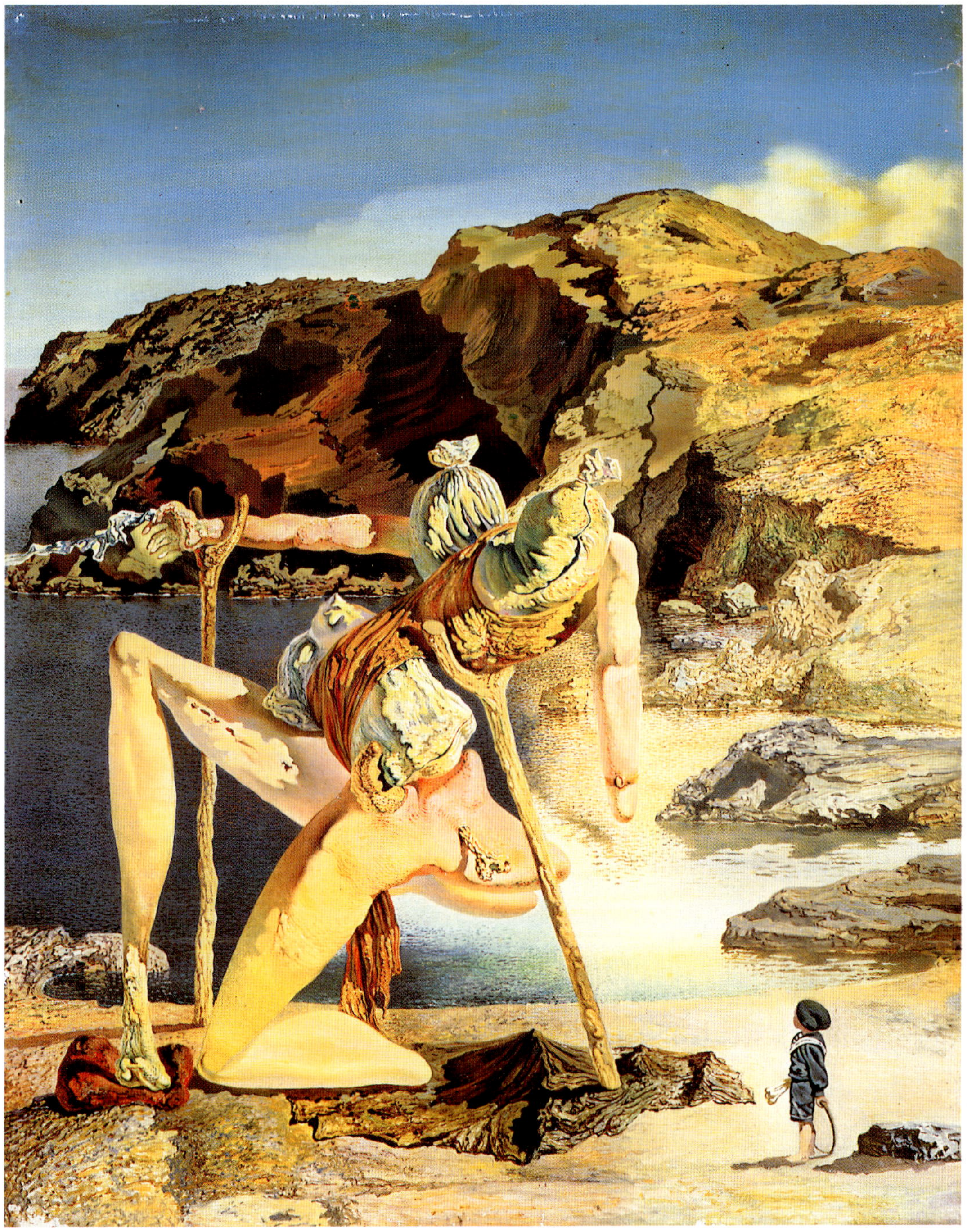

The Birth of Liquid Desires

Painted 1932
94.9 × 112 cm
Peggy Guggenheim Foundation, Venice

This oil painting constitutes one of Dalí's most hallucinatory images, with the gigantic, polymorphic form in the centre for once not acting as a self-portrait of Dalí but instead approximating far more closely to the type of rock formation seen near Cadaqués that had inspired it in the first place. The rock appears thin in the middle, judging by the hole in it, but nearby it deepens to become the mouth of a cave into which a virtually nude man is stepping.

As a partially obscured woman hides her face and pours a heavy, sperm-like liquid into the bowl in which the man in the centre (who enjoys very female breasts) is resting his foot, another woman with a head composed of flower petals embraces him. Springing from the phallic loaf resting on the man's head is a huge form that at the top metamorphoses into cypress trees, of the type that Dalí remembered from his schooldays, while liquid pours copiously from the base of a broken cupboard nearby.

The sexual meaning of all this imagery is purposefully opaque, but therein lies its strength, for it can easily bear the viewer's interpretation in the light of his or her own sexual responses. The imaginative charge engendered by the picture is analogous to the type of response sparked off by the best Surrealist poetry, wherein meaning and expressivity are communicated on a subliminal level, without the intervention of reason.

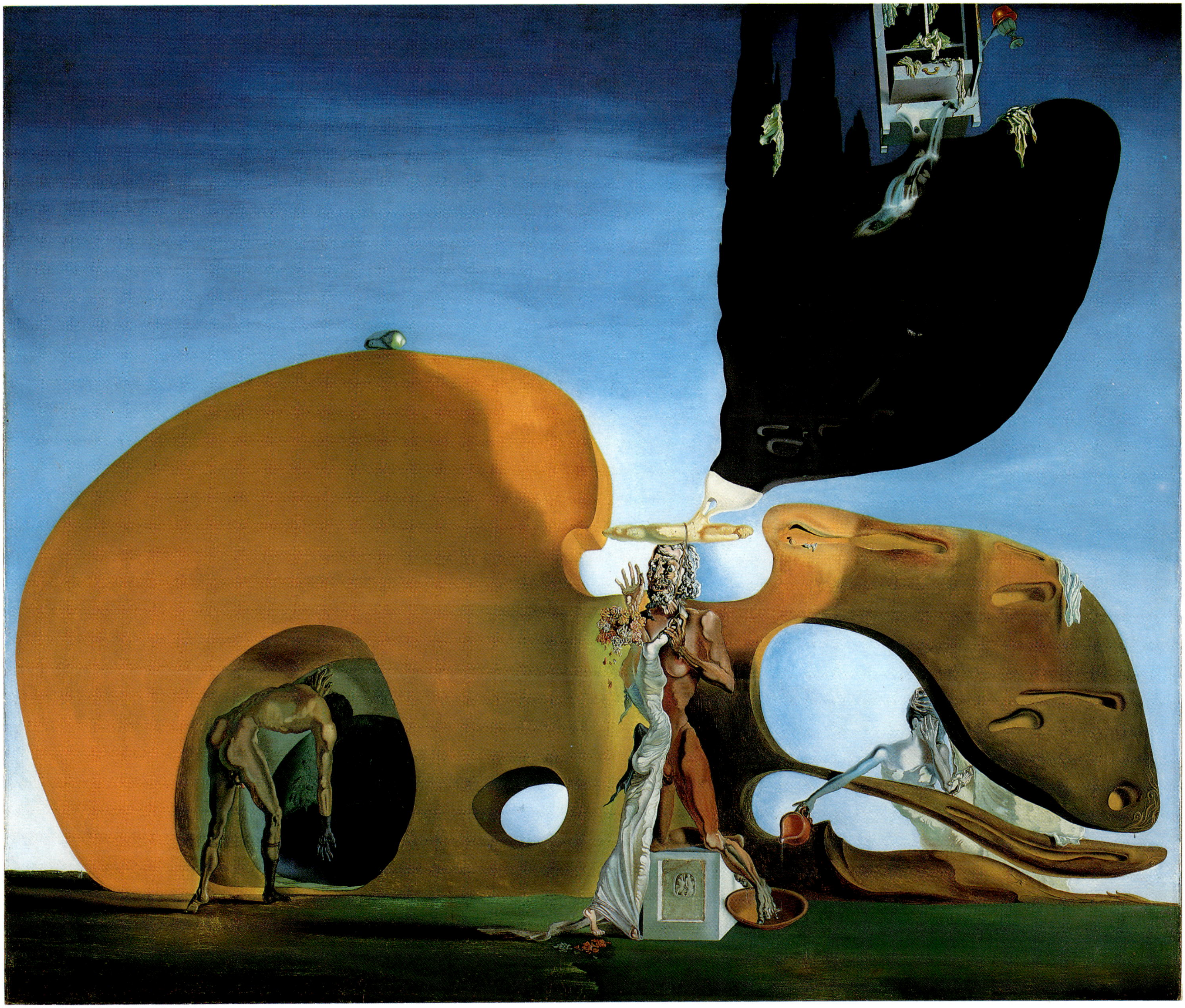

The Enigma of William Tell

Painted 1933

201.6 × 146 cm

Moderna Museet, Stockholm

If Dalí dealt with sexual dominance and emasculation in the 1930 *William Tell* (Private Collection), here he debunked the authority of a father-figure by making his William Tell look like Vladimir Ilyich Lenin, the father-figure of the Russian Revolution and therefore a hero to the Marxist leader of the Surrealist movement, André Breton. By such means Dalí not only demonstrated his wholehearted identification with the irrationality of Surrealism but equally he fulfilled its revolutionary aims by demonstrating that he was no respecter of persons or of Surrealist orthodoxy, for a representation of William Tell as a hideously distorted Lenin was calculated to enrage Breton. The picture certainly achieved that aim when it went on display at the 1934 Salon des Indépendants, for when Breton saw the work he attempted to destroy it, although he failed, for it had been hung too high on the wall for him to reach it. Later that year Breton put Dalí on 'trial' for his political and intellectual unorthodoxy but, faced with the sympathy that was expressed for Dalí's free thinking by his fellow Surrealists René Crevel, Paul Eluard and Tristan Tzara, he was eventually forced merely to caution the painter, instead of expelling him.

On the plinth in front of Tell/Lenin is one of Dalí's soft watches. Both the peak of the hat of Tell/Lenin and one of his buttocks extend enormously outwards, with the peak of the hat eventually resembling an extended tongue, and the buttock looking like a huge phallus. On the buttock/phallus is a piece of raw meat, which also resembles a piece of excreta, and this lump of meat or faecal matter respectively furthers the animalism and linkage of sexuality with excretion that so obsessed Dalí.

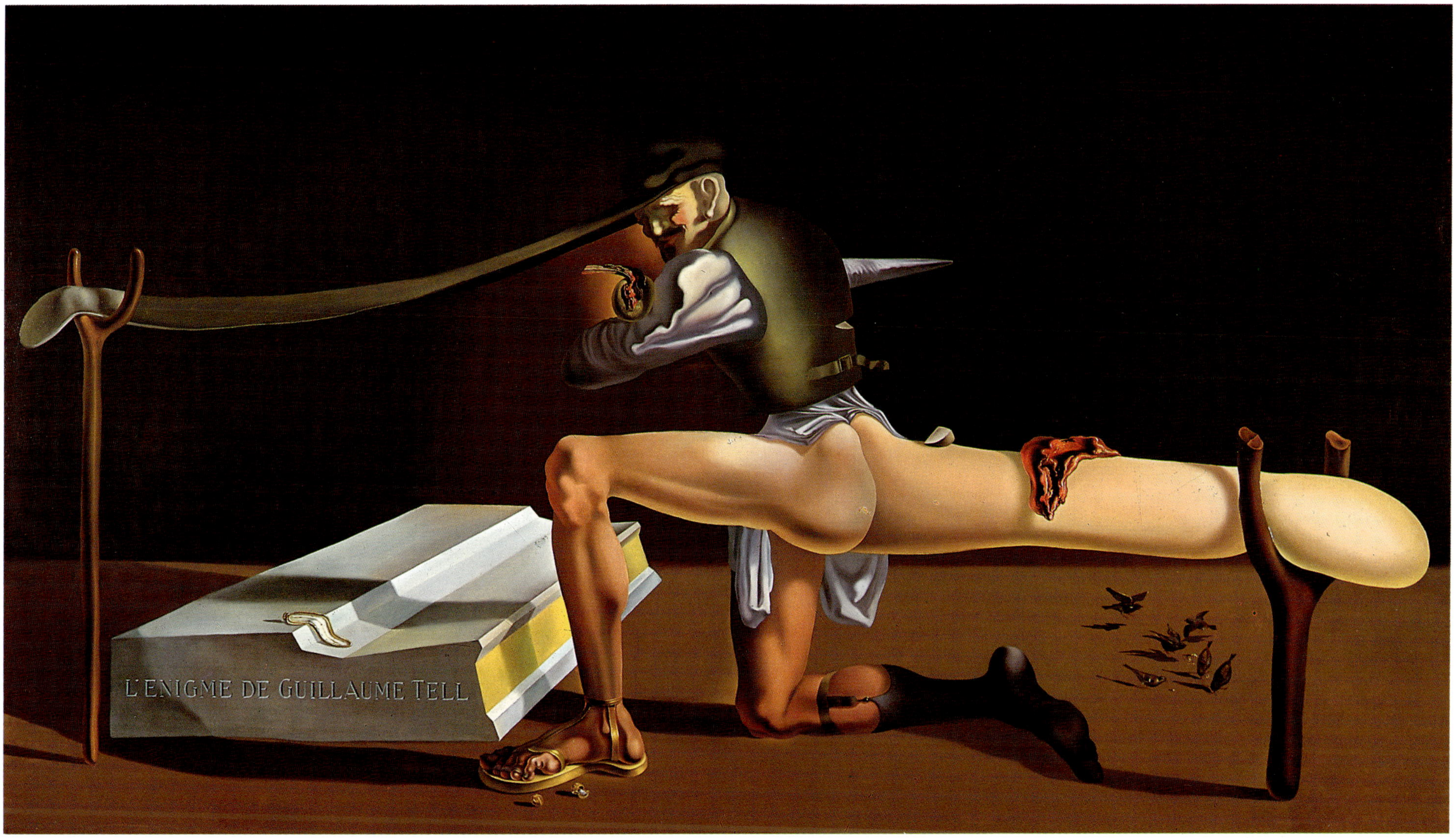
L'ENIGME DE GUILLAUME TELL

Jean-François Millet's painting *The Angelus* (see page 6) fascinated Dalí all his life. He had first seen a reproduction of it as a schoolboy in Figueras, and the two figures and wheelbarrow in that painting reappeared in a great many of Dalí's pictures. Dalí also wrote an essay on the work entitled 'The Tragic Myth of Millet's *Angelus*, Paranoiac-Critical Interpretation', which was first published in Paris in 1963.

Whereas the Millet is a dawn scene, here Dalí has set his peasants (who, according to the title, harken back to their remote ancestors) at the opposite end of the day. The male figure in the Millet has been transformed into a thin rock, with a skull for a head, out of which rises the wheelbarrow. This strange emanation is balanced by the thin rod that projects from the woman's arm. The harsh lighting gives the picture an hallucinatory intensity that is far removed from Millet's calm pastoralism.

Atavism at Twilight

Painted 1933–34

14.4 × 16.9 cm

Kunstmuseum, Bern, Switzerland

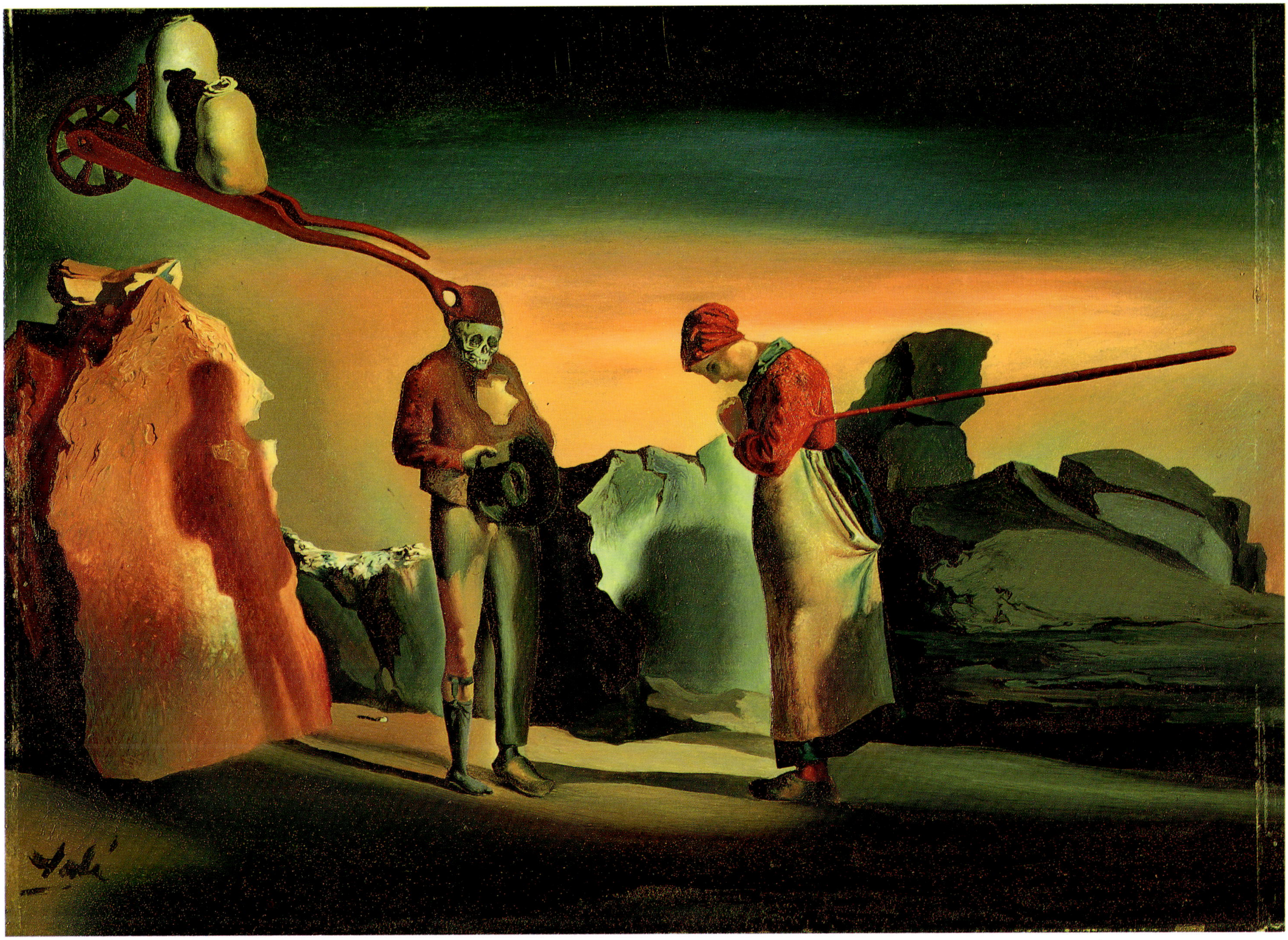

Civilization and animalism meet on the beach at Cadaqués, in one of Dalí's most strikingly simple but powerful oil paintings, an image that was inspired by a dream. The strangeness of seeing a piano bent out of shape as it is attacked by a hideously alive fossilized skull is augmented immeasurably by those objects being set far back in the fictive space of the image, and therefore surrounded by so much highly realistic detail: Dalí's stated intention to use 'the most imperialist fury of precision' to 'materialize the images of concrete irrationality' here seems triumphantly realized.

Atmospheric Skull Sodomizing a Grand Piano

Painted 1934

13.9 × 17.7 cm

Salvador Dalí Museum, St Petersburg, Florida

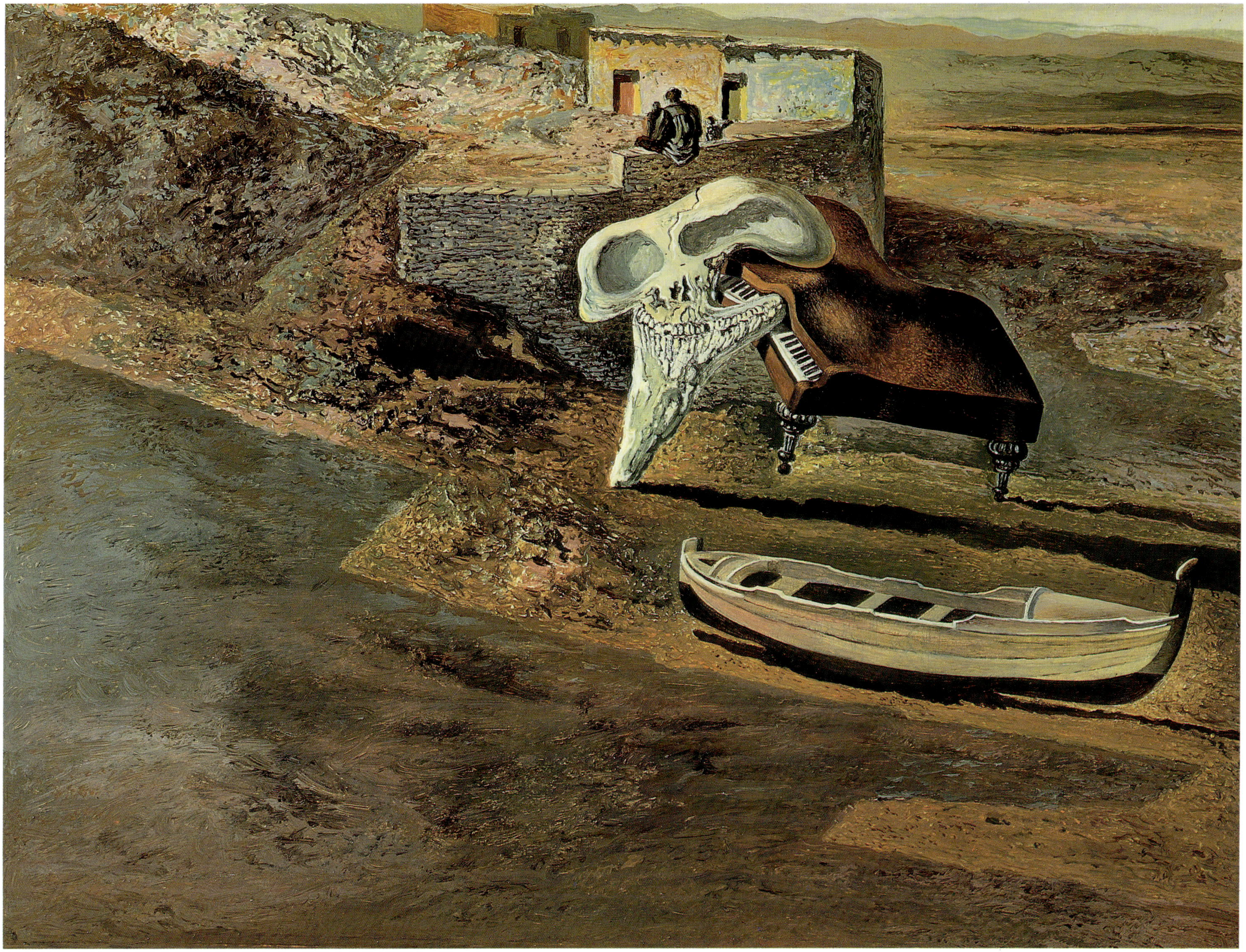

This drawing, in gouache on newspaper, demonstrates one of Dalí's most inventive and witty employments of dual and composite imagery. It needs no verbal explanation, just careful scrutiny.

In the 1970s the 'apartment' was actually realized in the Teatro-Museo Dalí in Figueras by a Catalan architect working under Dalí's direction, but the result is not nearly as effective as this design, principally because in being realized three-dimensionally the imaginative level of the image was sacrificed, while spatial distortion also robbed the components of something of their dualism. However, the sofa of Mae West's lips that Dalí made in 1936 (Private Collection), in which the lipstick was represented by shocking pink satin, retains the witty appeal of the original, and the object anticipated the picture of Marilyn Monroe's lips (Hirschhorn Museum, Washington D.C.) created in the early 1960s by another genius of the absurd, Andy Warhol.

The Face of Mae West (Usable as a Surrealist Apartment)

Drawn 1934–35
29.2 × 17.8 cm
Art Institute of Chicago

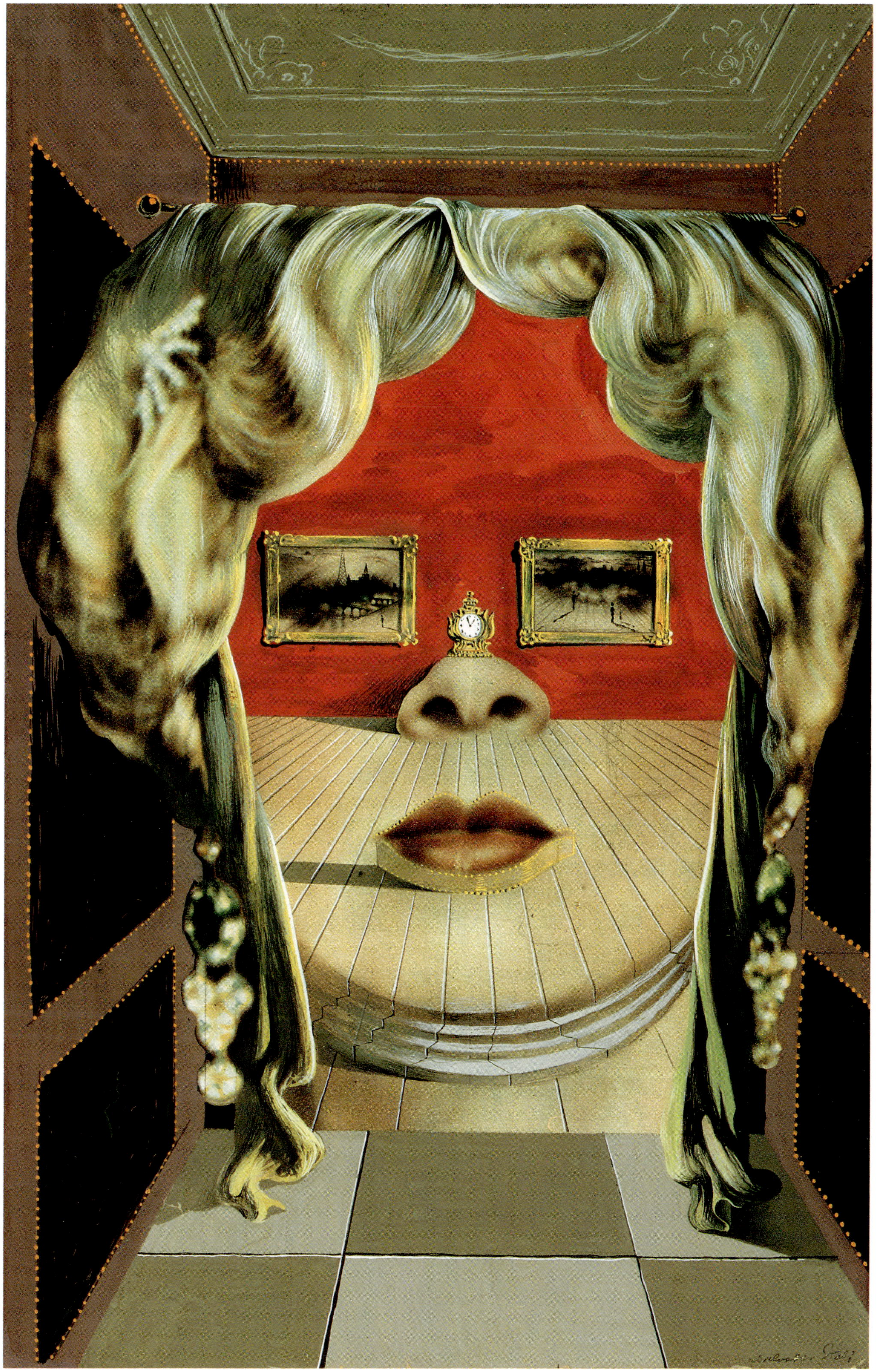

Here Dalí explored visual coincidence and opposition. The hole in the rock formation on the right neatly interlocks with the shape of the screen, doortop and soft bonnet of the car, while on the left a section of rock that is identical in shape and depth to the hole on the right extends outwards from the rock face, into which is also set a depression that reiterates the exact outline of the car. Confronted with the debris on the ground below the rock face on the left, one is forced to ask whether the car has been cut out of the façade and placed on the right, in exchange for the rock removed from the hole behind it. But who or what could have effected these changes? And why is the car bestrewn with tendrils and flowers? The answers hang in the air, in true, poetic Surrealist fashion . . . .

Paranoid-Critical Solitude

Painted 1935

19 × 24.4 cm

Private Collection

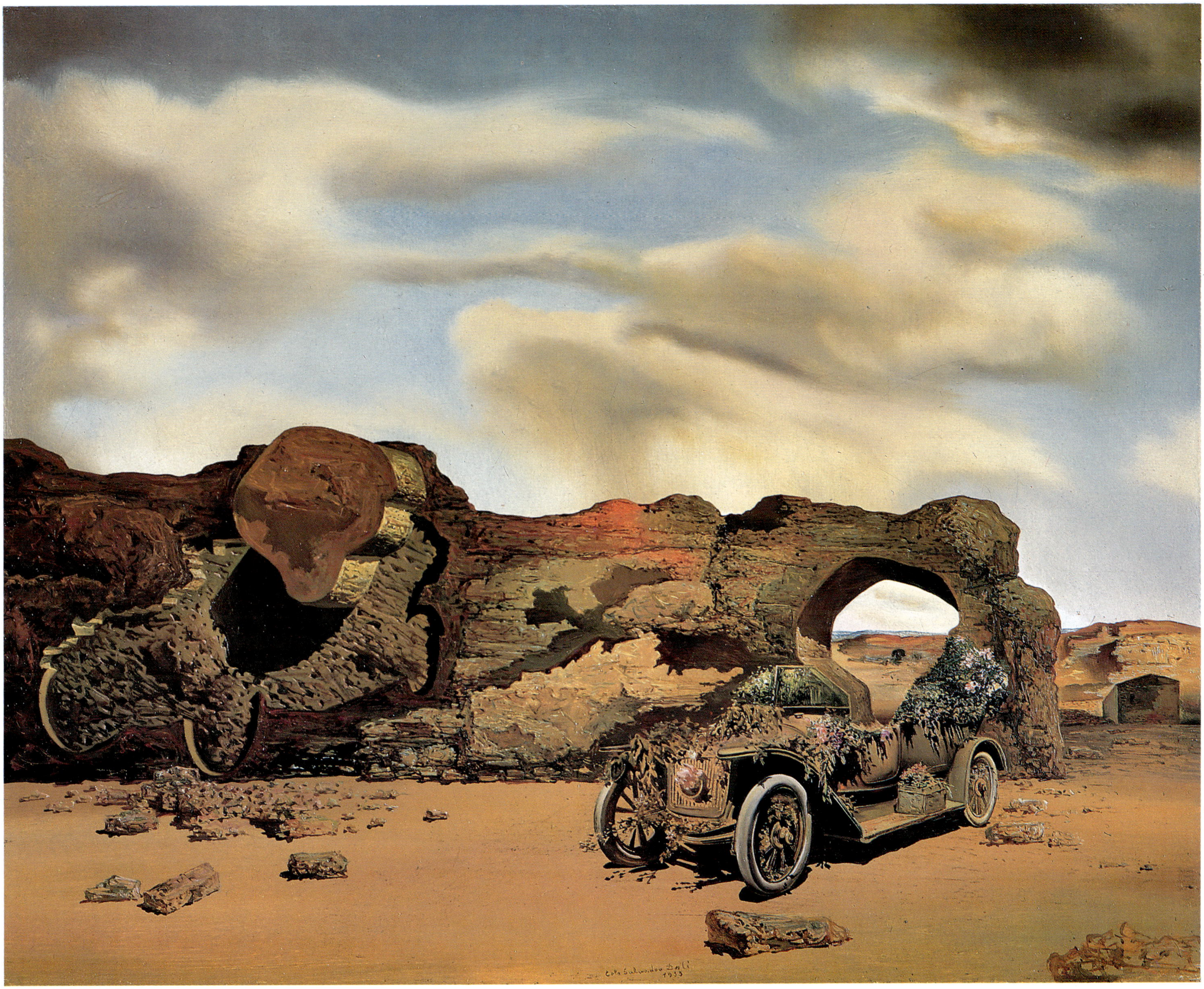
Salvador Dali

Soft Construction with Boiled Beans: Premonition of Civil War

Painted 1936
100 × 99 cm
Philadelphia Museum of Art

The direct ancestor of this picture was undoubtedly Goya's *The Colossus (Panic)*, which was possibly painted around 1812 and which shows an immense landscape filled with panic-stricken people and animals fleeing in all directions beneath the apparition of an immense nude man with raised fists in the sky. Dalí surely knew the Goya from his student days, for it hangs in the Prado Museum in Madrid.

As civil strife was no new phenomenon in Spain, especially in the twentieth century, Dalí's claim that he had a premonition of the coming civil war when he painted this picture some six months before the outbreak of hostilities was therefore not as prescient as it might seem. Even so, this is still one of the most startling images of our epoch, with its low viewpoint enabling the hideously distorted, hag-like creature to tower over us, a dominance that also allowed Dalí to paint one of the finest and most immense skyscapes in all art.

In *The Secret Life of Salvador Dalí* the painter wrote of this work:

In this picture I showed a vast human body breaking out into monstrous excrescences of arms and legs tearing at one another in a delirium of autostrangulation. As a background to this architecture of frenzied flesh devoured by a narcissistic and biological cataclysm, I painted a geological landscape, that had been uselessly revolutionized for thousands of years, congealed in its 'normal course'. The soft structure of that great mass of flesh in civil war I embellished with a few boiled beans, for one could not imagine swallowing all that unconscious meat without the presence (however uninspiring) of some mealy and melancholy vegetable.

Dalí also adorned the repast with the outcome of eating so many beans, namely a huge lump of excreta, to be seen draped over the thigh on the right. Just beyond the hand at the lower left is a figure from another picture that Dalí also painted in 1936, *The Pharmacist of Ampurdán in Search of Absolutely Nothing* (Folkwang Museum, Essen). This represents the father of a famous author from Figueras, and the figure itself was taken from a newspaper photograph.

Dalí's use of transformation is quite brilliant in this picture, for the squeezed teat on the left is grasped by a hand that emanates from an arm which is joined to another arm that becomes a thigh, then a buttock supporting a foot which eventually again becomes an arm; Dalí's long study of the similarities of things paid off handsomely here, for it allowed him to effect effortless anatomical transitions.

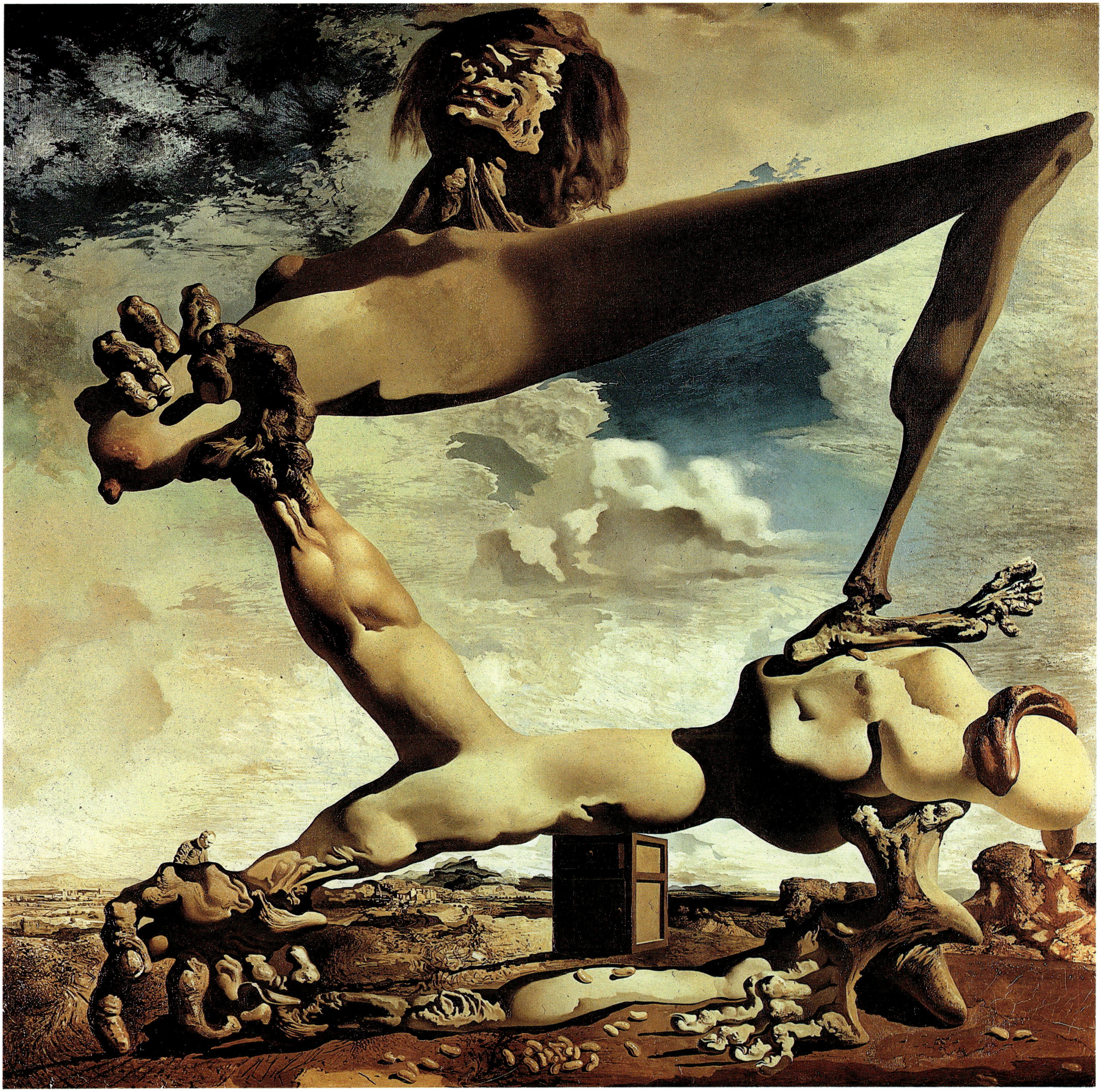

In the *Soft Construction with Boiled Beans* (page 79) Dalí responded to the impending cataclysm in Spain in terms of a single creature tearing itself apart; here we see two creatures dining off each other's flesh, an even more disturbing metaphor for civil war. Dalí later contrasted this approach with Picasso's 1937 treatment of the Spanish Civil War in his great painting *Guernica*:

These Iberian beings mutually devouring each other correspond to the pathos of civil war considered as a pure phenomenon of natural history, as opposed to Picasso who considered it a political phenomenon.

The heads of Dalí's cannibals are clearly related to those of his earlier polymorphic self-portraits, and yet his creatures do not enjoy any red-blooded human fleshiness; instead (as the correspondence with the partially peeled apple in the centre foreground suggests), in places they are like fruit on the inside – note the hole with peeling skin that is surrounded by ants on the head of the left-hand cannibal – while in other places their flesh approximates to milk or cheese, as where the spoon on the left dips into it. The culinary associations are garnished by various nuts, pieces of bread, meat patties and chops. The contrast between the intense detailing of the landscape and the vague forms of the clouds adds to the unreality of the setting, and the long shadows, which may be cast by a setting sun, further the sense of things coming to an end. That is fitting, given that the title tells us we are looking at an autumnal scene.

Autumn Cannibalism

Painted 1936
65 × 62.5 cm
Tate Gallery, London

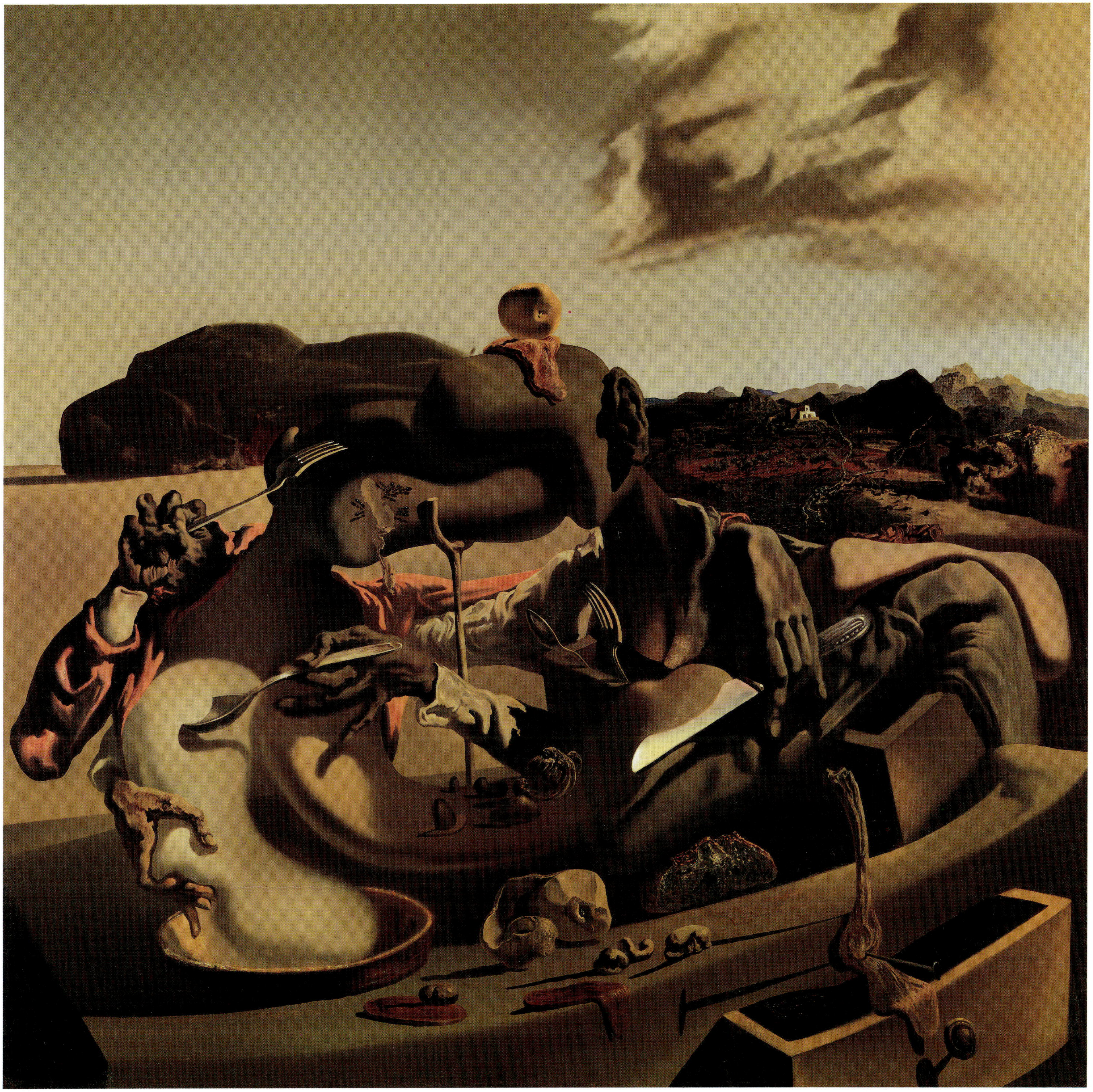

The Great Paranoiac

Painted 1936

61.9 × 61.9 cm

Boymans-van Beuningen Museum, Rotterdam

Dual imaging was central to Dalí's 'Paranoiac-Critical Method' but rarely did he achieve with it the complete congruence of form and content that we see here. Not only does the eye easily construct a complete head out of the various writhing figures, but equally the writhing itself vividly projects a sense of twisting nervous energy that wholly communicates the mental state referred to in the title (paranoia being a condition characterized by hallucinations or delusions).

The exaggeratedly irregular contours of the shadows on and around the figures augment the constancy of motion throughout, and they also subtly further the notion that we are looking at a surreal image, for in places they melt softly into their surroundings, thus imparting a sense of floating detachment from reality.

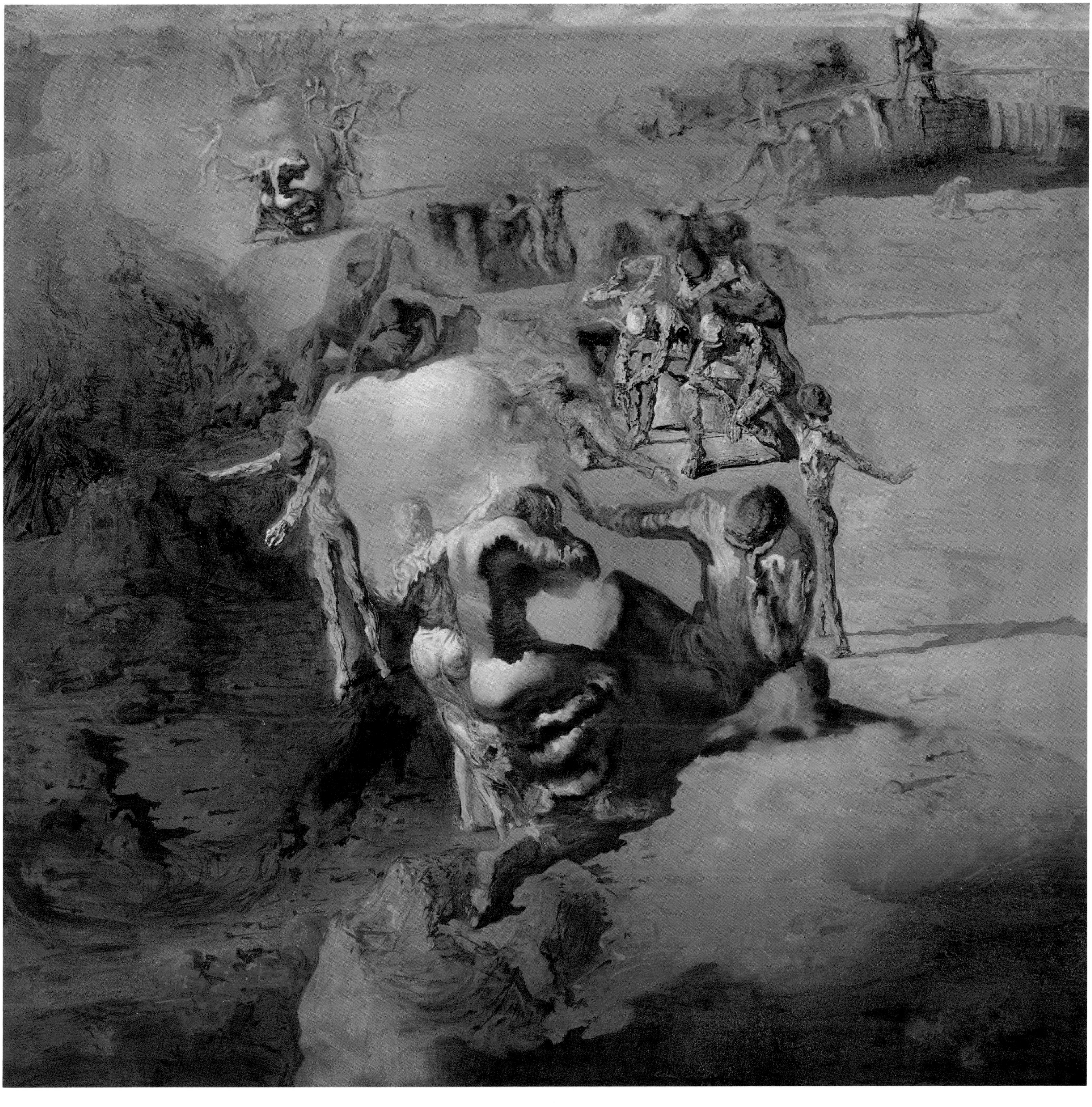

The Anthropomorphic Cabinet

Painted 1936

25.4 × 44.1 cm

Kunstsammlung Nordrhein-Westfalen, Düsseldorf

As the title tells us, this is no ordinary cabinet. Dalí had painted an open drawer in the 1932 *Birth of Liquid Desires* (page 67), but by 1936 he became especially concerned with placing such drawers in various anatomical positions in his figures, as can equally be seen in *The Burning Giraffe* (page 91) of that year. Moreover, in 1936 he also cut such drawers into the chest of a plaster statue of the *Venus de Milo*, in which task he was assisted by Marcel Duchamp. And Dalí had earlier wrought a similar change to the chest of a stuffed polar bear. In his memoirs, Edward James relates that members of his family had

. . . brought back far too many trophies from their hunting expeditions . . . There was even a polar bear from Greenland which was eight feet tall. He was mounted holding a silver salver, that poor bear, and in the end he got moth in his chest so, in 1934, I gave him to Salvador Dalí and shipped him over to Paris, where Dalí had him dyed mauve. He had drawers put in the bear's chest to keep his cutlery in.

Here the drawers are empty, with one exception, and the woman with her head buried in the topmost drawer seems utterly despondent. At the top right Dalí has carefully recreated the appearance of a *fin-de-siècle* view of a city and, judging by the woman's gesture, withered skin and vacant drawers, her despair seems to be caused as much by the loss of the past as by her inner emptiness.

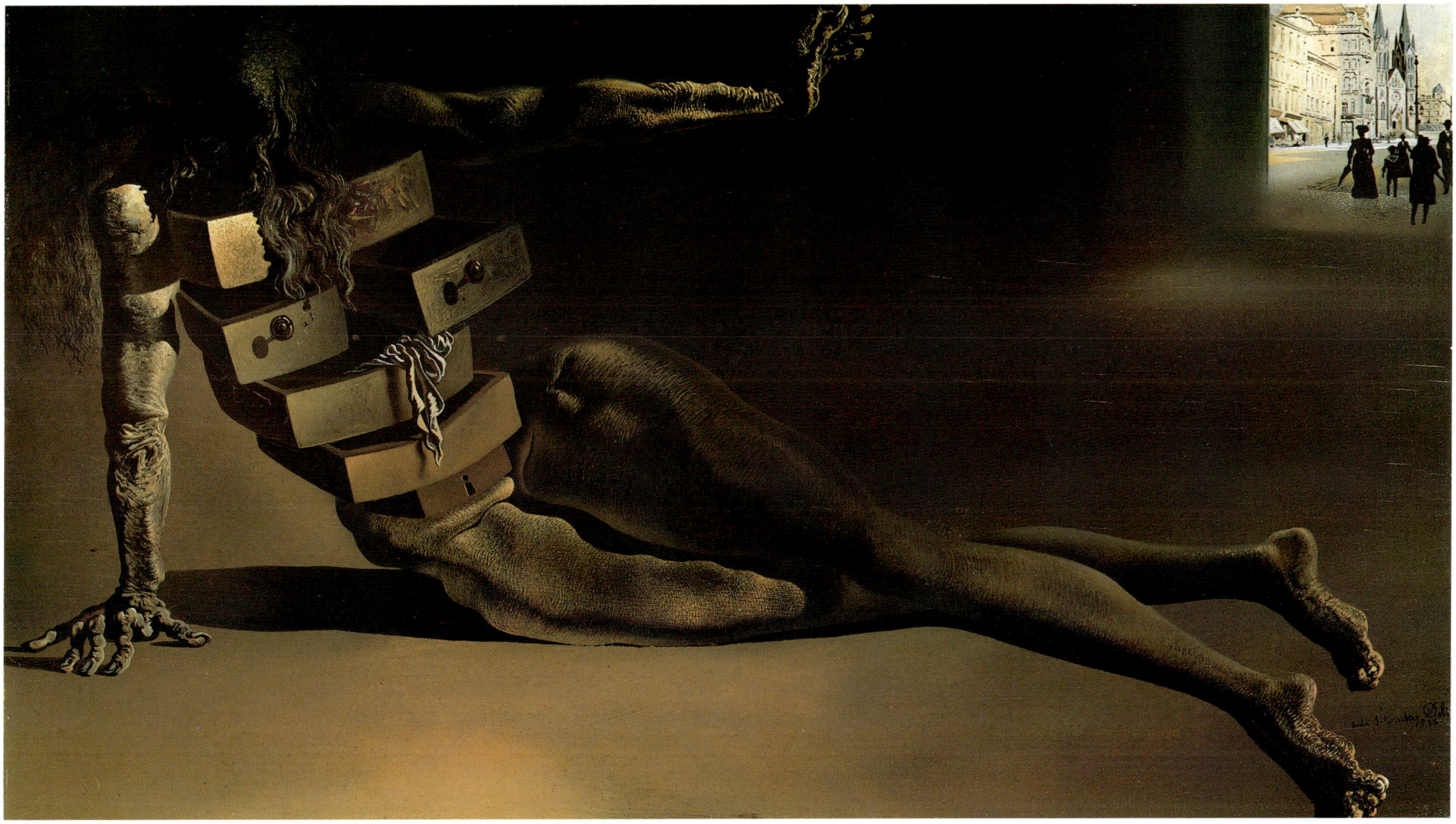

The Metamorphosis of Narcissus

Painted 1936–37
50.8 × 76.2 cm
Tate Gallery, London

In Ovid's *Metamorphoses*, Narcissus is an unusually handsome youth who is punished by Nemesis by being made to fall in love with himself when he sees his own reflection in a pool; in turn he is loved by the nymph Echo, whose punishment by Juno dictates that she is only ever able to repeat the last words that are spoken to her.

Here Dalí represented Narcissus gazing downwards on the left and, by creating a complete visual correspondence between the body on the left and the hand and bulb sprouting a narcissus flower on the right, equally he suggested Echo's verbal repetitiousness. The warm colour of the body and the cool tones of the hand add to the sense that we are looking at complementary forms, and thus they advance the Narcissus and Echo theme, while the group of distant nudes between the figure and hand amplify the sexual undertones of the original myth. Moreover, soon after this painting was completed, Dalí published a poem and essay entitled 'The Metamorphosis of Narcissus' in which he related that in Catalonia the phrase 'To have a bulb in the head' means to have a psychological complex. The painter then went on to state that 'If a man has a bulb in his head it might break into flower at any moment. Narcissus!', which is probably why we see the narcissus springing forth here. And in the far distance on the right may be seen the tips of further fingers holding another bulb. Before them is a youth (or perhaps a statue of a youth) standing on a plinth; this too may be Narcissus.

When Dalí visited Sigmund Freud in London in 1938 he showed him this painting and was purportedly told:

It is not the unconscious I seek in your pictures, but the conscious. While in the pictures of the masters – Leonardo or Ingres – that which interests me, that which seems mysterious and troubling to me, is precisely the search for unconscious ideas, of an enigmatic order, hidden in the picture, your mystery is manifested outright. The picture is but a mechanism to reveal it.

In fact, this response was surely wishful thinking on Dalí's part, for by 1938 Freud had difficulties in speaking due to his throat cancer. But in a letter that the psychoanalyst wrote to Stefan Zweig directly after the meeting he did make it clear that Dalí had changed his attitude to Surrealism, which he had previously thought to be foolish, for 'This young Spaniard, with his ingenuous fanatical eyes, and his undoubtedly technically perfect mastership has suggested to me a different estimate.'

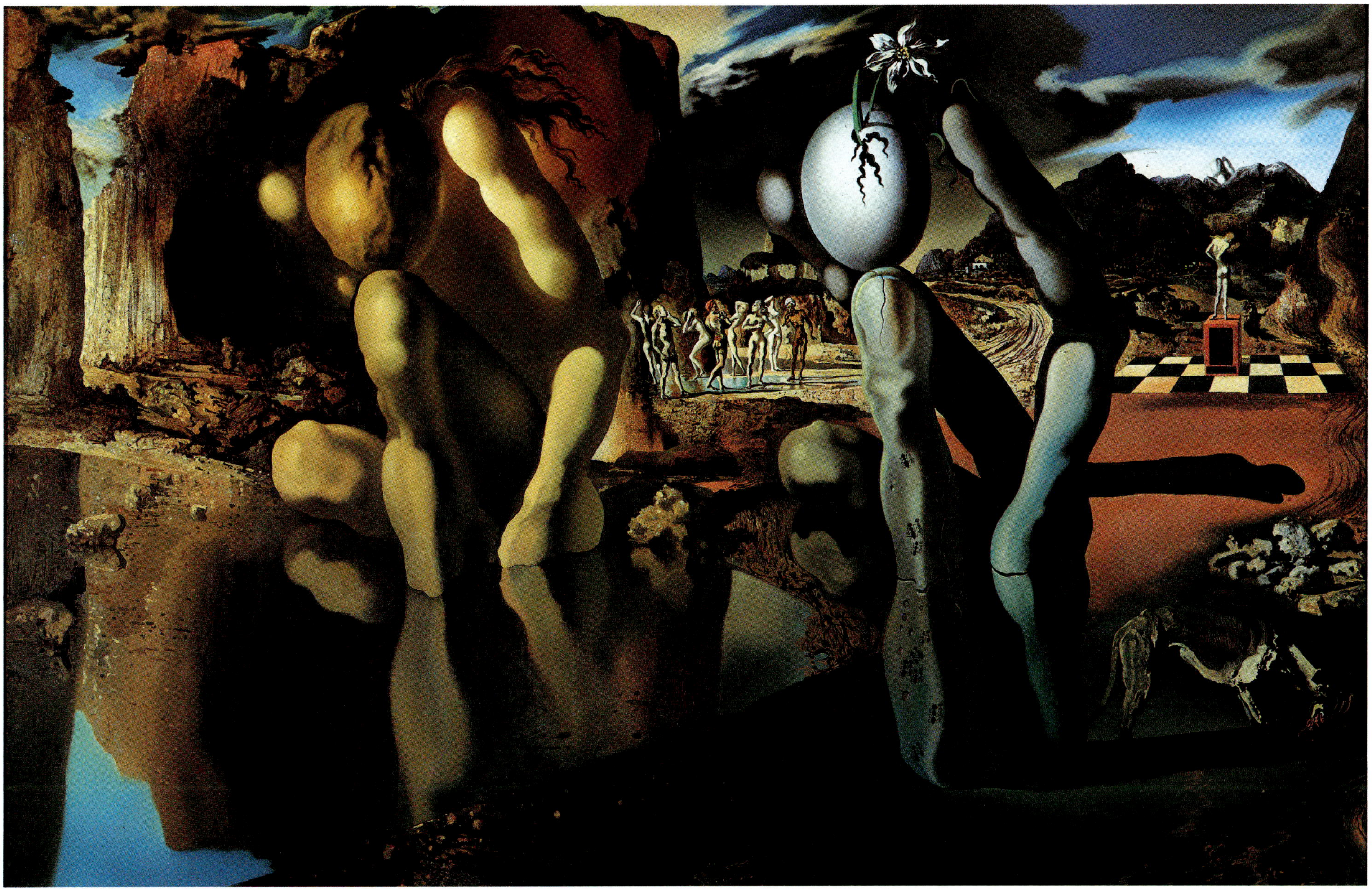

Morphological Echo

Painted 1936
30.4 × 33 cm
Salvador Dalí Museum, St Petersburg, Florida

In 1936 Dalí painted landscapes in oil on panel within the framed shapes of the heads and shoulders of a man and a woman, pendant panels that he gave the joint title of *A Couple with Their Heads Full of Clouds* (now in the Museum Boymans-van Beuningen, Rotterdam). In both images a table shrouded with a tablecloth appears in the foreground, and the tablecloth in the 'female' of the two works is identical to the tablecloth pictured here.

Dalí exploited spatial ambiguity in this tiny oil painting on panel, for because the objects are vertically aligned and yet cast deep shadows, we can either see them as rising above the table or as being regularly spaced out beyond it. The fact that the area beyond the table enjoys no horizon line furthers this ambiguity, and certainly that surround adds to the dreamlike, floating nature of the image. The warm colour-range introduces associations of a desert-like background, while the table and still-life equally evoke echoes of Spanish seventeenth-century still-life painting, in which case the empty area beyond the objects might be read alternatively as a blank wall with the objects floating in front of it.

The left-hand vertical line comprises a glass and spoon, a nursemaid and a tower; the centremost line a crust of bread, seated nursemaid and rock-formation, of the type seen near Cadaqués; and the right-hand line features a bunch of grapes, a reclining man wearing the type of soft worker's cap sported by Lenin in other pictures by Dalí (for example, see the 1933 *Enigma of William Tell*, page 69), and a brick wall. The 'morphological echoes' of the title are not difficult to discern, for on the left the glass, nursemaid and tower share their verticality, while in the centre line the bunched nursemaid's skirt serves visually to connect the crusty bread to the encrusted rockface, and through their overall similarities of form one can easily apprehend the 'echoes' of the objects on the right.

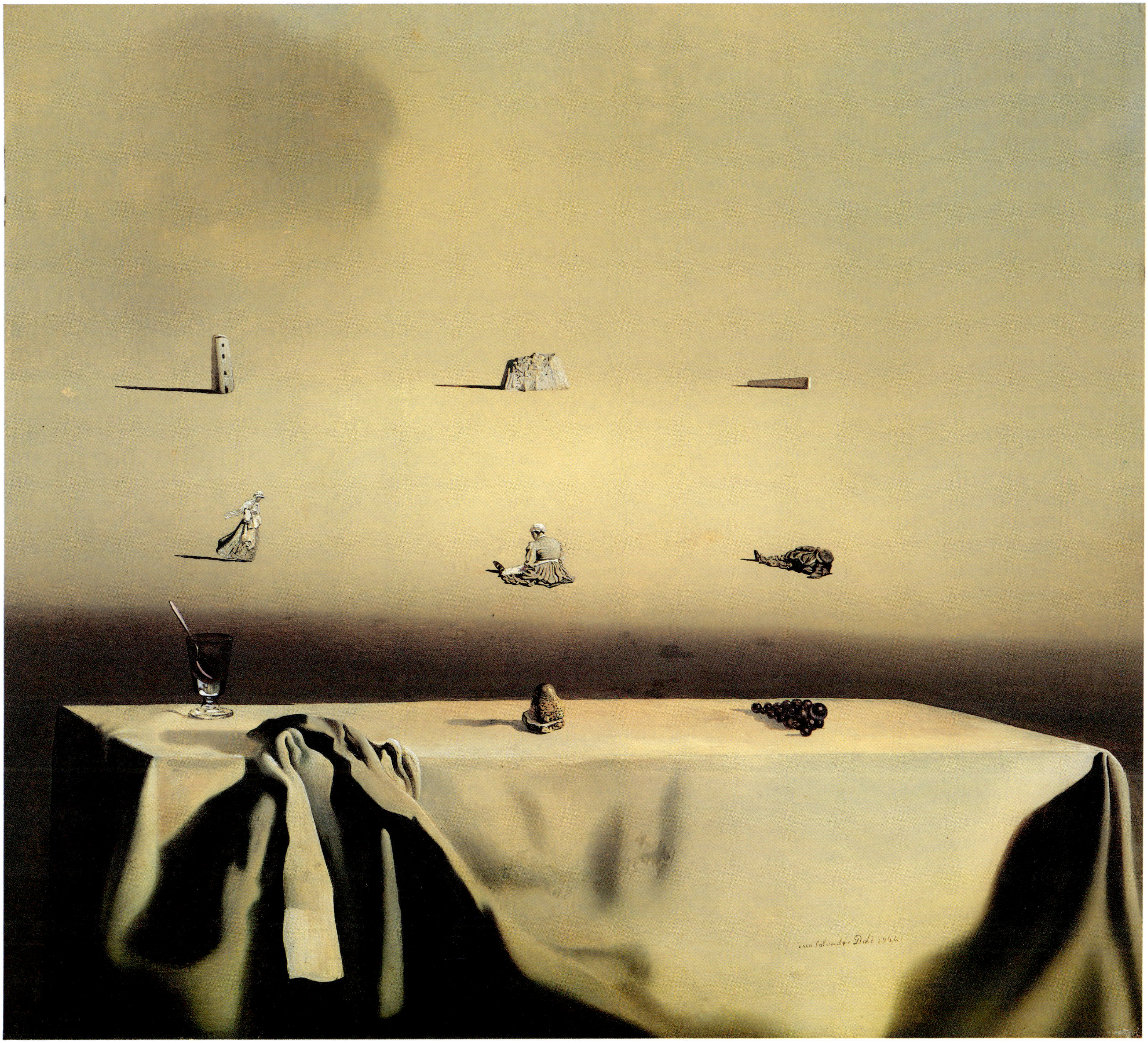

Sleep

Painted 1937
51.1 × 78.1 cm
Boymans-van Beuningen Museum, Rotterdam

In an article published in the Surrealist review *Minotaure* in the winter of 1937, Dalí stated that, when sleeping, 'It is enough for one lip to find its exact support in a corner of the pillow or for the little toe to cling imperceptibly to the fold in the sheet for sleep to grip us with all its force.' This declaration helps us understand the presence of so many supporting crutches in this oil painting. In the essay Dalí also drew attention to the dog on the extreme left leaning on his crutch, opening one eye and then going back to sleep again, in addition to 'the well-known summering town' (seen on the right) that had appeared 'in the boring dream of Piero della Francesca', a reference to Piero's *Legend of the True Cross* fresco cycle in the Church of San Francesco in Arezzo, wherein may be found the image of the Emperor Constantine lying asleep in his tent.

Dalí also later described this work as a 'painting in which I express with maximum intensity the anguish induced by empty space' and stated that 'I have often imagined the monster of sleep as a heavy, giant head with a tapering body held up by the crutches of reality. When the crutches break we have the sensation of "falling".' On the right the elongated and utterly limp form resembles a spent balloon, while the area where we would expect to see an ear is covered by a cloth, suggesting that all sound has been shut out. The limpness of the head projects the exhausted nature of sleep, while in the far distance a beached boat induces associations of being cut off from a normal environment. The huge empty space and detachment of the head from direct earthly support also fully project our disembodiment from a conscious state when asleep.

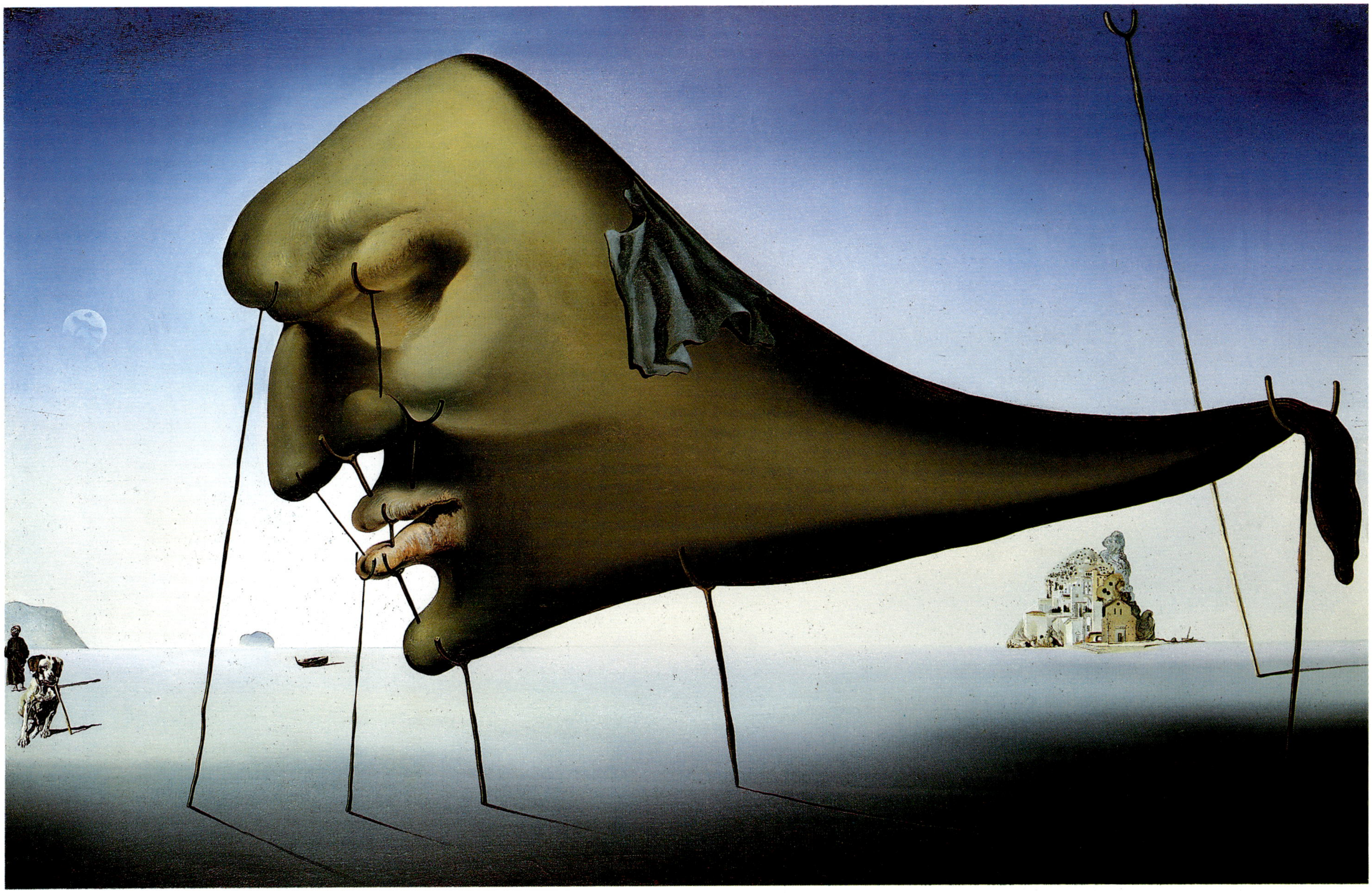

The elongation of forms clearly preoccupied Dalí in this painting, which projects one of his most surrealistic and wholly inexplicable but memorable images. The picture is unusually sketchy, but its predominantly blue colouring serves to accentuate the warmth of the fire in the distance, whilst adding to the unreal mood. The pose of the nearest woman is shared by a woman in a drawing by Dalí entitled 'an imaginary costume for a "dream ball",' the hands representing the yearnings of aviators' which was published in *The American Weekly* in March 1935.

The Burning Giraffe

Painted 1936–37

34.9 × 26.9 cm

Emanuel Hoffmann Foundation, Kunstmuseum, Basle, Switzerland

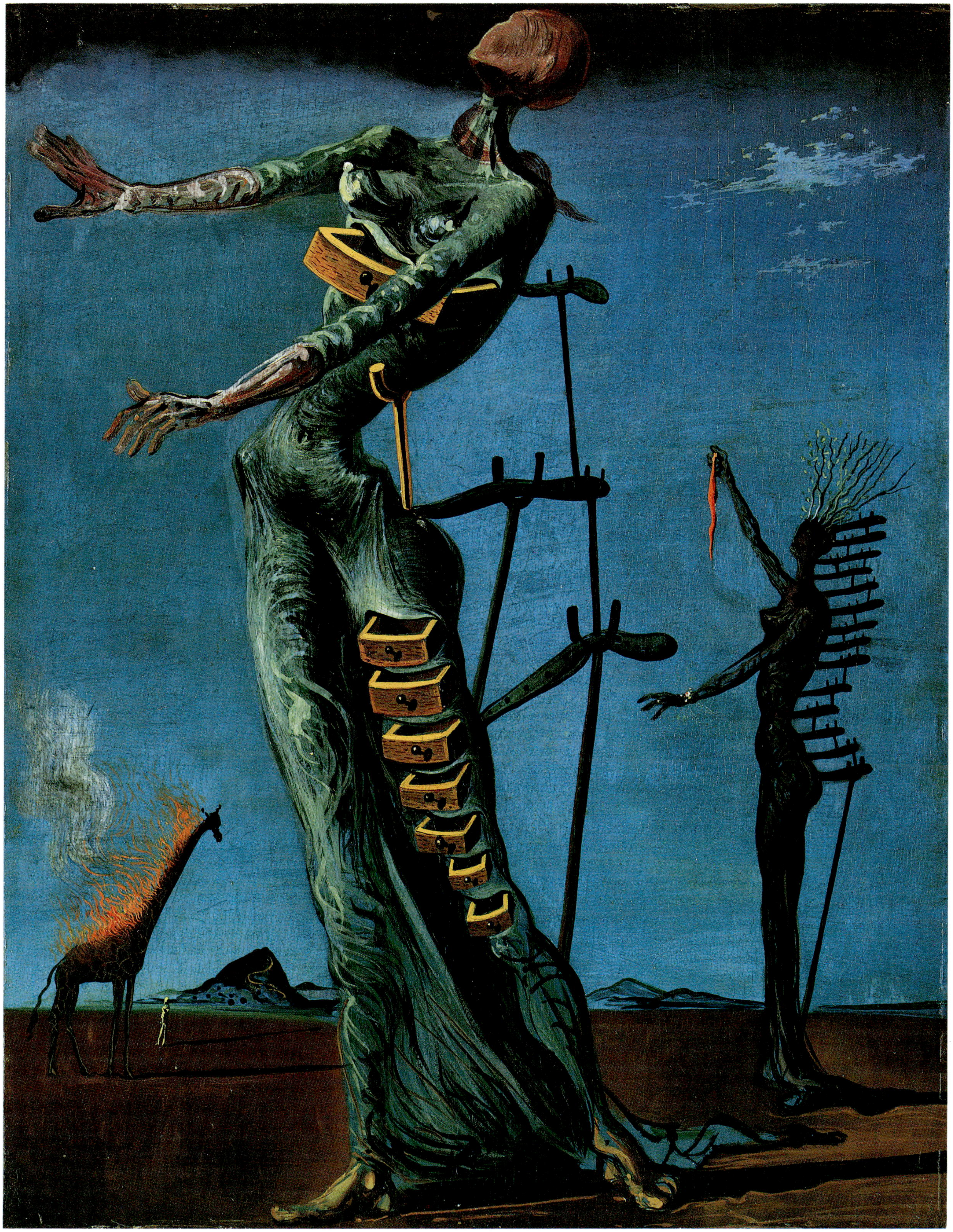

Here again we encounter a highly poetic, inexplicable universe whose strangeness is greatly heightened by the sharp contrasts of 'furious precision' and loose areas of form. And in reproductions of this picture, unlike reality, one can easily enjoy Dalí's inventiveness to the full, for if the colour plate is turned upside down the elephants that support the swans in the centre will themselves be transformed into swans and the swans into elephants: Dalí has not only perceived their similarity of form but doubled the number of times he played upon it, using the stumps of trees beyond the swans to provide the legs of the upside-down elephants. The sinuous curve of a branch above the leftmost swan counterpoises the sweeps of neck and/or trunk below it, and in the far distance on the left appears a strange rock formation and hill town that Dalí clearly appropriated from early Italian painting (see page 27), of the type that may also be seen in the *Sleep* (page 93), painted in the same year.

Swans reflecting Elephants

Painted 1937

51.1 × 77.1 cm

Private Collection

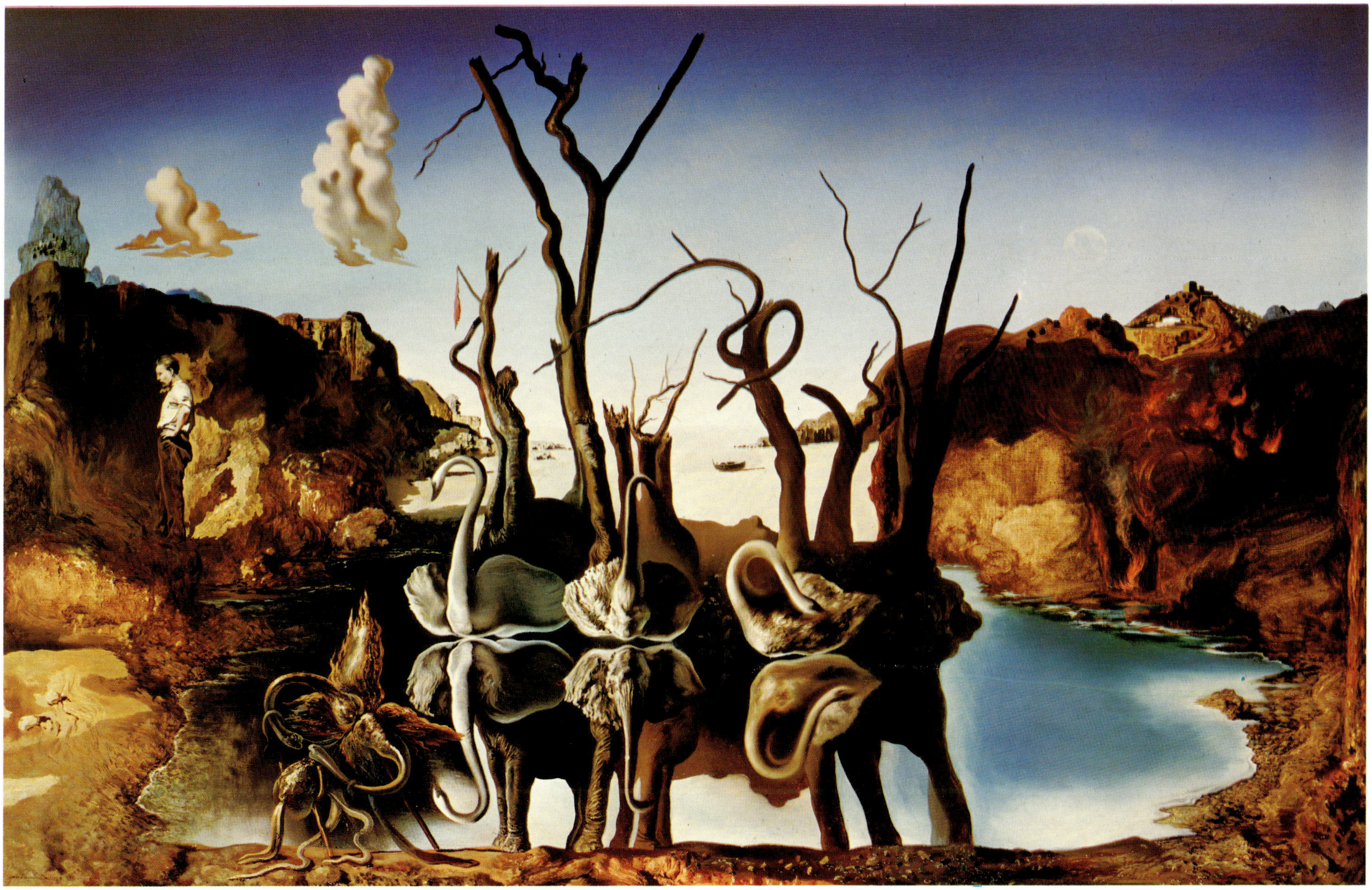

As well as looking carefully at early Italian paintings on his trips to Italy in the mid-1930s, Dalí also studied the works of Leonardo da Vinci, and that influence can easily be perceived in the distant figures in this picture. Such an assimilation was of course apt, for Leonardo himself had advocated the apprehension of things in other things, much as Dalí often forces us to do, and does again here. In overall terms the painting is reminiscent of Leonardo's unfinished *Adoration of the Magi* in the Uffizi Museum, Florence, as well as some of its related drawings, and facially Dalí's leaning woman is markedly similar to many of Leonardo's women. But Dalí's leaning woman is formed compositely out of the distant struggling figures, and her face appears only as an alternative to the struggling figures who form it – we cannot see *both* the face and the figures at once, as we might with many of Dalí's other dual images; we have to read one set of images or the other. And the painting also forces us to question the nature of illusion and reality in other ways as well, for the chest, drawer, foot and arm in the foreground are more tangible than the sketchier forms elsewhere, being more highly modelled, and yet they are themselves merely illusions within an overall illusion.

By 1938 Spain was approaching the climax of its Civil War, so it seems highly appropriate that Dalí epitomized that country as both a desolate plain peopled with struggling figures, animals and odd bits of furniture, and equally as a fragmented woman composed of many warring creatures.

Spain

Painted 1938

91.7 × 60.3 cm

Boymans-van Beuningen Museum, Rotterdam

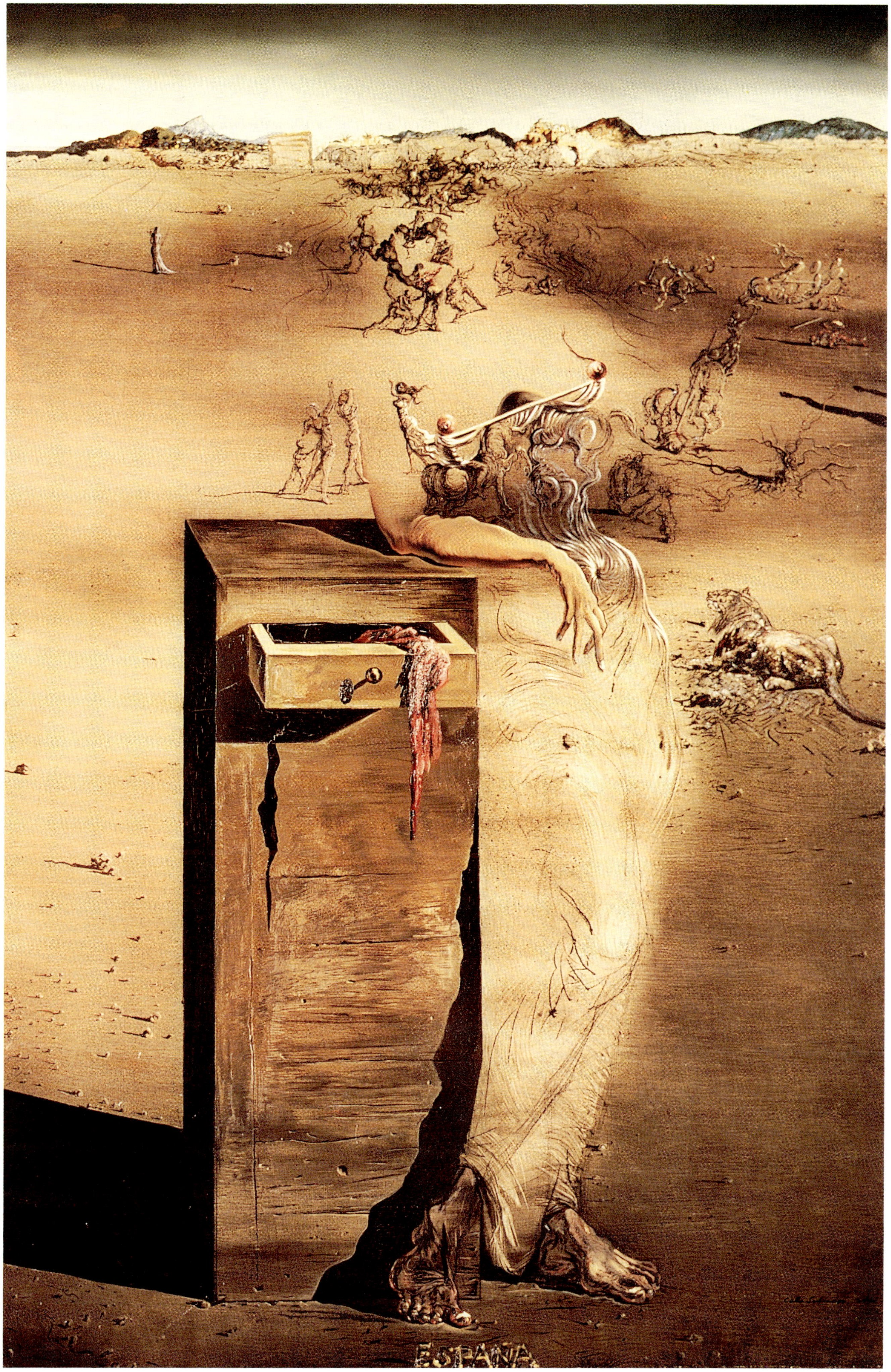
ESPAÑA

For Dalí, the playwright Raymond Roussel (1877–1933) was 'the greatest French imaginative writer', and it was from a play by Roussel entitled *Impressions of Africa* that he obtained the title of this picture, for by 1938 he had never been to Africa (he painted the work in Rome after a visit to Sicily, wherein he had found 'mingled reminiscences of Catalonia and of Africa'). Roussel was very fond of playing games with words and meanings, which is why his work greatly appealed to Dalí, and the painter similarly played around with illusion and reality here, as well as with intense contrasts of broadness and minuteness. On the left is Dalí himself, with Gala behind him. The shadowed areas around her eyes are exactly aligned with some adjacent Moorish archways, and the emptiness and dreaminess of the central area of the image are greatly augmented by the contrasting crowded and fragmented areas to either side, while the wide tonal shifts and hot colours certainly project the heat and dust of Africa.

Impressions of Africa

Painted 1938

91.1 × 117.4 cm

Boymans-van Beuningen Museum, Rotterdam

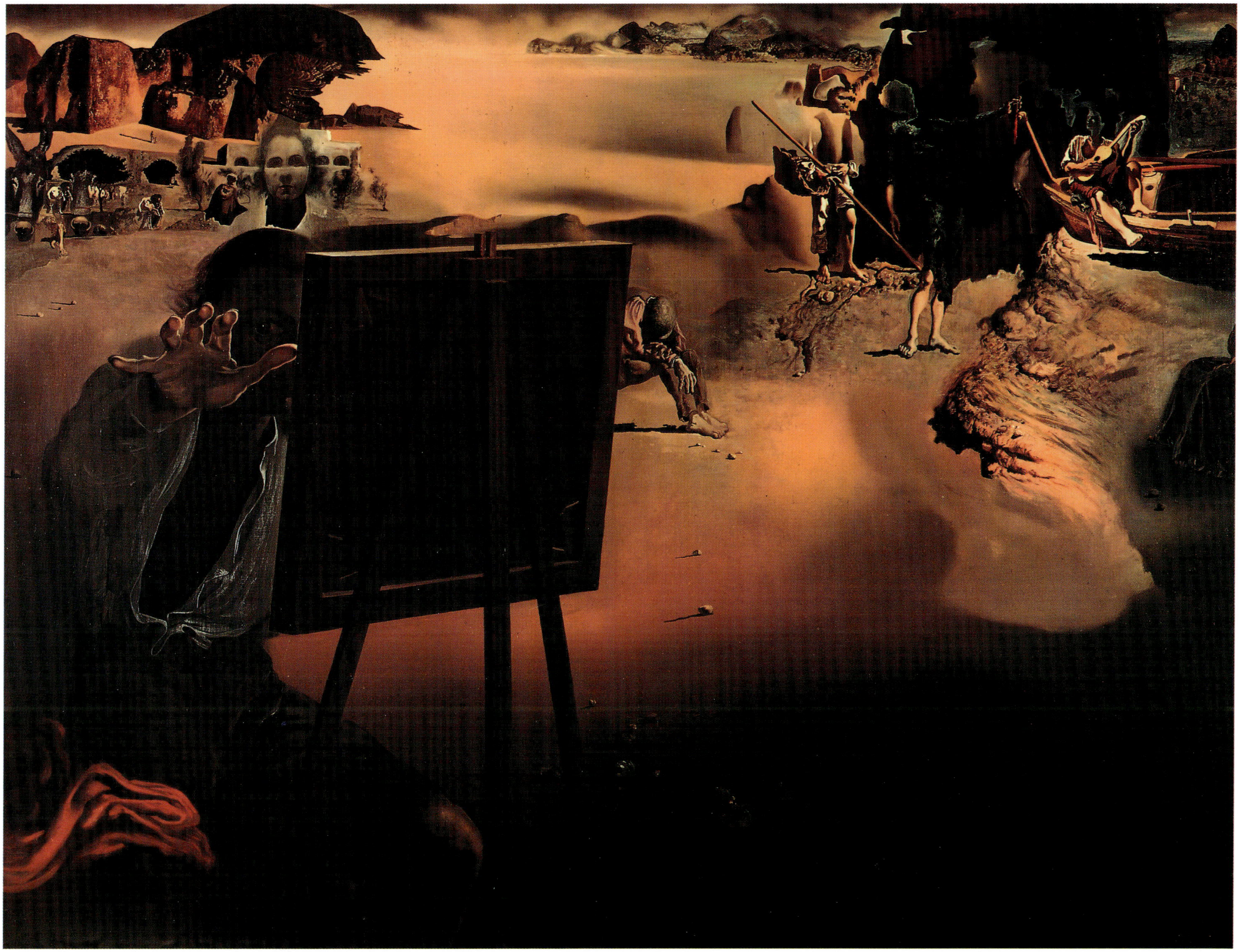

Apparition of Face and Fruit Dish on a Beach

Painted 1938

114.9 × 143.8 cm

Wadsworth Athenaeum, Hartford, Connecticut

Here again Dalí cleverly created a composite image out of differing objects, whilst simultaneously imbuing a picture with visual poetry through his manipulations of space and scale, emptiness and crowding. The face is easy to recognize, even if it is slightly more difficult to apprehend its nose, mouth and jaw as equally standing for the bulbous projections and flutings of a fruit dish. Above the face/fruit dish the imagery even becomes reversed, so that hair assumes the shapes of pears, while to the left of the face/fruit dish a wall of water also resembles hair and towers over a pool that enjoys the elongated shape of a fish lying on its side, a visual pun that Dalí frequently employed elsewhere.

The nearest object to the eye is a small circular pebble in the right foreground, and its rotundity is picked up and amplified at the top left by the moon, the most distant object in the image. The spatial transitions are especially fine in this painting, with the eye gradually being led off into the far distance, and with the moon acting as the climactic form, both spatially and poetically.

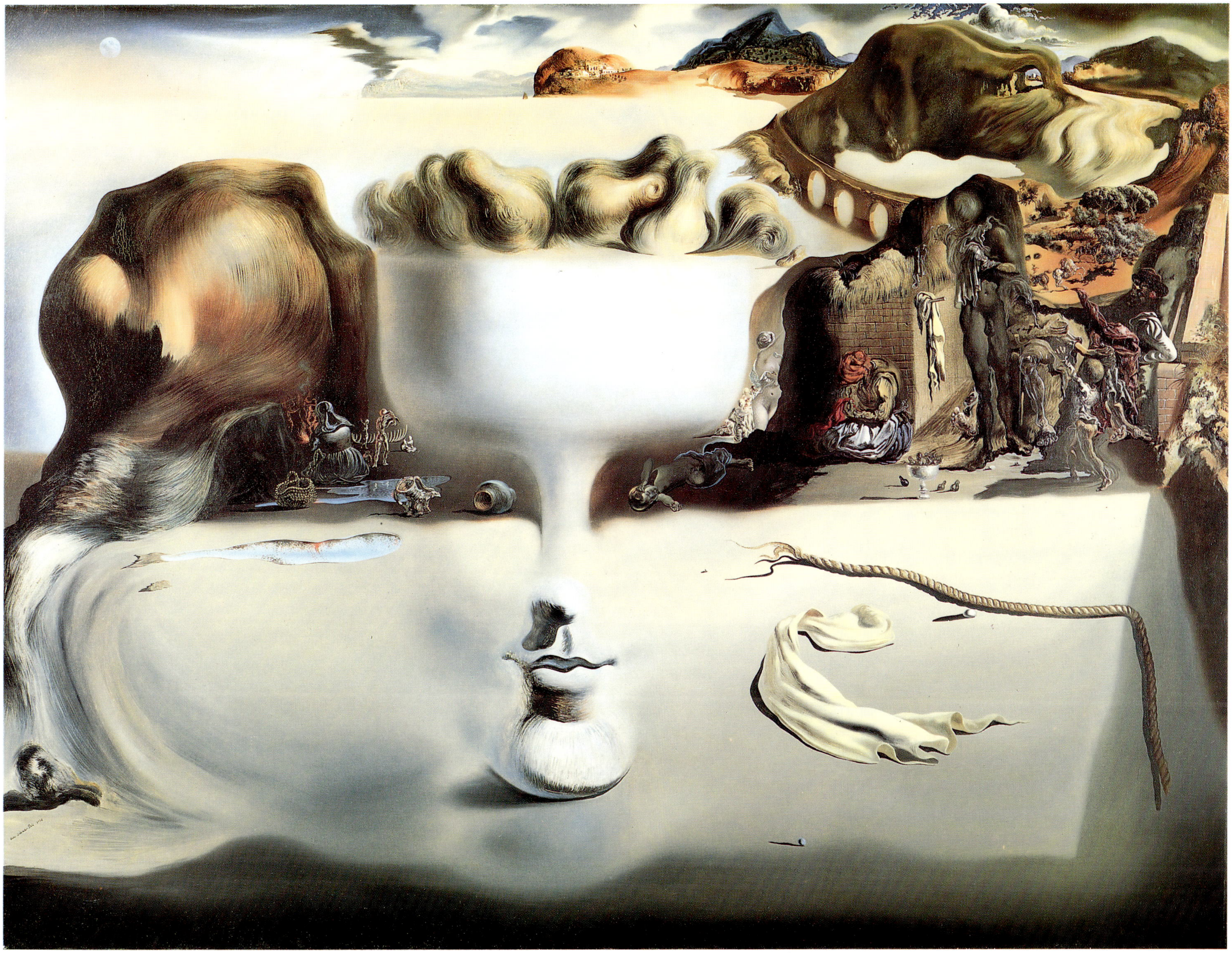

On the left is Gala; beyond her is the slave market where two people dressed in seventeenth-century black-and-white formal costume are framed by an archway. These figures and the arch may alternatively be read as forming the head of Voltaire, in a monochromatic rendering of the well-known portrait bust by Houdon. To the right of these figures is another person dressed similarly but who does not enjoy any alternative visual appearance.

For Dalí, Voltaire epitomized reason, and thus embodied an opposite approach to life from that of the Surrealists; as the painter wrote in his *Unspeakable Confessions*:

The illustrious Monsieur de Voltaire possessed a peculiar kind of thought that was the most refined, clearest, most rational, most sterile, and misguided not only in France but in the entire world. Voltaire did not believe in angels or archangels, nor in alchemy, and he would not have believed in the value of the 1900-style entrances to the Paris Métro . . . .

Voltaire's dedication to reason explains why Dalí set him in a slave market, for here the slavery is clearly a subservience to rationalism. On the right, visual confusion is purposefully created by the juxtaposition of some fruit in a bowl with a girl holding a circular object (which doubles as the bald head of her companion), and the crowding of the entire central part of the picture is heightened by contrast with the placid and virtually empty landscape beyond, as well as by Gala's languid and contemplative pose.

The Slave Market with the Disappearing Bust of Voltaire

Painted 1940

46.3 × 65.4 cm

Salvador Dalí Museum, St Petersburg, Florida

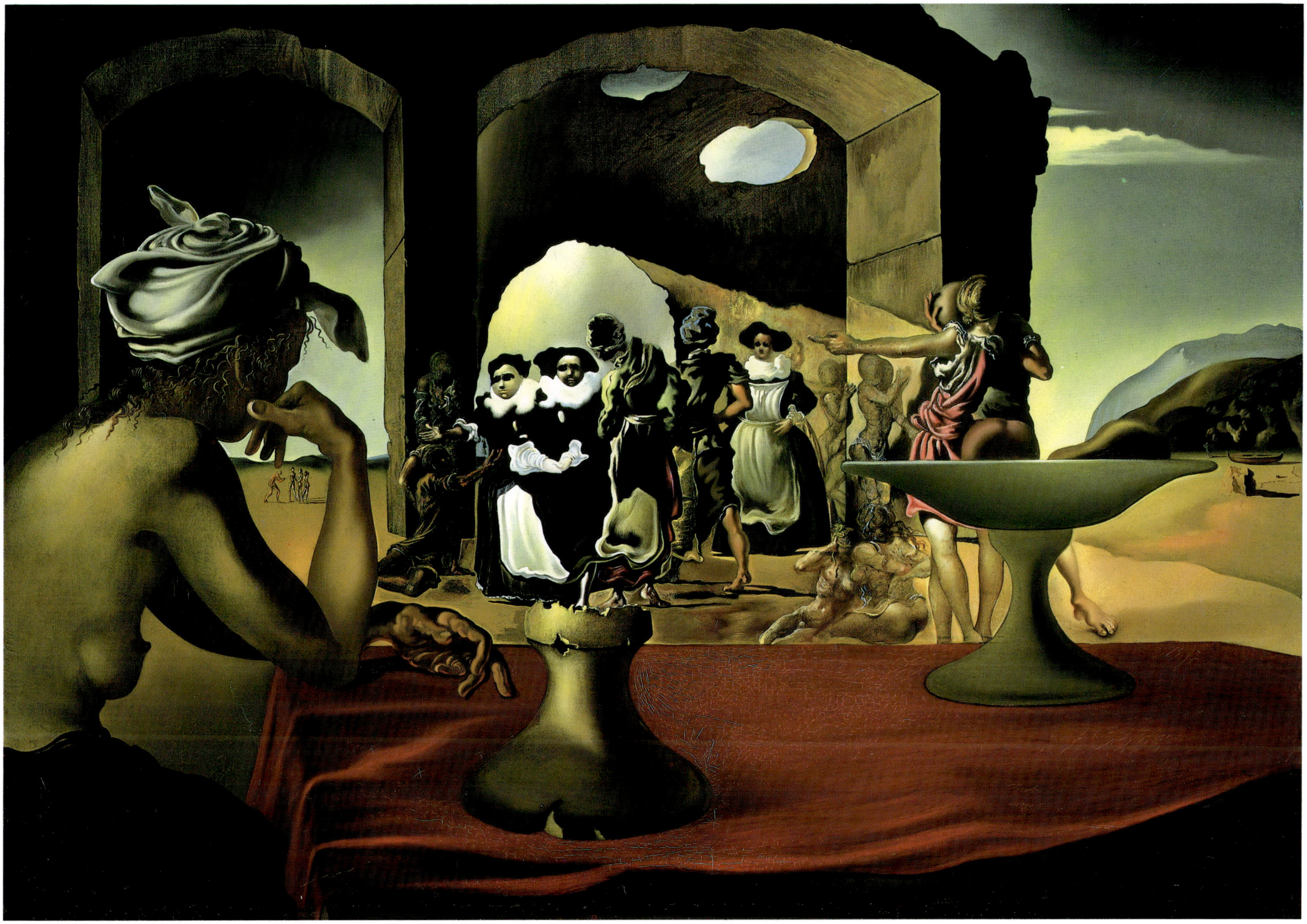

For Dalí, the eyes in this picture were 'stuffed with infinite death', but although it is undeniably a visually effective image, it is also a work that demonstrates the degree to which a certain obviousness, if not even banality, had begun to enter Dalí's art by 1940. The head is entirely explicable in symbolic terms, and therein lies its weakness, for whilst Dalí could imbue irrational-looking imagery with intense poetic feeling, when it came to rational meanings – and symbolism is a decidedly rational process, involving the matching of image to meaning – then his touch could easily desert him, as here: we are only one remove from a propaganda poster, of the type that was becoming common by 1940.

Visage of War

Painted 1940

64.1 × 79 cm

Boymans-van Beuningen Museum, Rotterdam

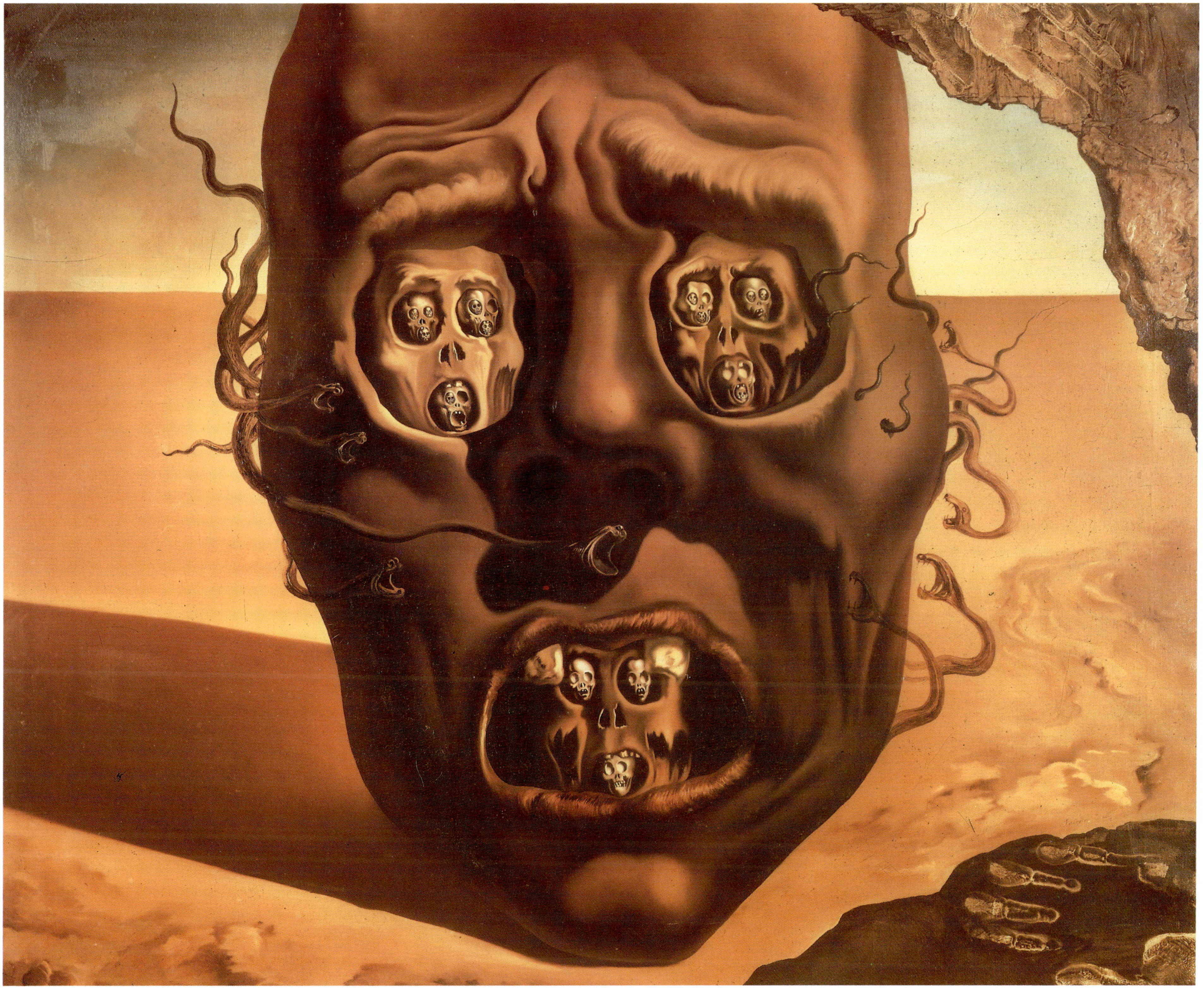

Here Dalí was more imaginatively at home than in the previous work discussed. The strip of grilled bacon before this witty self-portrait adds to the culinary associations of the supported form, brown and soft though it is.

As in his earlier 'soft' self-portraits, Dalí rejected the notion of affording a window into his own soul, and instead employed his elliptical approach to reality, whereby soft pieces of matter reminiscent of food or excreta could represent other objects and emphasize their physicality in the process. Moreover, the ants that congregate at the corners of Dalí's eyes and mouth, and the well-worn crutches, add a subtle note of decay to the proceedings, thus making a further comment on the painter's own physicality.

Soft Self-Portrait with Grilled Bacon

Painted 1941

61.2 × 50.8 cm

Teatro-Museo Dalí, Figueras

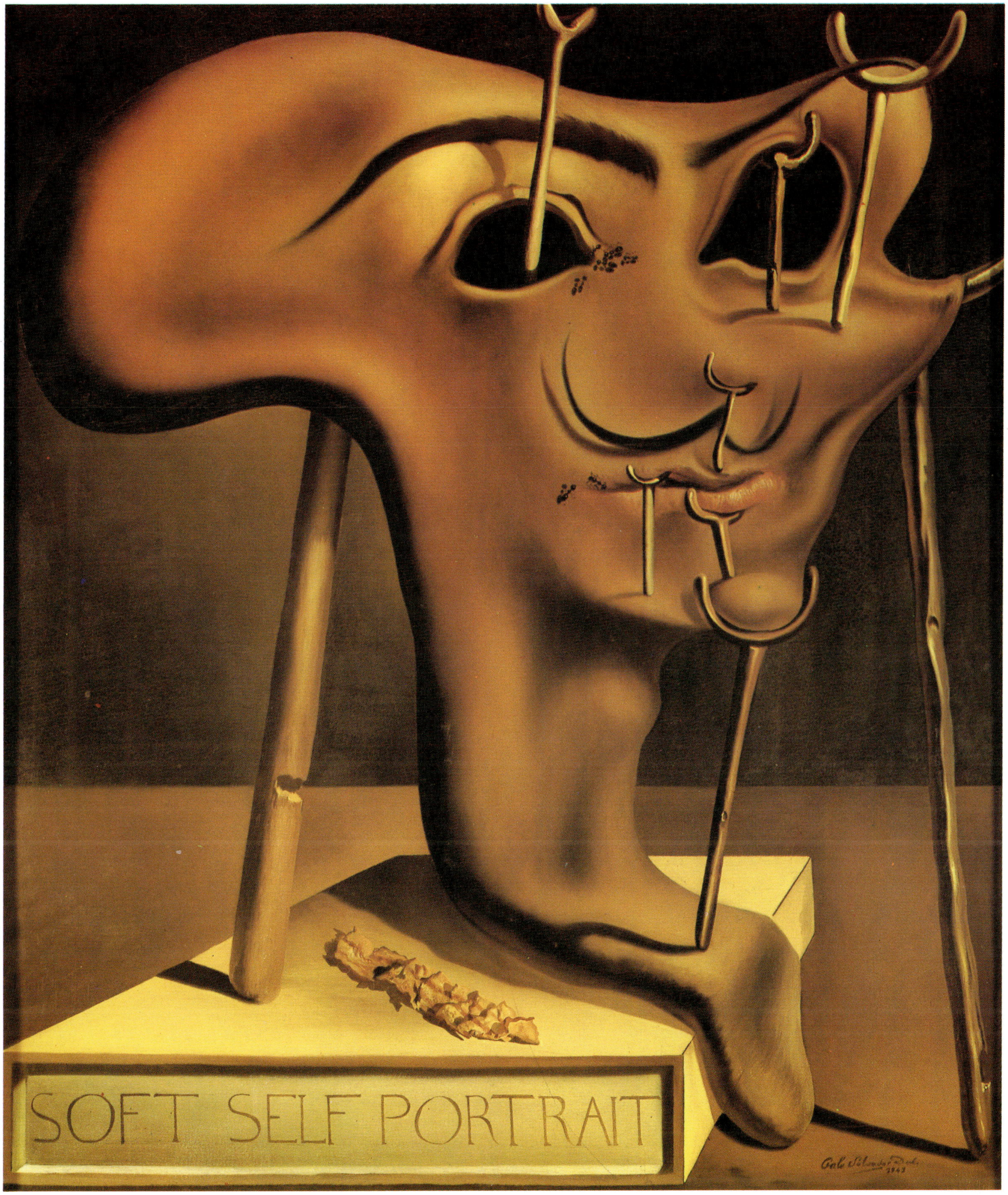
SOFT SELF PORTRAIT

This is one of Dalí's wittier works of the early 1940s. It was made in gouache watercolour over a chromolithographic reproduction of an oil painting by a minor creator of animal kitsch named Schenk; Dalí superimposed the floor in the foreground and all the background furniture, fittings, bookcases and wall, as well as adding the reclining woman and the golden, decorative 'feet' to those of the sheep. The light that appears above the amusingly Dalinian lampholder is the wan sun from the original winter scene, as are the bird perched on the woman's head and the shepherd supporting a superimposed dish or ashtray on his head. Yet although the sheep, birds and shepherd were all in this picture first, such was Dalí's visual inventiveness and technical fluency that they seem to be invading the safe cosy world of the library instead.

The Sheep

Drawn 1942

22.8 × 34.2 cm

Salvador Dalí Museum, St Petersburg, Florida

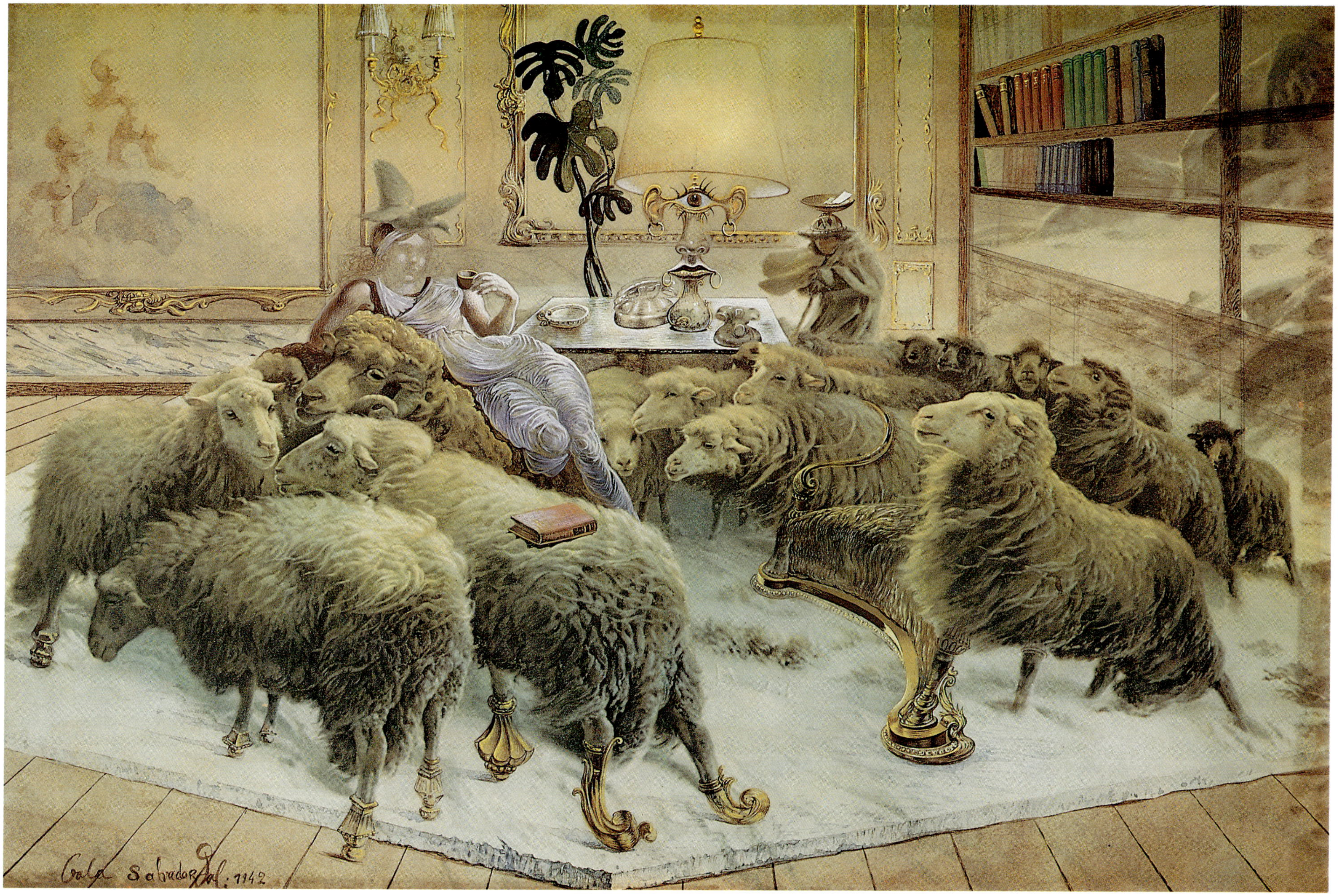

Helena Rubinstein's Head Emerging from a Rocky Cliff

Painted 1942–43

88.9 × 66 cm

Helena Rubinstein Foundation, New York

If in the previous work Dalí wittily superimposed his own particular brand of disorder upon kitsch, here he came perilously near to producing kitsch himself. In order to survive economically when in American exile during the war years – and for Dalí and Gala 'survival' meant leading a very affluent lifestyle indeed – the painter took to producing society portraits. But the people he painted did not want their visages replicated in soft, culinary or excretory terms; evidently what they required was to be flattered and surrounded by merely a little safe surrealism. This certainly made for financial success but unfortunately it did not make for good paintings, as here.

Helena Rubinstein created her fortune in the cosmetics industry, and Dalí was extremely scathing about her in his *Unspeakable Confessions*. In this picture he represented her as Andromeda chained to a rock by her emeralds, with a further female form beyond her bearing the Andromedan burden so that she can continue to look quite unperturbed. As always, Dalí's technique and attention to the appearances of things is impressive, but the portrait seems slick and artificial in its lack of any convincing intensity of vision or authentic Dalinian insanity.

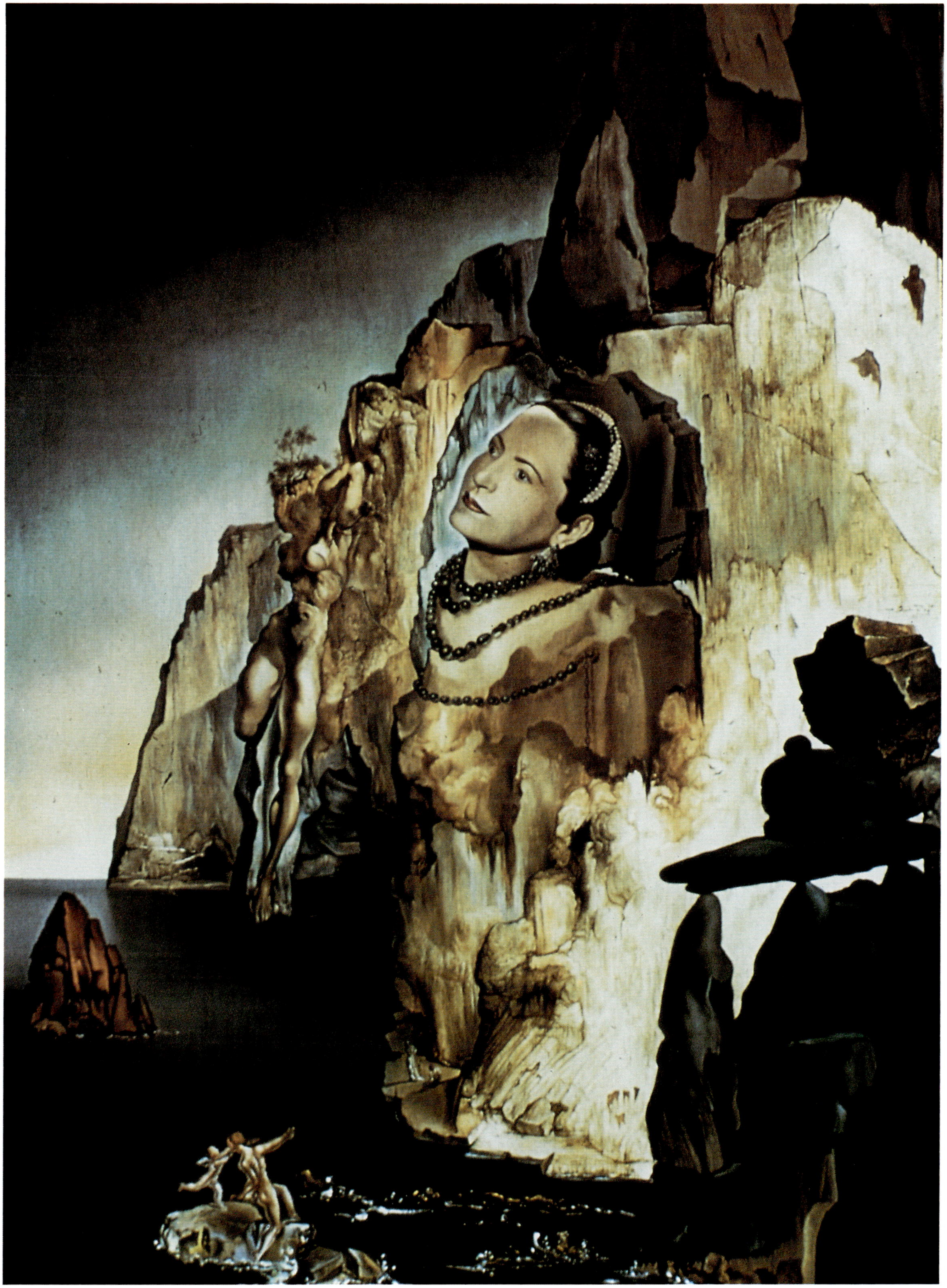

Dalí appropriated the tigers in this work from a circus poster and, indeed, the entire image has the look and visual immediacy of a poster, which perhaps accounts for its popularity. But ultimately this picture is Surrealism made easy, for because the events of the dream take place around someone sleeping, we tend to see them as occurring in that person's mind, as the manifestation of *her* dream rather than as the projection of a dream *per se* that we need to fathom wholly in terms of our own non-rational experience. Moreover, both title and imagery enjoy a sense of connection and sequence – in the foreground are the bee and pomegranate, while a further pomegranate bursts on the left, disgorging fish, tigers and a rifle whose bayonet is about to prod the prostrate form of Gala awake in a second's time – and connection and sequence are rational processes that make the proceedings very approachable conceptually. Here we are a long way from 'the depths of the subconscious' because it is so easy to understand things in rational terms. By the mid-1940s Dalí's Surrealism was becoming a little too pat and predictable. Although there are undoubtedly memorable images here – the elephant with extended legs is a superbly imaginative conceit – nonetheless there are not enough of those images to push the work into that ineffable imaginative dimension that lies beyond mere illustration.

Dream Caused by the Flight of a Bee around a Pomegranate One Second before Awakening

Painted 1944

51.1 × 40.6 cm

Thyssen-Bornemisza Collection, Madrid, Spain

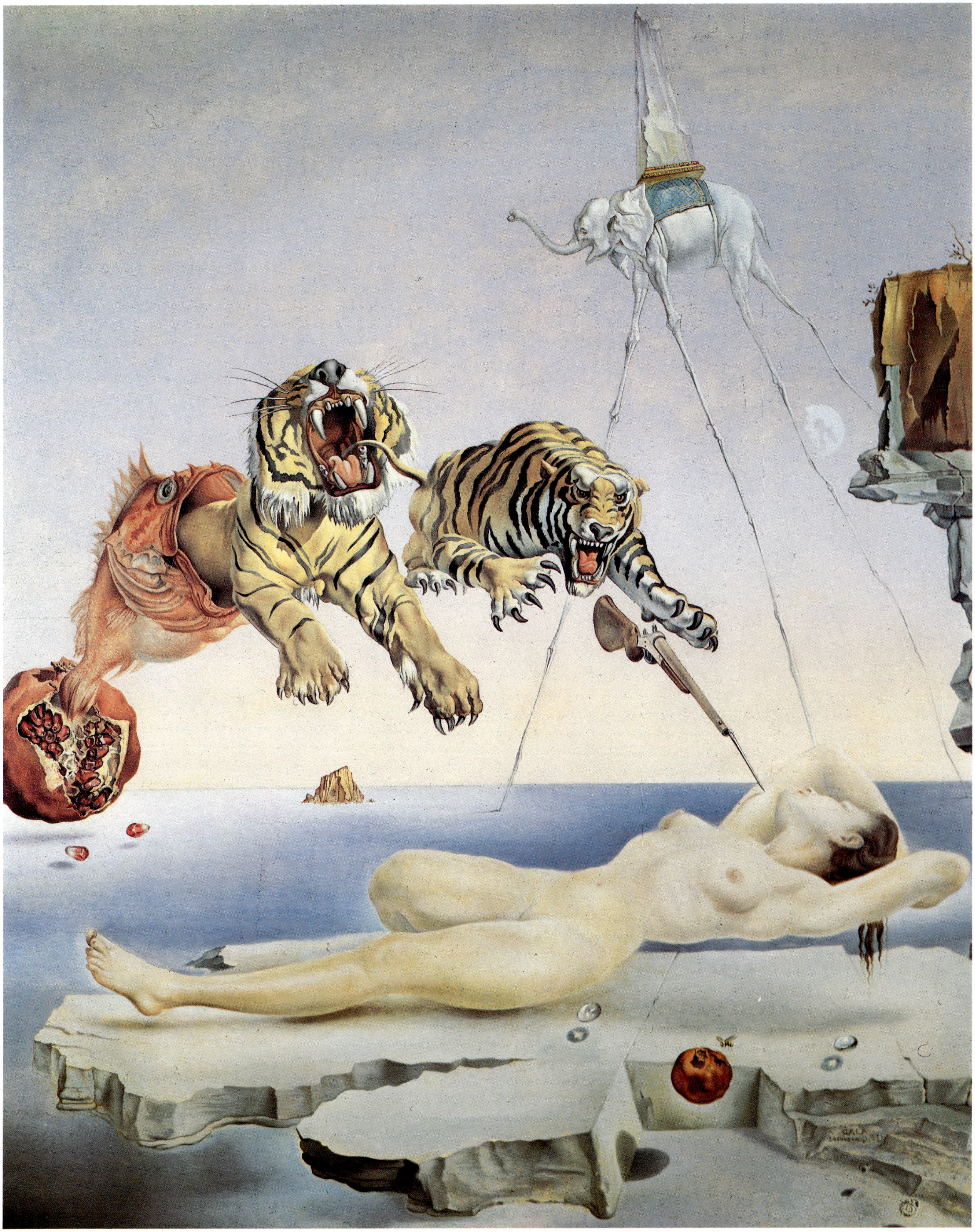

This is one of the last works in which the manic Dalí still shone forth with his old imaginative intensity. The painting enjoys the subtitle *Diurnal Dream of Gala*, and Gala is stretched out on the right. Although the picture thus also projects someone else's dream (as does the previous work discussed), nonetheless here the imagery does enjoy all the authentic disconnection of a dream – it is impossible to relate the objects and occurrences to one another. A preliminary drawing for this picture was made in 1943 (now in a private collection), and it looks rather like a work by Nicolas Poussin in its figures and landscape. But in this oil painting the calm classicism of the drawing has been replaced by a truly surreal and rather nightmarish intensity of mood, with a baroque and somewhat Poussinesque chariot rising up in the middle distance and all kinds of unrelated cultural fragments placed in seemingly random spatial relationships around and before it.

The Apotheosis of Homer

Painted 1944–45

64.1 × 118.4 cm

Staatsgalerie Moderner Kunst, Munich

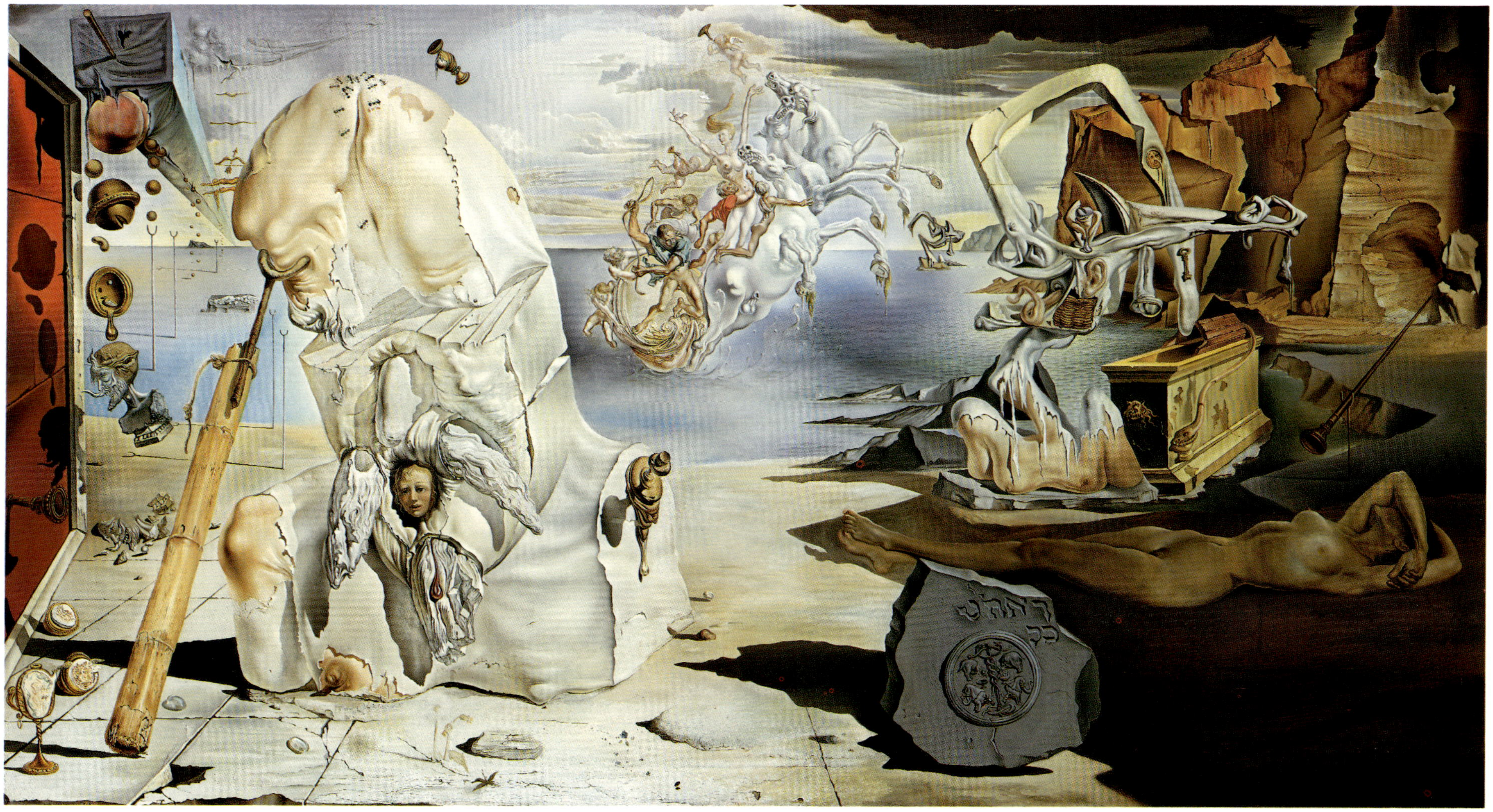

Although Dalí wrote disparagingly of Piero della Francesca in 1937 (see *Sleep*, page 92 above), nonetheless his comment shows that he had been looking carefully at the Italian painter's works by then, and in this oil painting on canvas such analysis paid off, for it is one of the better society portraits of the period. Although there is little sense of surrealism to the image (despite the blossoming crutches in the centre-distance, and the hair on a pendant upswelling into a miniature tree on the sitter's chest), the work does enjoy a modicum of visual and art-historical wittiness that offsets such a deficiency.

The obvious model for the basic layout of the work was Piero's dual portrait of Federico da Montefeltro and his wife in the Uffizi Museum in Florence (see page 30), a picture in which that Duke of Urbino faces his duchess across the frame pretty much as Isabel Styler-Tas confronts a rock formation here. It must have caused Dalí little imaginative effort to perceive in the sitter's hat the beginnings of a related form, and by making the rock look vaguely human, Dalí was also building upon the influence of Giuseppe Arcimboldo, a sixteenth-century Italian painter who was popular with the Surrealists for his composite heads fashioned out of disparate objects such as fruit, vegetables, fish and shells.

Portrait of Isabel Styler-Tas

Painted 1945

64.1 × 86 cm

Nationalgalerie Staatliche Museen Preussischer Kulturbesitz, West Berlin

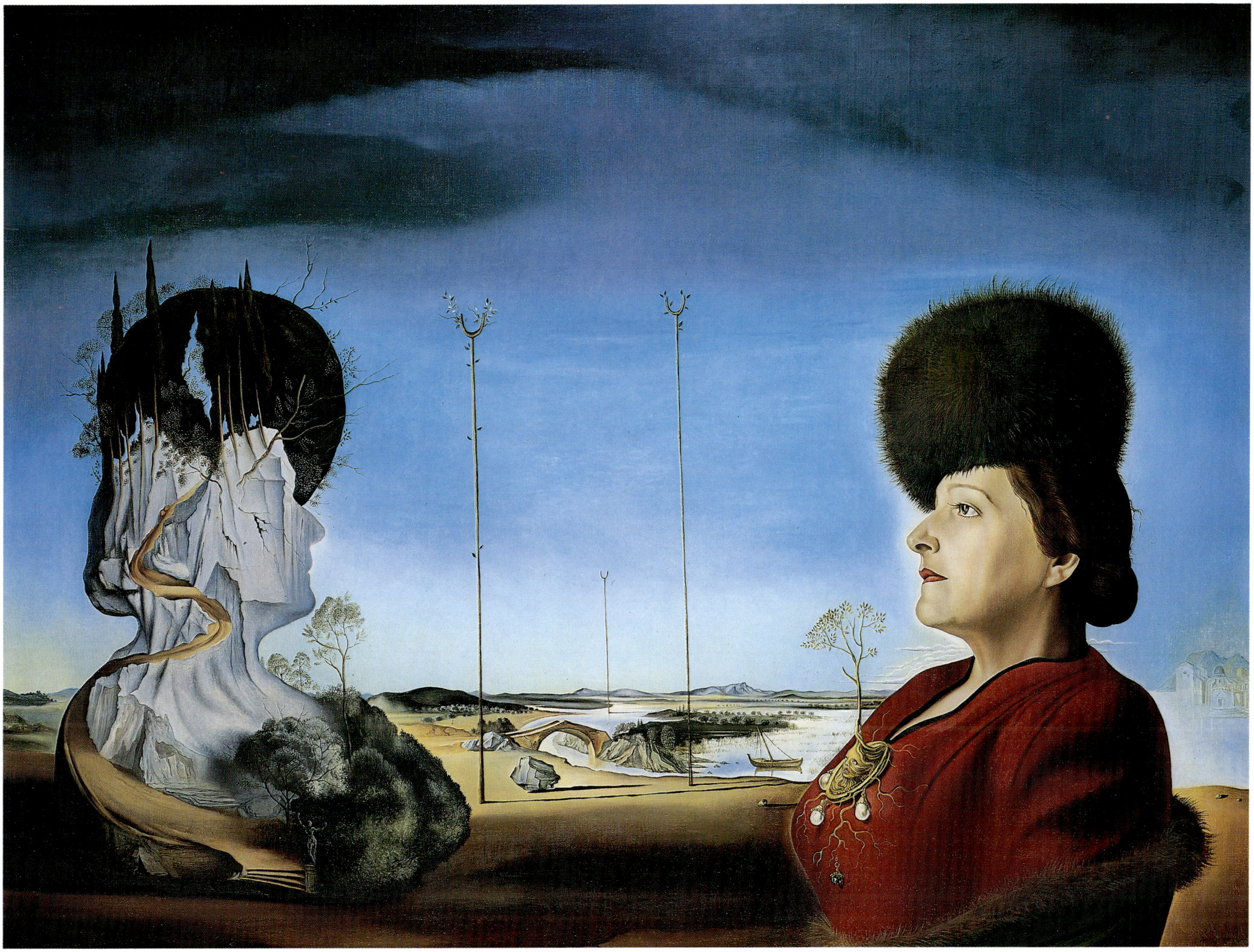

Dalí painted this picture for a competition organized by Albert Lewin in connection with his film of Maupassant's *Bel Ami*; the competition was won by Max Ernst.

Here again we see the illustration of someone else's state of mind rather than the projection of a state of mind in itself, for we look over St Anthony's shoulder and therefore see the phantasms before him through his eyes. The painter has merely employed his vivid imagination to project the saint's mystical experience, and that brings the picture very close to being a mere illustration because of the subservience of the imagery to some extra-visual programme. (As we shall see, such a criticism may also be levelled at many of Dalí's later religious pictures.)

The Temptation of St Anthony

Painted 1946

89.5 × 119.3 cm

Musées Royaux des Beaux-Arts de Belgique, Brussels

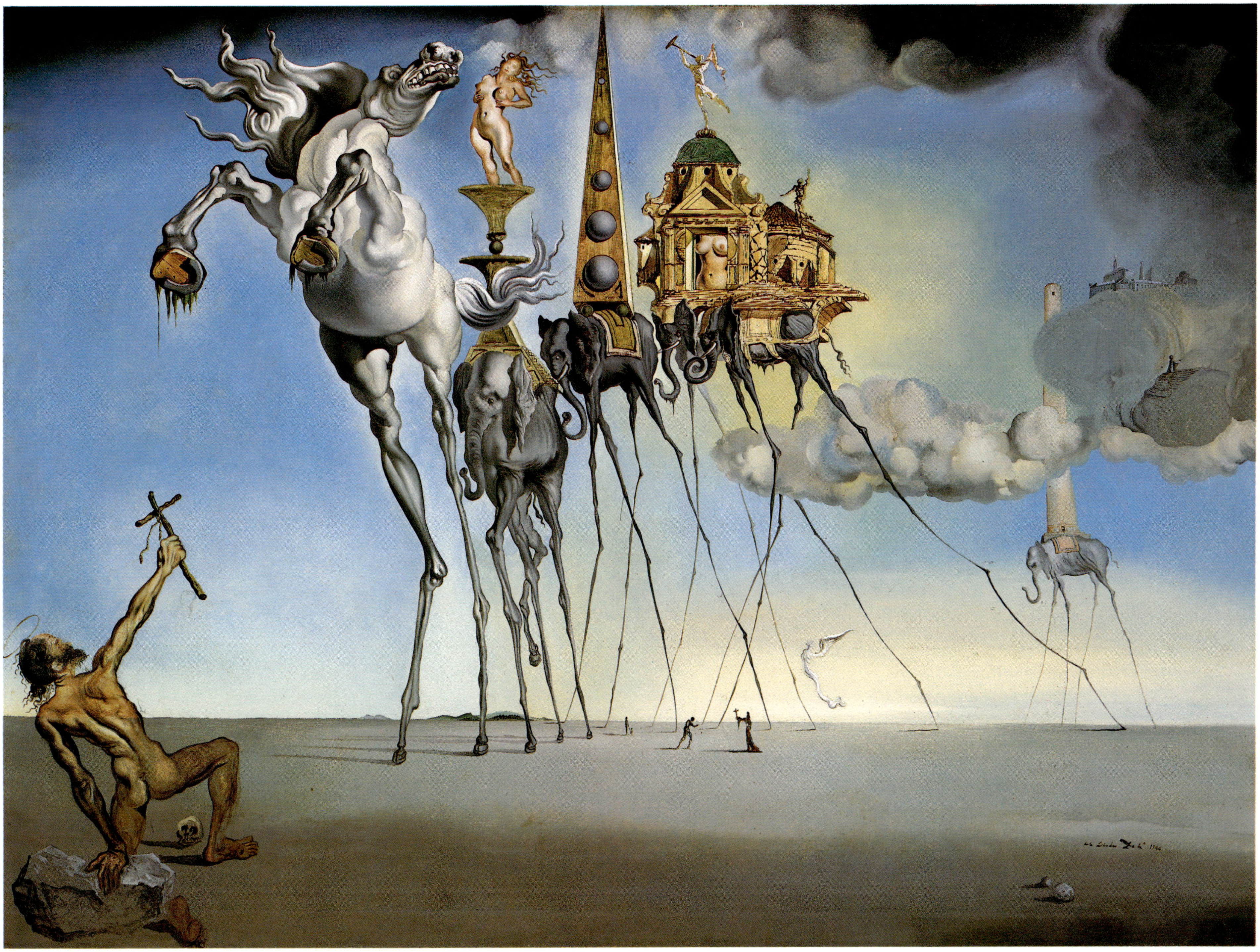

Although Dalí looked up to Picasso when young, by 1947 he had turned against him, as this portrait makes abundantly clear. Moreover, the picture was painted at the height of the Cold War, by which time Dalí had become violently anti-Communist, and after Picasso had joined the Communist party in 1944 Dalí felt as much alienated by Picasso's politics as by his long-acknowledged supremacy as a modern artist, a position that Dalí felt was his by right.

We can perceive this change in Dalí's attitude to Picasso in a passage in his second volume of autobiography, the *Unspeakable Confessions*:

Picasso is doubtless the man I have most often thought about after my own father. He was my beacon when I was in Barcelona and he was in Paris. His eye was my criterion. I have come across him at all the high points of my reign. And when I left for America, once again he was there: without him I would have had no ticket. I thought of him as the apple-crowned boy thought of William Tell taking aim. But he was always aiming at the apple, not at me. He radiated prodigious Catalan life. When the two of us were together, the spot at which we were must have become heavier and the noösphere assumed special density. We were the highest contrasts imaginable and conceivable. My superiority over him lay in my name being Gala-Salvador Dalí and knowing that I was the saviour of modern art that he was bent on destroying, while his name was simply Pablo. I was two and predestined. He was so alone and desperate that he had to become a Communist. He never ceased cuckolding himself.

The downside of Dalí's latterday love–hate relationship with Picasso may be seen in this portrait. Once again it is a work that draws upon the visual example of Arcimboldo for its imagery, with Picasso's 'head' composed of an array of disparate objects such as molluscs and amphora handles, and its brain reemerging through its mouth as an elongated tongue. Dalí obviously remembered the particular shape of Picasso's mouth, for that part of the head rather resembles it.

Portrait of Picasso

Painted 1947

64.1 × 54.6 cm

Teatro-Museo Dalí, Figueras

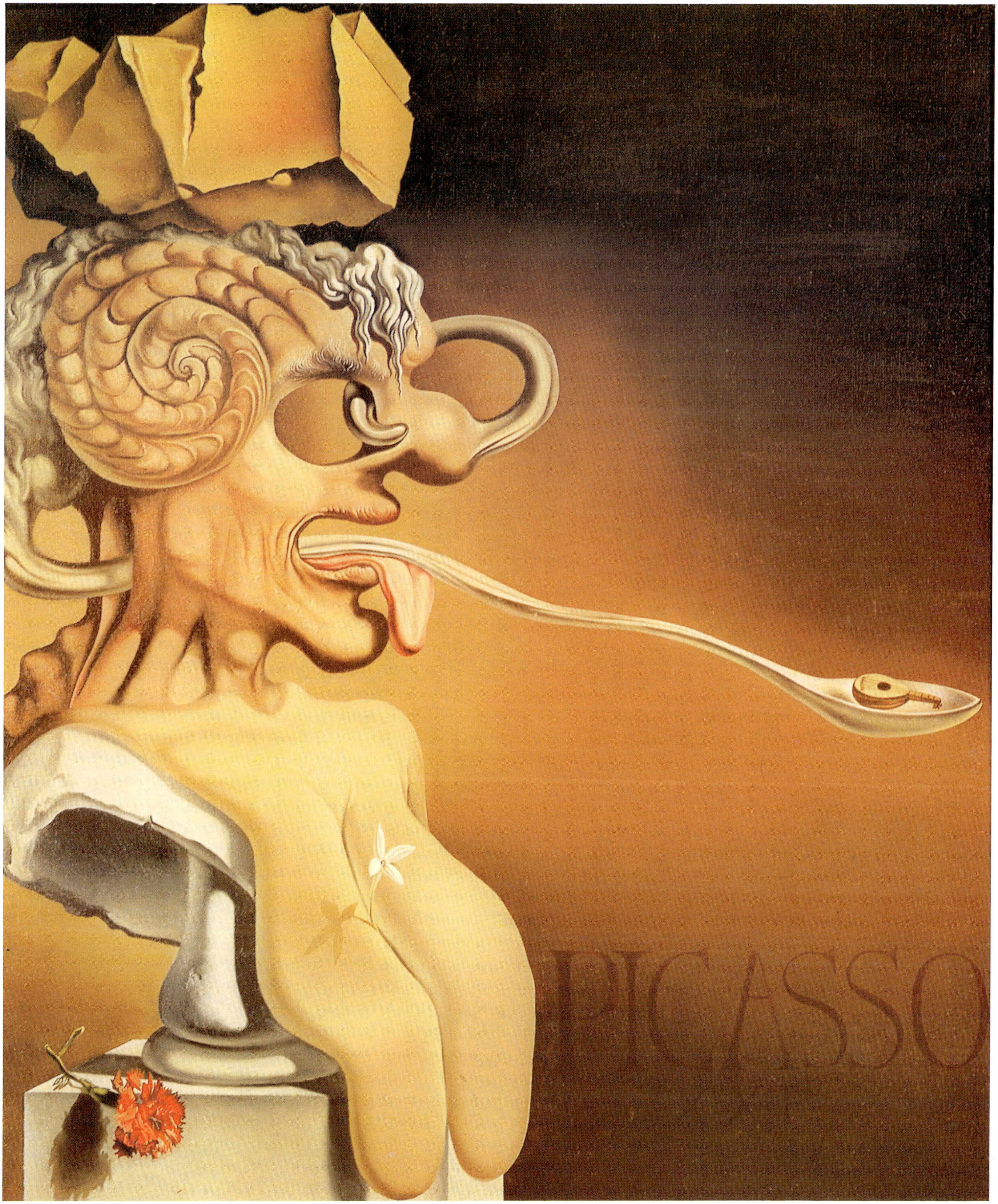
PICASSO

The Madonna of Port Lligat

Painted 1949
49 × 38.5 cm
Haggerty Museum of Art, Marquette University, Milwaukee

Dalí produced two versions of this work; this is the preliminary oil study for the final oil painting, and he received the Pope's blessing for it when he was presented to the religious leader in 1949. An obvious model for both images was Piero della Francesca's *Madonna and Child Enthroned with Angels and Six Saints, Adored by Duke Federico of Urbino* (in the Brera Museum, Milan), for the egg suspended from a conch shell above both of Dalí's Madonnas is virtually identical to one that appears in the work by the Italian master; Dalí has simply reversed Piero's conch and diminished it in size. As we have seen earlier, Dalí looked carefully at Piero's works when touring Italy in the 1930s, and although publicly he disparaged them verbally, clearly they made a profound impression upon him visually. In the Piero painting the suspended, unbroken egg probably symbolizes the act of divine fertilization by which Jesus was sired, although it is not known what Dalí made of it.

The moral absurdity, touching on blasphemy, of representing Gala Dalí as the Virgin Mary is discussed in the Introduction (see page 36), but by the late 1940s Dalí not only regarded his wife as divine; by that time he was also no longer capable of enjoying sexual relations with her, which possibly added to the virginal associations she enjoyed for him, despite the fact that she was constantly making herself sexually available to other men.

Dalí projected fragmented imagery such as we see here in a number of religious pictures painted during the late 1940s and 1950s, and it grew directly from his new-found interest in nuclear physics after 1945; later he explained this fragmentation as standing for 'dematerialization, which is the equivalent, in this atomic age, of divine gravitation'. The image undeniably enjoys an impressive sense of scale, even if it skirts (or perhaps crosses) the borders of kitsch because of the bogusness of representing Gala as the Virgin and its overall lack of visual originality; by the late 1940s (if not much earlier) this kind of religious imagery looked very hackneyed indeed, and increasingly does so.

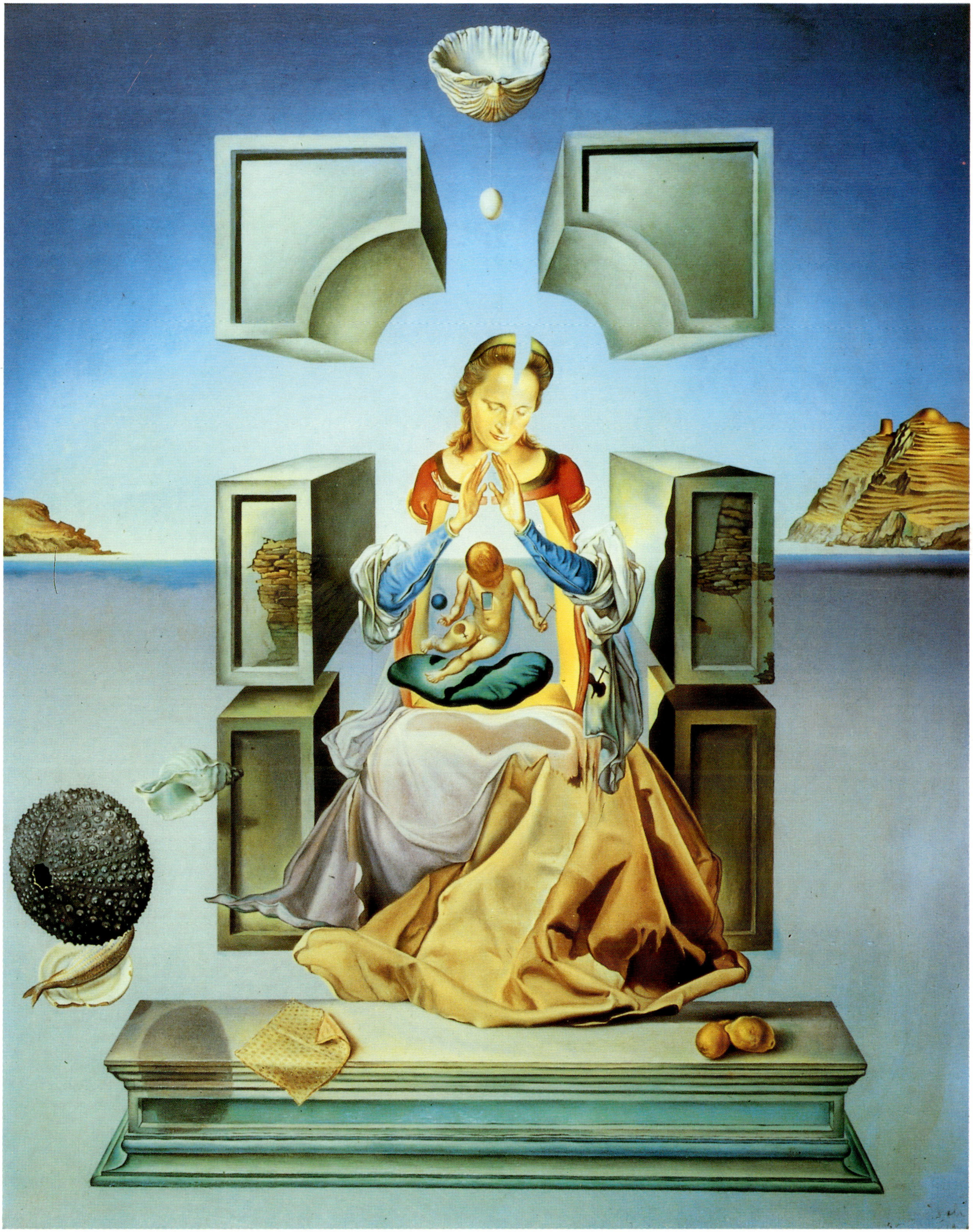

Christ of St John of the Cross

Painted 1951
205.1 × 115.8 cm
Glasgow Art Gallery

This is one of Dalí's most popular works, and the painter received the inspiration for it from a drawing that was supposedly made by St John of the Cross in which the crucifixion is viewed from above, as here, although from an oblique rather than a frontal angle. And on a study for this picture (now in a private collection), Dalí also wrote

When . . . I saw the Christ drawn by St John of the Cross, I geometrically decided upon a triangle and a circle, which 'aesthetically' *summed up all my previous experiments . . . AND PUT MY CHRIST IN THAT TRIANGLE.*

The triangulation is very evident, and clearly relates to the Trinity. Moreover, Dalí also appears to have been aware that triangles relate to a Platonic tradition in European thought, whereby basic forms like triangles and circles were deemed to enjoy metaphysical powers, being universal constants. Naturally, such a form is highly appropriate to the representation of a religious figure who supposedly enjoyed or enjoys universal powers.

This is amongst the most successful of Dalí's religious paintings, and much of its appeal derives from its visual simplicity and acute attention to detail, the anatomical representation of Christ and the *chiaroscuro* or sharp division between light and shade being particularly felicitous. But here we are not witnessing Surrealism at all; by 1951 Dalí had replaced it with religious mysticism, which is something different and which, for better or worse, has to be accepted on its own terms. Usually Dalí's late mysticism does not ring true, and this is not surprising, for the painter was anything but a mystic. But in works like this he successfully projected some modicum of genuine religious belief, whilst avoiding his more usual tendency to make such offerings look like something straight out of a Hollywood movie.

Glasgow Art Gallery paid £8,200 for this painting in 1952, a price that caused outrage at the time, leading one furious protestor to slash the work. By 1958, however, the museum had already made a profit on the picture through the sale of entry fees to view it and royalties and reproductions of the work, thus justifying its investment.

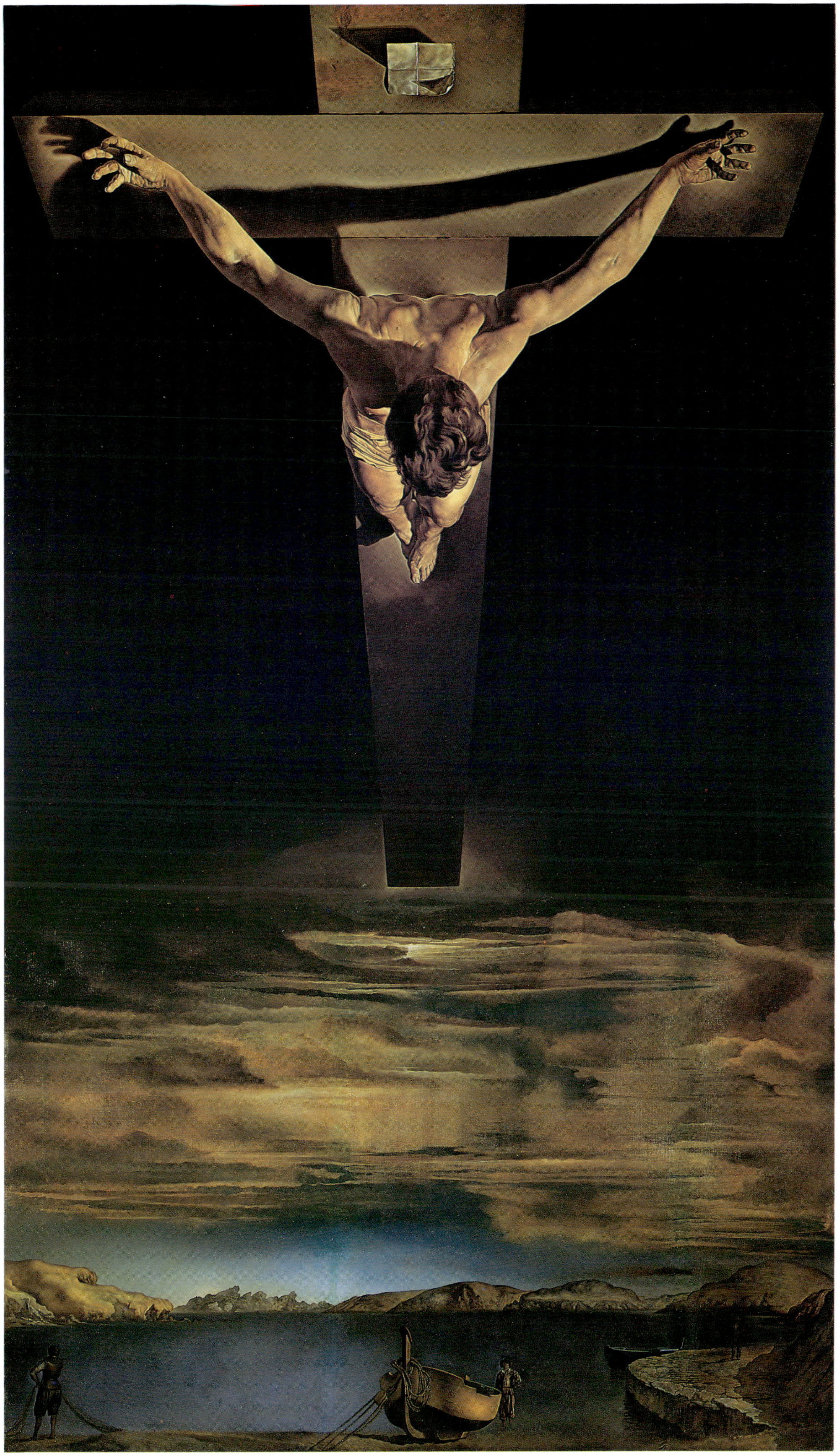

By the mid-1950s Dalí suffered from the occupational hazard of successful painters: he had begun to repeat himself, although this oil painting does mitigate that defect by recycling Dalí's most famous image in terms of his post-war interest in physics and metaphysics. Dalí said of the work:

After twenty years of total immobility, the soft watches disintegrate dynamically, while the highly coloured chromosomes of the fish's eye constitute the hereditary approach of my pre-natal atavisms.

The Dalinian 'soft' self-portrait is located immediately below the fish, while the sea is represented as a skin that can be lifted, a conceit that Dalí would frequently employ elsewhere after it appeared here.

The Disintegration of the Persistence of Memory

Painted 1954

25.4 × 33 cm

Salvador Dalí Museum, St Petersburg, Florida

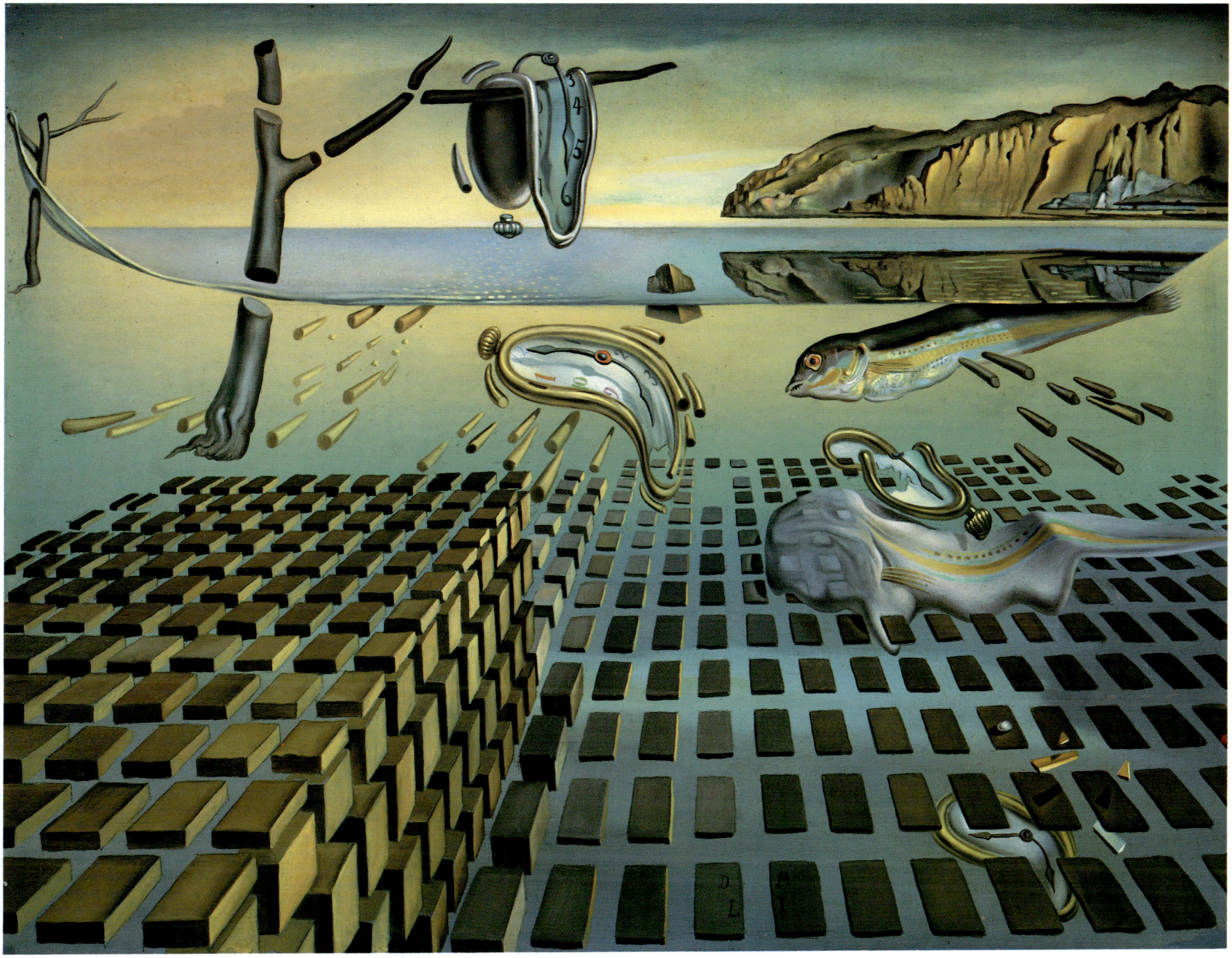

From his earliest years Dalí was profoundly drawn to the works of nineteenth-century historical painters such as Meissonier, but usually such an attraction merely affected the degrees of verisimilitude and detailing in his works and was thus easily reconciled with his Surrealism. However, from the 1950s onwards, and obviously because he had begun both to falter imaginatively and to become more reactionary as far as art was concerned, Dalí frequently painted purely historical subjects that are barely modified by any Surrealistic input whatsoever.

Nothing could better typify this aspect of his work than the present small canvas. Naturally, the low viewpoint emphasizes the towering height of the colossus, and a vaguely surrealistic touch is afforded by the fact that the giant statue of the sun god Helios is shielding its eyes from the sun. Yet in all other respects the image does not differ very much from a Hollywood film poster. As always Dalí created a convincing fictive space and demonstrated his enormous skills as a landscapist, albeit rather slickly.

The Colossus of Rhodes

Painted 1954

68.8 × 39 cm

Kunstmuseum, Bern, Switzerland

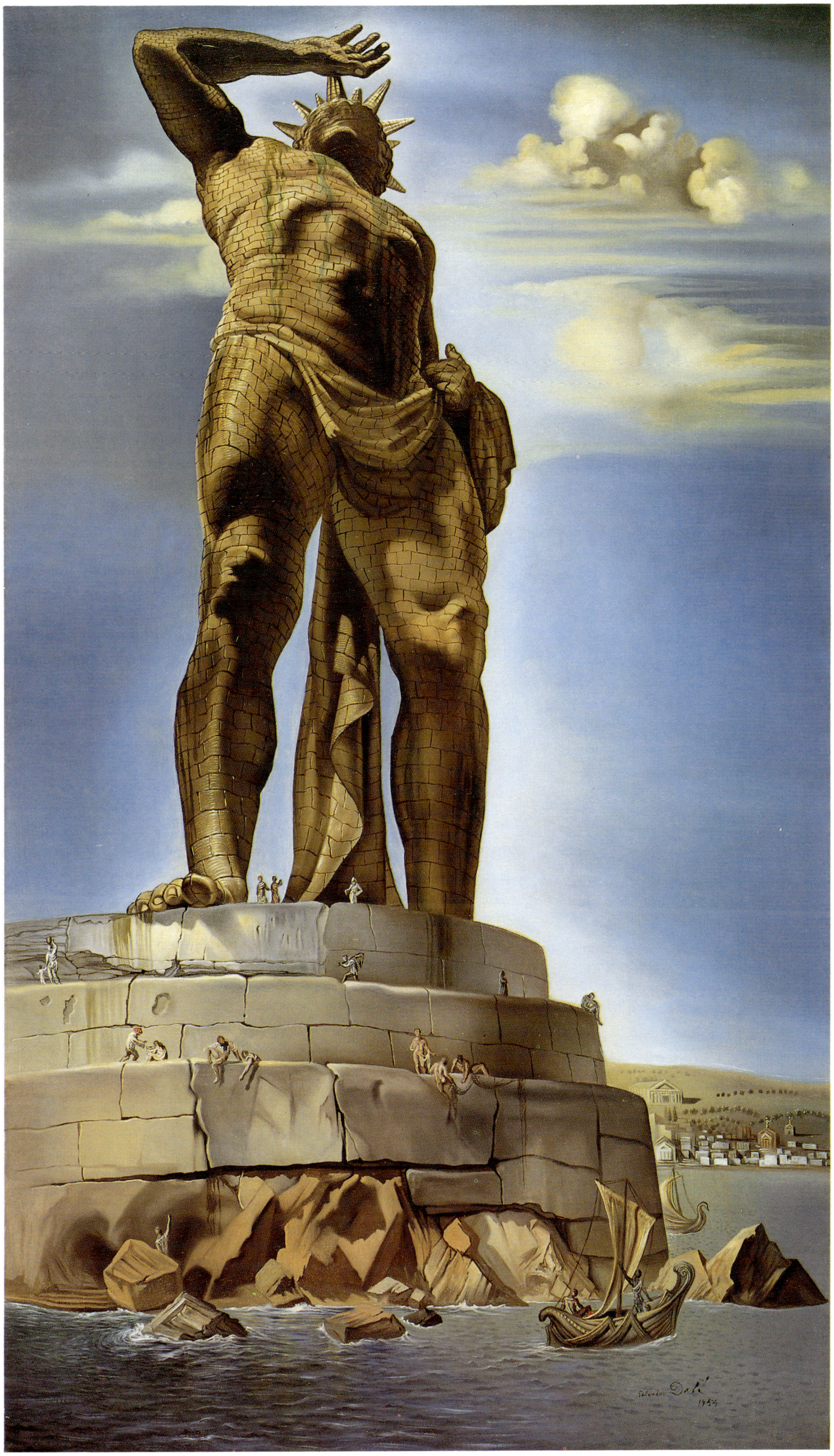
Salvador Dalí

The Last Supper

Painted 1955

165.7 × 267.3 cm

National Gallery of Art, Washington DC

It took Dalí about three months to paint this picture, and for much of the material he employed photographs, stating later that

I almost always use photographic documents. It's traditional. Praxiteles made direct casts of arms, legs, and anything he was going to reproduce. For someone who draws as I do, a photograph is an extremely useful element.

And elsewhere he added that the painting embodies an

arithmetical and philosophical cosmogony, founded on the paranoiac sublimity of the number twelve – the twelve months of the year, the twelve signs of the Zodiac around the sun, the twelve apostles around the Christ, the twelve pentagons in the celestial dodecahedron, the pentagon containing the microcosmic man, Christ. (Thanks to Lorca who told me that the Apostles were as symmetrical as the wings of butterflies.)

With its football-hero-type Christ (for which Dalí employed a handsome male model) and approachable symbolism, as well as its Hollywood sense of scale, naturally this painting soon became one of the most popular modern pictures in the National Gallery of Art, for which institution it was bought by Chester Dale in 1959. Equally, however, it caused disgust in some religious quarters for its sentimentality, which was deemed to border on kitsch, and it is difficult not to concur with that judgement.

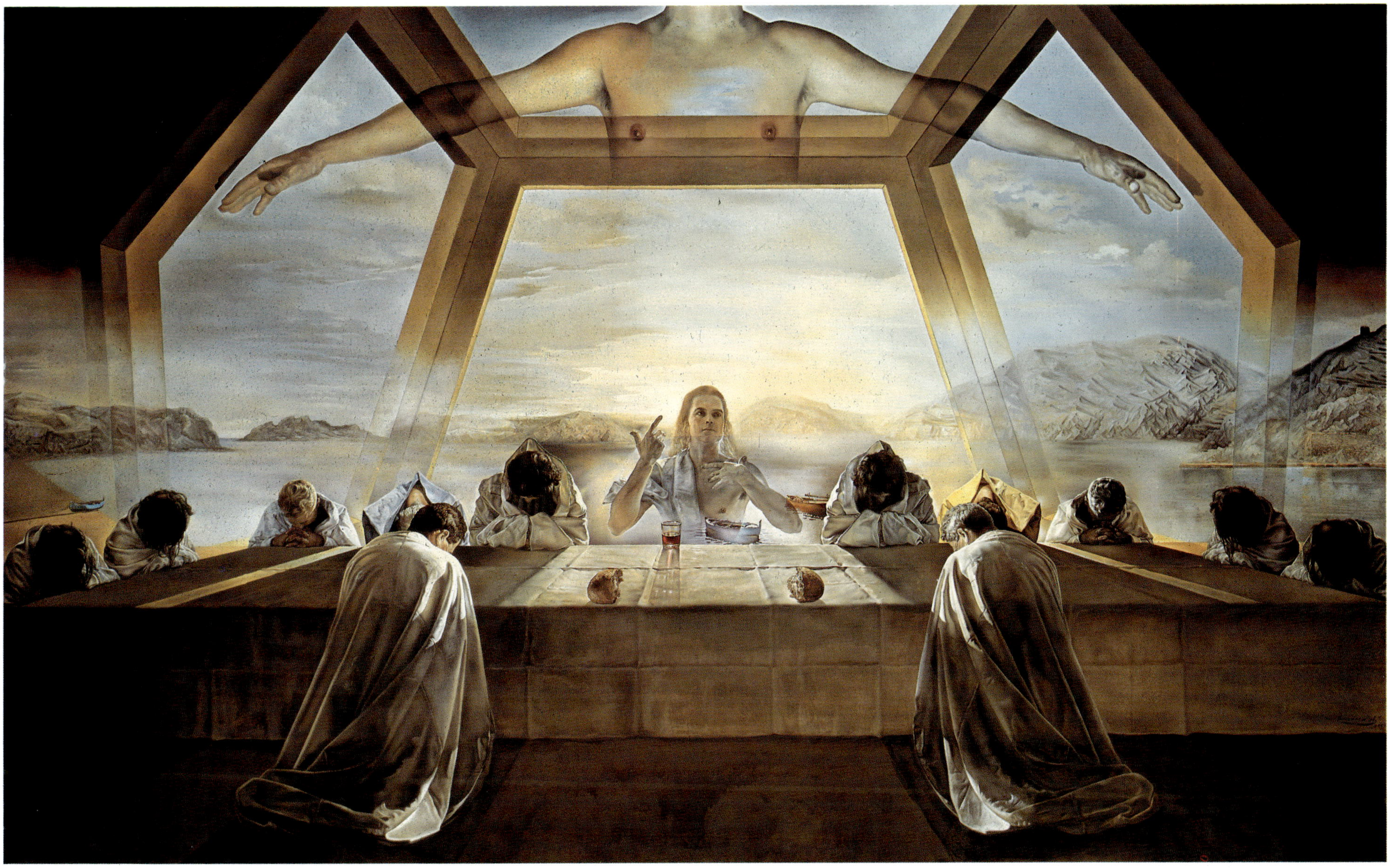

This painting embodies Dalí's latterday quasi-mystical attitude to time and space, and its creator wrote of it in those terms in his *Secret Confessions*:

When in my 1956 Nature morte vivante *(Unstill Still-Life; or, literally: Living Dead Nature) I show the fruit bowl floating in space with the fan and fruits and a cauliflower and a bird and a glass and a bottle emptying itself and a knife, in front of a window through which there is an endless moiré sea, while a hand holds a rhinoceros horn, I am defining and communicating a notion of time-space expressed through the vision of a levitation that shatters entropy. With the rhinoceros horn as maximum energy in minimum space, facing the infinite spaces of the sea, the picture becomes the privileged locus of a geometry that translates not only the loftiest scientific and philosophical speculations, but allows me, Dalí, existentially to know the truth of time-space and by that very fact a Dalinian truth of my person and my situation in the world.*

Here again we see Dalí's old-fashioned hyper-realism being validated as modernistic imagery through his unorthodox treatment of subject matter – if these objects were situated normally upon the table instead of flying around it, then the work would be little more than a conventional, almost photographic still-life.

Unstill Still-Life

Painted 1956
125 × 160 cm
Salvador Dalí Museum, St Petersburg, Florida

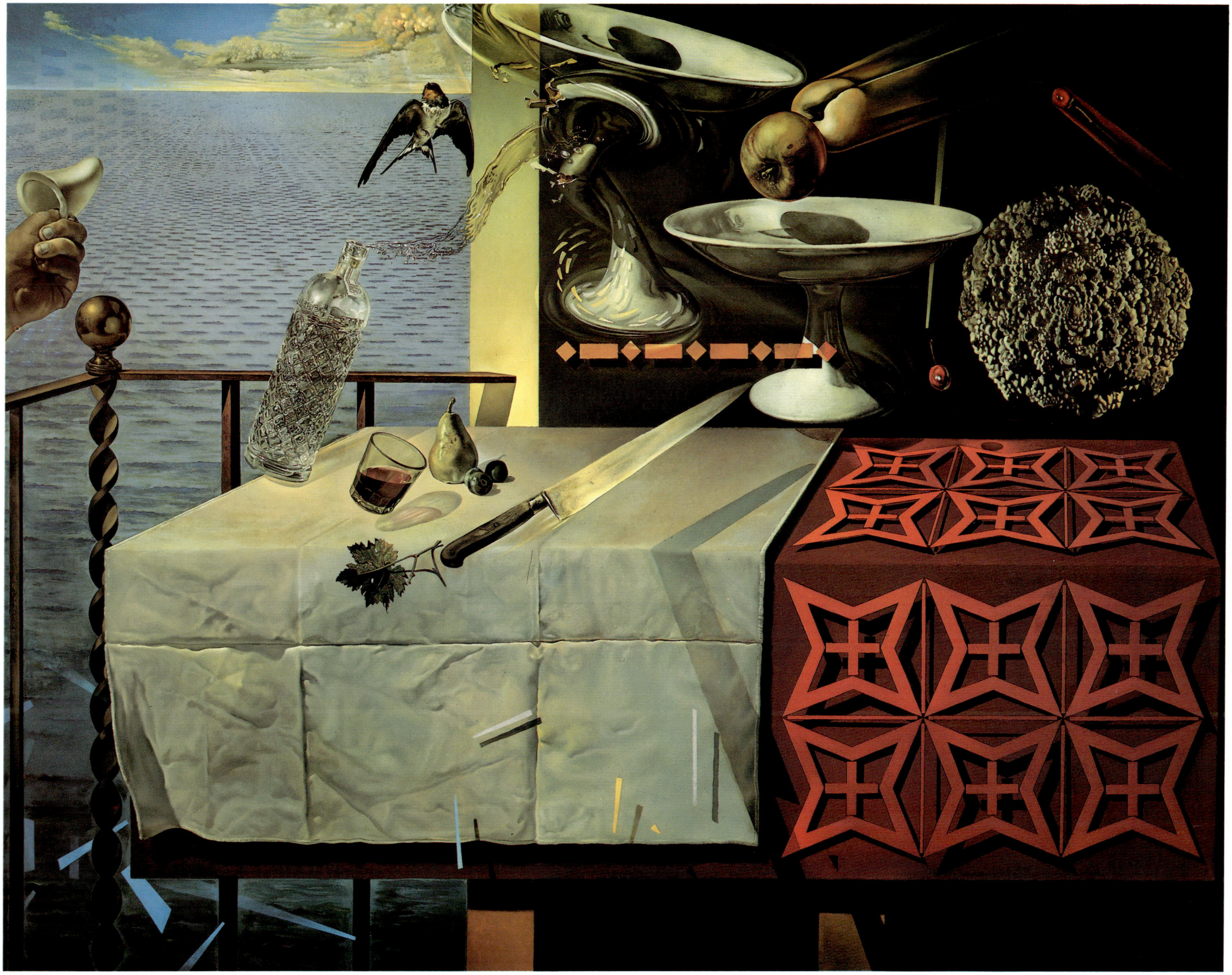

Dalí related the genesis of this large oil painting on canvas in his *Unspeakable Confessions*:

The day I planned to do a painting to the glory of St James, I happened to bump into the Vicomtesse de Noailles, who had just bought a book on Santiago de Compostela and showed it to me. Opening it, I was immediately struck by the shell-shaped architectural vault that is the palm tree of the famous shrine, which I decided to reproduce. I also looked until I found a photograph of a horse bucking and traced it in the same way.

It is perhaps not surprising, then, that the work looks very photographic. Beyond the bucking horse may be seen the base of an atomic mushroom cloud, while to the lower right Gala stands shrouded in the type of costume that was clearly intended to introduce biblical, if not even virginal, associations.

Santiago El Grande

Painted 1957

396.2 × 289.6 cm

Beaverbrook Art Gallery, Fredericton, New Brunswick

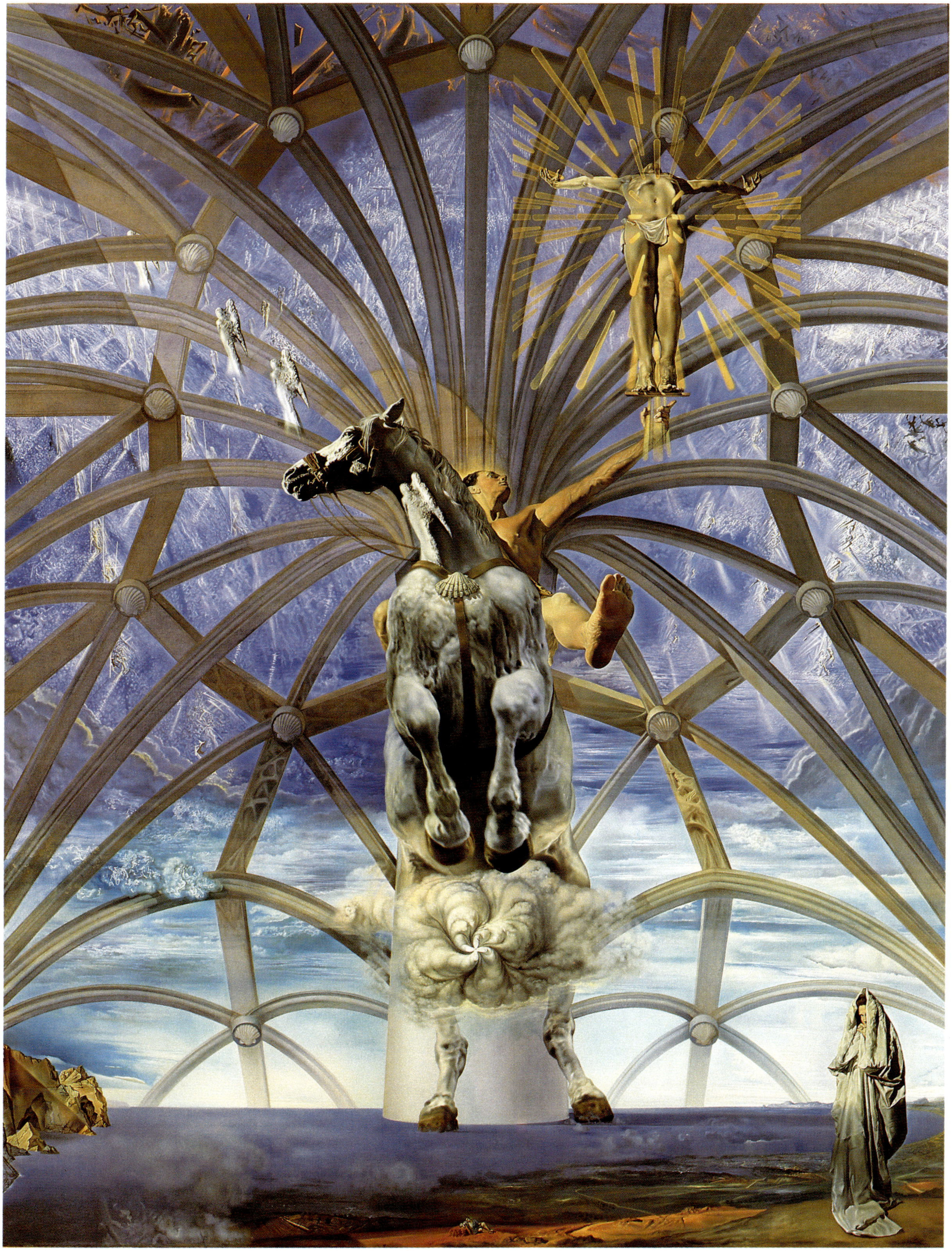

Dalí alternatively titled this painting *The Dream of Christopher Columbus*, and he also explained that the giant sea-urchin in the foreground is surrounded 'by the orbit of an artificial satellite' (in 1958–59 the Russians and Americans were just putting their first unmanned space vehicles into orbit around the earth). By such symbolic means Dalí was therefore obviously attempting to draw a parallel between recent new venturings into space and Christopher Columbus discovering America.

Gala emerges three-dimensionally from the banner on the left, while on the right Dalí has imitated the dot breakdown of mechanized newspaper reproduction, just as the American Pop artist Roy Lichtenstein would begin to do far more fully just three or so years later. Again, the high degree of verisimilitude was obtained by the faithful copying of photographs.

The Discovery of America by Christopher Columbus

Painted 1958–59

396.2 × 289.6 cm

Salvador Dalí Museum, St Petersburg, Florida

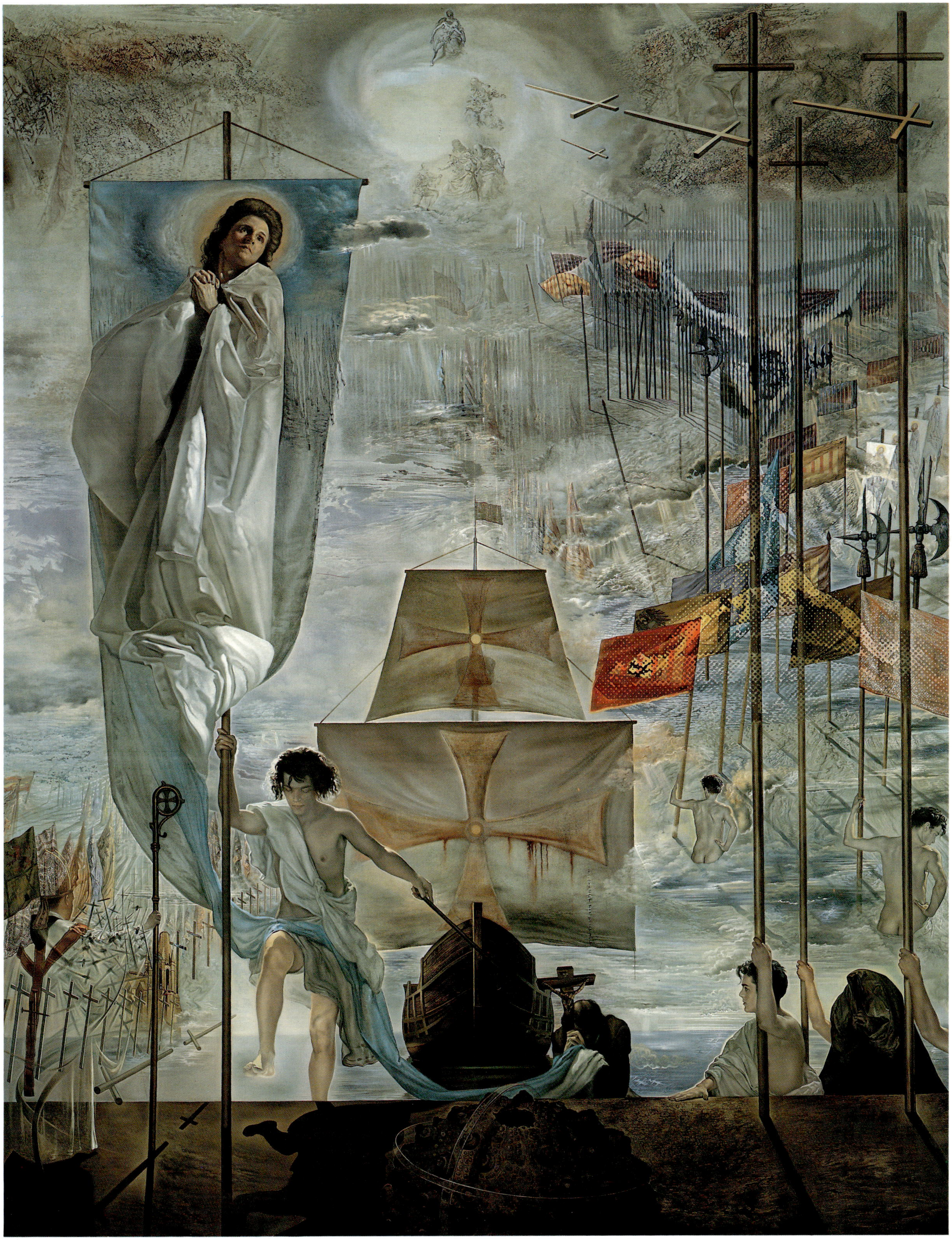

Hallucinogenic Toreador

Painted 1968–70

396.2 × 289.6 cm

Salvador Dalí Museum, St Petersburg, Florida

The inclusion of the Venus de Milo in this unusually large oil painting on canvas was prompted by seeing a reproduction of the Greek sculpture on a 'Venus'-brand pencil packet, in which image Dalí had simultaneously discerned the head of a toreador. Here that head can be made out in the shadows of the central Venus, shadows that are cast by the left side of her head, by her right-hand breast and by the folds across her midriff. Compositely these shadows respectively form the toreador's shaded left eye socket, the underside of his nose, and his mouth and chin. The curve of the arena beyond the sculpture gives us the contour of the toreador's hat, the green shadowed side of the Venus's lower garment forms his necktie, and the brilliantly coloured or monochromatic molecules to the left of the sculpture contribute his coat of lights. Beneath these molecules/lights, the shadowings of innumerable rock forms create an overall shape that was intended to represent the head of a dying bull, according to Dalí himself. And at the very bottom of the picture, in the centre, further disconnected shapes suggest an advancing wild animal. To the left of and slightly above the line of sculptures, the shadowed contours of a further representation of the Venus de Milo act equally as a figure twisting as it holds aloft a tambourine or possibly a *muleta*.

The distant terraces, walls and statues evoke echoes of de Chirico's deserted architectural surroundings, and from that setting a regular formation of small, shadowed ellipses advances to evolve gradually into a host of winged objects which at the bottom right finally turn into bluebottles. These common house-flies are watched unconcernedly by a little boy in a sailor's costume whom we have previously encountered in Dalí's work, for it is exactly the same portrayal of the painter himself that appears in *The Spectre of Sex Appeal* (page 65).

Elsewhere may be perceived a quasi-religious hallucinatory image of Gala at the top left; Dalí's arch-enemy of the irrational, Voltaire; and numerous heads or complete renderings of the Venus de Milo, including a head at the top left that enjoys a polarized colouring. When Dalí made this painting in the late 1960s, a similar colour polarization was very frequently encountered in popular graphics such as posters and the like, and it was commonly supposed to reflect the visual stimulus afforded by hallucinogenic drugs like LSD. Here and elsewhere in this work, Dalí was clearly building upon that familiar type of imagery so as to inject his rather tired Surrealism with the hallucinatory stimulus of the new drug culture.

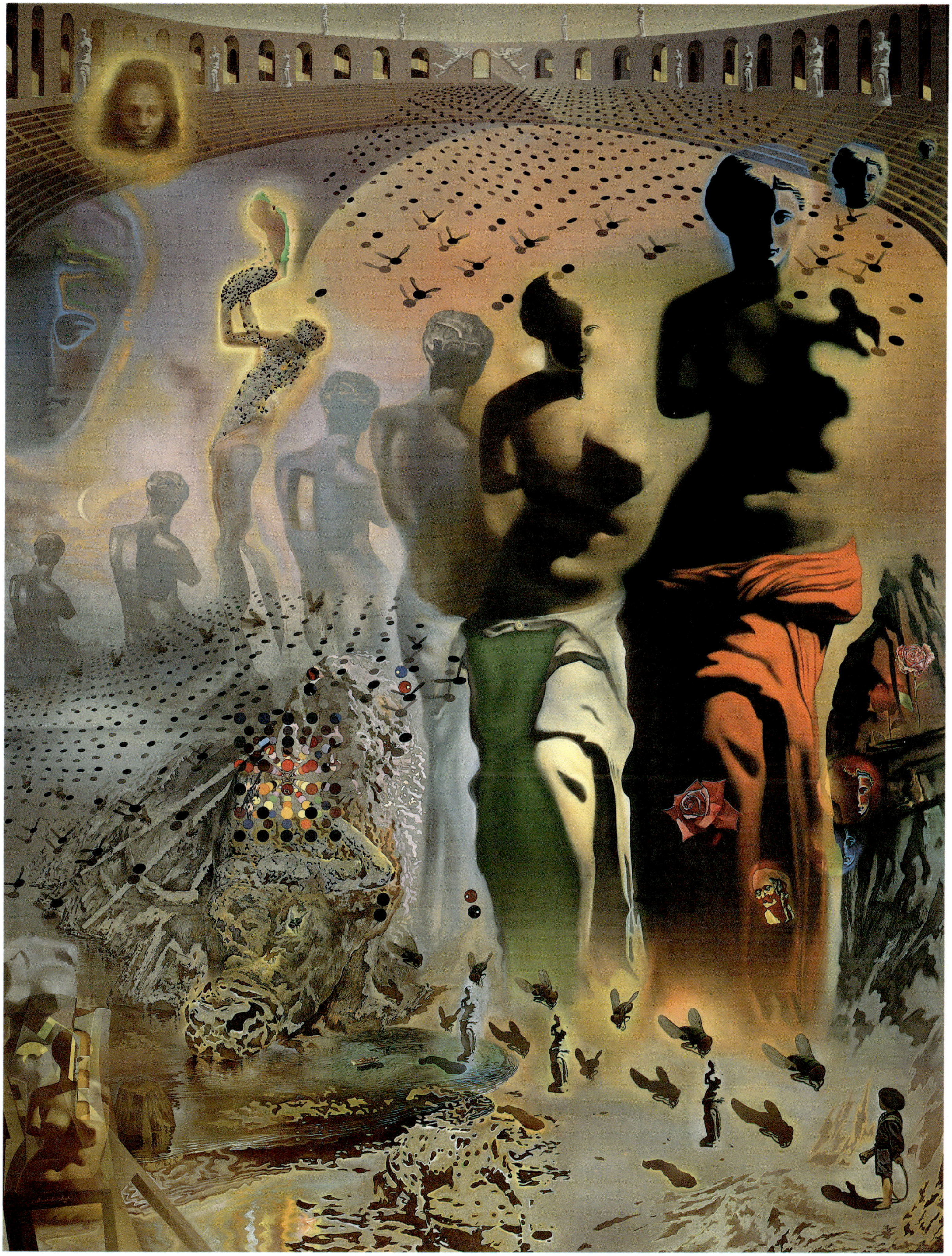

SELECTED BIBLIOGRAPHY

ADES, DAWN, *Dada and Surrealism Reviewed*, London, 1978.

—*Dalí*, London and New York, 1982.

BOSQUET, ALAIN, *Conversations with Dalí*, New York, 1969.

DALÍ, SALVADOR, *Diary of a Genius*, London, 1966.

—*The Secret Life of Salvador Dalí*, fourth edition, London, 1973.

—*The Unspeakable Confessions of Salvador Dalí*, London, 1976.

DESCHARNES, ROBERT, *The World of Salvador Dalí*, London, 1962.

—*Salvador Dalí, The Work, The Man*, New York, 1984.

ETHERINGTON-SMITH, MEREDITH, *Dalí–A Life*, London, 1992.

EXHIBITION CATALOGUE: *Salvador Dalí*, Centre Georges Pompidou, Musée National d'Art Moderne, Paris, 1979.

GERARD, MAX, *Dalí*, New York, 1968.

GIBSON, IAN, *Federico García Lorca, A Life*, London, 1989.

LEVY, JULIEN, *Memoirs of an Art Gallery*, New York, 1977.

MANILA, PHILIPPINES, *Telephone Directory*, 4th edition, 1938.

McGIRK, TIM, *Wicked Lady: Salvador Dalí's Muse*, London, 1989.

MORSE, REYNOLDS, *Dalí, A Study of his Life and Work*, New York, 1958.

ROGERSON, MARK, *The Dalí Scandal*, London, 1987.

SECREST, MERYLE, *Salvador Dalí, A Biography*, New York, 1986.

SERNA, RAMÓN GOMEZ DE LA, *Dalí*, London and Sydney, 1977.

WILSON, SIMON, *Salvador Dalí*, London, 1980.

CHRONOLOGY

1904
Birth of Salvador Felipe Jacinto Dalí y Domenech in Figueras, Catalonia, Spain, on 11 May.

1918
Shows first works in local art exhibition held in the Municipal Theatre, Figueras.

1921
Gains admittance to the San Fernando Academy of Fine Arts in Madrid and lives in the University Residence where he becomes friendly with Luis Buñuel and Federico García Lorca.

1923
Suspended by the Academy of Fine Arts for a year on account of his supposedly subversive behaviour.

1925
Between 14 and 17 November holds first one-man show at the Delmau Gallery in Barcelona.

1926
Makes first trip to Paris, where he visits Picasso. Is permanently expelled from the San Fernando Academy of Fine Arts. Holds second one-man exhibition at the Delmau Academy.

1927
Performs military service. Designs sets and costumes for Lorca's drama *Mariana Pineda* in Barcelona.

1928
Paints in Figueras. Contributes an attack on Catalan cultural provincialism and anti-modernism to the *Manifesto Groc* or 'Yellow Manifesto'.

1929
Between March and June visits Paris again, and collaborates with Buñuel on film *Un Chien andalou.* In summer is visited in Cadaqués by Gala and Paul Eluard, as well as by René Magritte. Officially joins Surrealist movement. In November holds first one-man show in Paris at the Goemans Gallery. Begins living with Gala Eluard.

1930
Is barred from family home in Cadaqués on account of relationship with Gala; with money provided by Vicomte de Noailles buys fisherman's cottage in Port Lligat, where he spends summer. Works on scenario of *L'Age d'or* with Buñuel.

1931
Holds second Paris one-man show, at Pierre Colle Gallery in June.

1932
Participates in Surrealist group shows in New York and Paris. Writes a third film scenario, *Babaouo* (never produced). Holds further show at Pierre Colle Gallery in Paris.

1933
Is promised a regular salary by a group of collectors and friends (the 'Zodiac' group) in exchange for right to choose works on a rote basis. Participates in show of Surrealist objects at Pierre Colle Gallery, where he also has further one-man show in June. First one-man exhibition in New York, at Julien Levy Gallery. Illustrates *Les Chants de Maldoror* for Swiss publisher, Albert Skira.

1934
30 January, marries Gala in Paris, with her ex-husband Paul Eluard as one of the witnesses. Holds six one-man shows (two in Paris, two in New York, one in Barcelona and one in London). November, visits United States.

1935
Lectures on Surrealism at the Museum of Modern Art in New York. Publishes major essay 'The Conquest of the Irrational'. Concludes agreement with English collector, Edward James, to sell him his most important works (agreement continues until 1939).
1936
Visits London in June–July for International Surrealist Exhibition, giving lecture in diving suit in which he nearly suffocates. Visits Spain in summer but forced to leave by outbreak of Civil War. December, revisits America for exhibition at Julien Levy Gallery, appears on cover of *Time* magazine, 14 December.
1937
February, visits Harpo Marx in Hollywood, and collaborates on film scenario entitled *Giraffes on Horseback Salad*. April, returns to Europe, spending month in Austria and Switzerland, then stays in Italy with Edward James and Lord Berners. Begins designing dresses and hats for Elsa Schiaparelli.
1938
Takes part in International Exhibition of Surrealism at the Beaux Arts Gallery in Paris, showing a mannequin inside a taxi. Visits Freud in London in July. In autumn visits Coco Chanel in Monte Carlo where he also designs ballet *Bacchanale*.
1939
January, returns to Paris. February, revisits New York for show at Julien Levy Gallery and is engaged by Bonwit Teller, a Fifth Avenue department store, to design shop windows; attracts wide publicity after dispute over the arrangement. Contributes *Dream of Venus* to New York World's Fair. Returns to France in autumn and eventually settles at Arcachon after outbreak of Second World War.
1940
After fall of France in June, flees to America via Spain and Portugal. Settles in Hampton, Virginia, at home of Caresse Crosby.
1941
Exhibits at Julien Levy Gallery in New York in April. Is attacked in print by André Breton who nicknames Dalí 'Avida Dollars' for propensity for making money. Designs ballet *Labyrinth*, with choreography by Léonide Massine. Writes autobiography, *The Secret Life of Salvador Dalí*. November, holds retrospective exhibition at the Museum of Modern Art, New York.
1942
Designs a calendar to benefit Free French cause.
1943
Holds exhibition of portraits of American personalities at Knoedler Gallery, New York. Designs apartment for Helena Rubinstein.
1944
Publishes only novel, *Hidden Faces*. Designs three ballets, *Sentimental Colloquy*, *Mad Tristan* and *El Café de Chinitas*.
1945
Holds exhibition at Bignou Gallery, New York, and publishes first issue of *Dalí News*. Creates dream sequence for Alfred Hitchcock's film *Spellbound*.
1946
Works in Hollywood with Walt Disney on unrealized project, *Destino*.
1947
Exhibits in Palm Beach, Cleveland and New York, where produces second edition of own self-promotional newspaper *Dalí News* containing first chapter of book on technique, *Fifty Secrets of Magic Craftsmanship*.
1948
Returns to Europe in July, and thereafter regularly winters in New York, spending rest of year in Paris and Port Lligat. Designs Shakespeare production for Luchino Visconti, Richard Strauss opera for Peter Brook, and begins to paint religious subject-matter. Terminates direct participation in Surrealist movement.
1949
Visits Pope Pius XII in Rome in November.
1951
With Gala attends Besteigui Ball in Venice in 7-metre-high costumes designed by Christian Dior.
1952
Lectures in United States on his 'new cosmogony'. Purchase of *Christ of St John of the Cross* by Glasgow Art Gallery for £8200 causes public outcry in Scotland.
1954
Completes series of 102 watercolours illustrating Dante's *Divine Comedy*.
1955
Lectures at the Sorbonne in Paris on 'The Phenomenological Aspects of the Paranoiac-Critical Method'. Paints portrait of Laurence Olivier dressed as King Richard III.
1956
Dalí's painting, *The Last Supper*, goes on view at the National Gallery of Art in Washington, DC.
1957
Develops ideas for 'living' nightclub in Acapulco, and for film of *Don Quixote* with Walt Disney who visits Dalí at Cadaqués, but both projects remain unrealized.
1958
Lectures at the Théâtre de l'Etoile in Paris with specially-baked loaf of bread almost 12 metres long. Remarries Gala in religious ceremony in Spain.

1959
Produces Ovicipede, a plastic bubble projecting the 'intra-uterine phantasm'.
1960
Exhibits *The Discovery of America by Christopher Columbus*, painted in 1958 for Huntingdon Hartford's Gallery of Modern Art in New York. Participation in Surrealist exhibition in New York leads to protests by fellow Surrealists. Exhibits *Divine Comedy* watercolours in Paris.
1961
Designs sets and costumes, and writes story for ballet with choreography by Maurice Béjart, the *Ballet de Gala*.
1962
Exhibits *The Battle of Tetuan* in the Palacio del Tinell in Barcelona alongside painting of same subject by Mariano Fortuny that inspired it.
1963
Publishes *The Tragic Myth of Millet's Angelus*.
1964
Publishes *The Diary of a Genius*, third volume of autobiography. Awarded the Grand Cross of Isabel la Católica by General Franco.
1965
Exhibits painting *The Perpignan Railway Station* at Knoedler Gallery in New York. Large exhibition of works held at the Gallery of Modern Art in New York.
1967
Shows painting of *Tuna Fishing* in Paris and contributes catalogue essay praising work of Meissonier and other 'Pompier' painters.
1970
Announces creation of Dalí Museum in Figueras.
1971
Dalí Museum of works from Morse Collection opens in Cleveland, Ohio; is later transferred to St Petersburg, Florida.
1972
Exhibits holograms at Knoedler Gallery in New York.
1974
September, Teatro-Museo Dalí inaugurated in Figueras.
1978
Exhibits first stereoscopic painting at the Solomon R. Guggenheim Museum in New York. Elected a Foreign Associate Member of the Academy of Fine Arts of the Institut de France.
1979
December, large retrospective exhibition opens at the Centre Georges Pompidou in Paris; later moves to London.
1982
March, presented with the Medal of Gold by the Generalidat of Catalonia. Gala dies 10 June in Pubol. Created Marquis de Pubol by the King of Spain on 26 July.
1983
Retrospective exhibition held at the Museo Español de Arte Contemporáneo in Madrid.
1984
30 August, seriously injured by fire while asleep.
1989
Dies 23 January in Figueras.

LIST OF ILLUSTRATIONS

All works are by Salvador Dalí unless otherwise specified.

(Photo: Bridgeman Art Library, London)

101 *Apparition of Face and Fruit Dish on a Beach*, 1938. Oil on canvas, 114.9 × 143.8 cm. The Ella Gallup Sumner and Mary Catlin Sumner Collection, Wadsworth Atheneum, Hartford, Connecticut.

103 *The Slave Market with the Disappearing Bust of Voltaire*, 1940. Oil on canvas, 46.3 × 65.4 cm. Salvador Dalí Museum, St Petersburg, Florida. © 1994 Salvador Dalí Foundation, Inc.

105 *Visage of War*, 1940. Oil on canvas, 64.1 × 79 cm. Boymans-van Beuningen Museum, Rotterdam. (Photo: Bridgeman Art Library, London)

107 *Soft Self-Portrait with Grilled Bacon*, 1941. Oil on canvas, 61.2 × 50.8 cm. Teatro-Museo Dalí, Figueras.

109 *The Sheep*, 1942. Gouache watercolour on chromolithograph, 22.8 × 34.2 cm. Salvador Dalí Museum, St Petersburg, Florida. © 1994 Salvador Dalí Foundation, Inc.

111 *Helena Rubinstein's Head Emerging from a Rocky Cliff*, 1942–43. Oil on canvas, 88.9 × 66 cm. Collection of Helena Rubinstein Foundation Portraits, New York.

113 *Dream Caused by the Flight of a Bee around a Pomegranate One Second before Awakening*, 1944. Oil on canvas, 51.1 × 40.6 cm. Thyssen-Bornemisza Collection, Madrid, Spain.

115 *The Apotheosis of Homer*, 1944–45. Oil on canvas, 64.1 × 118.4 cm. Staatsgalerie Moderner Kunst, Munich. (Photo: Artothek)

117 *Portrait of Isabel Styler-Tas*, 1945. Oil on canvas, 64.1 × 86 cm. Nationalgalerie Staatliche Museen Preussischer Kulturbesitz, West Berlin.

119 *The Temptation of St Anthony*, 1946. Oil on canvas, 89.5 × 119.3 cm. Musées Royaux des Beaux-Arts de Belgique, Brussels.

121 *Portrait of Picasso*, 1947. Oil on canvas, 64.1 × 54.6 cm. Teatro-Museo Dalí, Figueras.

123 *The Madonna of Port Lligat*, 1949. Oil on canvas, 49 × 38.5 cm. Patrick and Beatrice Haggerty Museum of Art, Marquette University, Milwaukee, Wisconsin. Gift of Mr and Mrs Ira Haupt.

125 *Christ of St John of the Cross*, 1951. Oil on canvas, 205.1 × 115.8 cm. Glasgow Art Gallery.

127 *The Disintegration of the Persistence of Memory*, 1954. Oil on canvas, 25.4 × 33 cm. Salvador Dalí Museum, St Petersburg, Florida. © 1994 Salvador Dalí Foundation, Inc.

129 *The Colossus of Rhodes*, 1954. Painted, 68.8 × 39 cm. Kunstmuseum, Berne, Switzerland.

131 *The Last Supper*, 1955. Oil on canvas, 165.7 × 267.3 cm. National Gallery of Art, Washington, DC. (Photo: Bridgeman Art Library, London)

133 *Unstill Still Life*, 1956. Oil on canvas, 125 × 160 cm. Salvador Dalí Museum, St Petersburg, Florida. © 1994 Salvador Dalí Foundation, Inc.

135 *Santiago El Grande*, 1957. Oil on canvas, 396.2 × 289.6 cm. Gift of the Sir James Dunn Foundation, The Beaverbrook Art Gallery, Fredericton, New Brunswick, Canada.

137 *The Discovery of America by Christopher Columbus*, 1958–59. Oil on canvas, 396.2 × 289.6 cm. Salvador Dalí Museum, St Petersburg, Florida. © 1994 Salvador Dalí Foundation, Inc.

139 *Hallucinogenic Toreador*, 1968–70. Oil on canvas, 396.2 × 289.6 cm. Salvador Dalí Museum, St Petersburg, Florida. © 1994 Salvador Dalí Foundation, Inc.